España Brit

España Britannia

ALISTAIR WARD

SHEPHEARD-WALWYN (PUBLISHERS) LTD

First published in 2004 by
Shepheard-Walwyn (Publishers) Ltd
Suite 604, The Chandlery
50 Westminster Bridge Road
London SE1 7QY

British Library Cataloguing in Publication Data
A catalogue record of this book
is available from the British Library

ISBN 0 85683 224 3

Typeset by Alacrity,
Banwell Castle, Weston-super-Mare
Printed through Print Solutions, Wallington, Surrey

Contents

For Susie, Isabella and Amelia

Acknowledgements

MY THANKS are due to the late Chris Thornycroft for providing me with a first-hand account of what is was like to fight with the International Brigade during the Spanish Civil War, and helping me understand the reasons behind British non-intervention.

I must thank Bill Carnaby for kindly reading my manuscript and correcting me on a number of points.

I am also grateful to Andrew Goodwin for accompanying me on three rewarding tours of the battlefields of the Peninsular War.

Finally I wish, especially, to thank my wife Susie for her loving support.

Preface

IN SEPTEMBER 1992, I travelled to the Spanish Basque country to take up an English teaching post at the Inlingua Idiomas language academy in Irún. One day the director of the academy mentioned that the Duke of Wellington had once passed through the area. I had always been very interested in history so was intrigued to find out more.

I had heard of a book called *A Guards Officer in the Peninsula* and asked my sister, who worked in London at the time, to buy it and send it out to me. The book, edited by Ian Fletcher, contains the letters of John Rous who, as a sixteen-year-old in 1812, had travelled to the peninsula to join Wellington's army, then busy trying to push Napoleon's army back into France. What fascinated me most was that five of the letters were written from a camp or lodgings near Irún. I decided that the next time I was in England I would go into Foyles in Charing Cross Road to see if there was anything else to read on the subject. When I got there, it was a beautiful sight. There was a whole bookcase crammed with books on the Peninsular War. I picked out four including Julian Paget's *Wellington's Peninsular War* which was destined to become my most-thumbed book.

After a year in Irún I moved to another Inlingua academy in Murcia, in the south-east of the country but in December 1994 felt the time had come to return home. I had thoroughly enjoyed my two years and three months in Spain. I had travelled about quite a lot and knew I would be back every year to see more of that fascinating and enchanting land.

Because I missed Spain, all my reading was now related to the country. There are a huge number of great books on the subject, from auto-biographical travel books like *As I Walked Out One Midsummer's Morning* by Laurie Lee to contemporary studies like *The New Spaniards* by John Hooper. However, I was most interested in reading about those events in history that involved both Britain and Spain. At first I thought such shared moments in history could be counted on the fingers of one hand – the Peninsular War, Catherine of Aragon, the Armada, pirates and Gibraltar – but, as I read on, other major events and personalities were added to the list until there were fifteen.

I started taking notes which, eight years on, have expanded into

España Britannia. I hope that after reading this book you will enjoy
your visits to Spain even more. I hope also that you will feel the urge
to leave the beaten track and view the more remote parts of that
beautiful country travelled by so many other Britons in such wildly
different circumstances so many years ago.

CHAPTER 1

The Eleanor Crosses

Ride a cock horse to Banbury Cross
To see a fine lady upon a white horse,
With rings on her fingers and bells on her toes,
She shall have music wherever she goes.

Traditional nursery rhyme

IN CENTRAL LONDON, only yards from the great square with the Spanish name, are a hotel, a station and a road that bear the name of Charing Cross. An imaginative reconstruction of the original thirteenth-century cross stands in the hotel and station forecourt. The original was the final of twelve crosses marking the night stops of the funeral cortège that carried the body of Queen Eleanor, the Spanish wife of Edward I, from Harby in Nottinghamshire to Westminster in 1290. The others were set up at Lincoln, Grantham, Stamford, Geddington, Hardingstone, Stony Stratford, Woburn, Dunstable, St Albans, Waltham and Cheapside. In time such crosses came to be seen as symbols marking the centres of villages and market towns, and places never visited by the cortège sprouted them. One of these, Banbury, is immortalised in the old nursery rhyme. The cross at Sledmere in Yorkshire was built only in 1895, then converted to a war memorial in 1919. Of the originals, only three remain: at Geddington (the best example), Hardingstone and Waltham.

So who was this Spanish queen whose loss was so mourned that her warrior husband strove to ensure she would never be forgotten?

Eleanor was born in northern Spain in 1244 to King Ferdinand III of Castile and Joan of Ponthieu. Her father was a great crusader who united Castile and León and accelerated the pace of reconquest from the Moors. Soon after her birth she would have been taken south as her father moved his base to Andalusia. When he died in 1252, he was succeeded by Eleanor's half-brother Alfonso X. It would have been expedient for Eleanor to marry the English Edward, eldest son of Henry III. The English king's lands in Gascony were adjacent to Castile so marriage would secure the borders for both parties. It would also

1

deal with her brother's spurious claim to that part of Aquitaine. The claim was based on the supposition that the English sovereign Henry II had pledged Gascony to Alfonso VIII of Castile as part of the deal that took Henry's daughter Eleanor to Castile as queen in 1170.

The marriage negotiations included an Anglo-Castilian treaty by which the kings of Castile and England became allies against all enemies. Edward was to be knighted and would assist in the Castilian struggle to reduce Navarre. Interestingly, for a time when the reconquest was not yet complete, Henry also agreed to assist Alfonso in an invasion of North Africa.

In October 1254 Prince Edward arrived in Burgos for the wedding. The venue was the monastery of Las Huelgas de Burgos, founded by Alfonso VIII of Castile and Eleanor of England in 1187 as their future mausoleum. The ceremony most likely took place on 1 November. The groom was fifteen, his bride just ten. Later that month they travelled to Gascony where they spent a year before journeying to England the following October. It was an arranged marriage between two very young people from vastly different backgrounds but it was to last for thirty-six years and produce more children than the union of any other king and queen of England before or since.

During the next ten years, Henry III's inept rule provoked the barons to take government into their own hands. For a time Edward supported the rebels, led by Simon de Montfort, Earl of Leicester. Later he turned to support his father and was captured during the royal defeat at the Battle of Lewes in 1264, after which Eleanor fled to France. Edward escaped a year later to lead royalist forces back to victory at the Battle of Evesham in August 1265 and Eleanor returned to join her husband, who became effective ruler.

Edward was the archetypal medieval king. His tall and powerful physique gave him an advantage in tournaments in that age of chivalry. He hunted stag, practised falconry, patronised minstrels and heralds and played chess. But no knight's record was complete without a crusade. And so it was that, in August 1270, Eleanor left with her husband on the long and dangerous journey to the Holy Land. The Fifth Crusade did little to help the fortunes of Jerusalem. One of its few legacies was a tale that was long recounted as proof of Eleanor's selfless devotion to her husband. The story goes that, whilst in his chamber at Acre, Edward was visited by a Moslem who attacked him with a poisoned dagger. Edward fought back and killed the would-be assassin before Eleanor dutifully sucked the deadly poison from his wound. It is a nice story but unlikely to be true: it first appears in a work written by an Italian Dominican friar no less than a century and a half later. That he was from an order that Eleanor supported suggests ulterior motives for embellishing a less remarkable account of what actually happened.

Eleanor and Edward left the Holy Land in September 1272. In Sicily they received the dramatic news that they were king and queen, Henry III having passed away. England was stable enough for them not to rush home. Eleanor had good reason not to travel on: she was pregnant with her eighth child.

One of the frustrations of medieval history is the difficulty of establishing facts. How many children did Eleanor actually have? Most likely fourteen, but we have only twelve names – four boys, called John, Henry, Alfonso and Edward, and eight girls, Katherine, Joan (two), Eleanor, Margaret, Bernagaria, Mary and Elizabeth. It is possible that there were more. The tragedy is that only six lived to adulthood.

Four of Eleanor's children had already died when she gave birth to a boy in Aquitaine in November 1273. She invited her brother Alfonso X to the baptism in Bayonne. Amazingly for a child second in line to the English throne, he was given a very foreign name – Alfonso, after his godfather and uncle. When the baby's elder brother died the following year, he became first in line until his own untimely death at the age of ten. Eleanor must have suffered a great deal, both physically, during years of pregnancy and childbirth, and mentally, having to cope with the illness and death of so many of her children. It appears that she mourned Alfonso the most, decreeing that, when she died, his heart should be buried with her own.

Queen Eleanor and King Edward I arrived at Dover on 2 August 1274. Seventeen days later they were crowned in Westminster Abbey. Queen Eleanor was a sophisticated cosmopolitan woman who coped well with the cultural shock of thirteenth-century England. She owned and commissioned literary works and was very interested in education. She enjoyed embroidery and weaving, and kept dogs. Notably, she did not bring in Castilian relatives and hangers-on, but she did introduce carpets to England in 1255 and, apparently, the first merino sheep. There are also records of her purchasing olive oil, pomegranates, figs, oranges and lemons, either from abroad or directly from Castilian ships calling at English ports. She was obviously supportive of her husband but the notion that she had a calming influence on him is probably untrue. Like so many others, Eleanor had a reputation in death that differed considerably from that in life. As Edward's wife, many people in England denounced her as a foreign-born land-grabber who caused her husband to rule harshly. Such a view would have been aggravated by her not speaking English, if that was indeed the case. She and her husband both had French mothers, and French was spoken at court. Unless you planned to speak to peasants and tradesmen, there was no point in learning English.

Financial arrangements at the time did not allow the queen to have all her expenses covered by the king. Instead, Edward encouraged Eleanor to augment her own income through the acquisition of land. The stewards she employed to act for her in this earned her much crit-icism as they went about their work with some ruthlessness. One of her methods was to take over debts to Jews, who were struggling due to arbitrary Crown taxes, then charge the same exorbitant interest rates whilst enjoying the protection of her position. Her stewards were quick to seize manors and other assets if there was any default on payment – it was the manors they really wanted. Knights who had borrowed money for the crusade were incensed to lose their property by such underhand methods. Most of her acquisitions, however, did not involve the Jews. Anyone with land, whether financially burdened or not, feared that their property could fall under the greedy gaze of her stewards, who would thus concoct some way of obtaining it. After she had acquired the land, her ruthlessness fell on the tenants. The Archbishop of Canterbury, John Pecham, was sufficiently outraged by her behaviour to warn her that she was committing mortal sin. Her husband's desire to give her a reputation not enjoyed in life might be one of the reasons why Edward arranged for three magnificent tombs, twelve beautiful crosses and a funeral procession and ceremony of unprecedented splendour.

In 1290 Edward expelled the Jews, a move that enabled him to raise substantial revenue in taxes from subjects who no longer had finan-cial obligations to the departed moneylenders. Late that year, Queen Eleanor was on her way to the Scottish border when she was taken gravely ill. The forty-six-year-old queen died in Richard de Weston's house at Harby, Nottinghamshire on 28 November. Her body needed three tombs as her intestines were to be buried at Lincoln Cathedral, her heart with that of her beloved son Alfonso at the London Domin-ican church and the rest of her in Westminster Abbey. The ceremony in the abbey on 17 December set a standard that would make the great building the focus of splendid regal ceremony through time to the coronation of Queen Elizabeth II, the funeral of Diana, Princess of Wales, and beyond. Besides the desire to give his wife a positive legend, and the ruling Plantaganets some excellent propaganda, Edward's devotions on his wife's death still owed much to the fact that he loved her deeply. In his own words she was a woman 'whom living we dearly cherished, and whom dead we cannot cease to love'.

Edward I went on to rule for seventeen more years. He married again and had four more children. During his thirty-three-year reign he strengthened the Crown and Parliament against the feudal nobility and oversaw great progress in administration and legal reform. After eight years of campaigning he succeeded in subduing Wales, his son Edward becoming the first Prince of Wales. He attempted to do the same to Scotland but, although he executed William Wallace and confiscated the Stone of Scone, the 'Hammer of the Scots', as he became known, never succeeded. He died on his way to put down a rebellion by Robert the Bruce.

Five hundred and seventy years after Eleanor's death, another great and powerful monarch was to be deeply saddened by the loss of her beloved spouse. After Queen Victoria's husband Prince Albert died in 1861, the leading architect of the Gothic revival, Sir George Gilbert Scott, sought inspiration for a lavish memorial to the prince consort. His design was a magnificent sculpted granite structure with a splendid gilded statue. His inspiration was the Eleanor cross.

CHAPTER 2

Man in Black

Because in his deeds in Spain he restored the true king to his throne after
his defeat, overthrowing the tyrant and making the kings of Navarre and
Majorca almost his subjects, his great power and qualities were such that
the Lord could have said to him, as to David, 'I have made thy name great
among the names of the great ones of the earth.'

Thomas Brinton, Bishop of Rochester, 1376

PEDRO I, KING OF CASTILE and León between 1350 and 1369,
was also known as Pedro El Cruel. You may be disappointed to
learn that, despite this label, he was probably not cruel at all. To
right the misnomer, the tag of his spiteful enemies, and call attention
to the firm execution of justice during his reign, some subsequent
historians have called him Pedro El Justiciero (the just or righteous).
During his reign his bastard half-brother Enrique de Trastamare was
desperate to get his hands on the throne. Enrique was supported by
Pedro IV of Aragon who, to confuse things, has also been called Pedro
El Cruel. He really did deserve the tag for the extreme malice he
displayed to anyone challenging his authority. Enrique bought Pedro
IV's support with a promise of one-sixth of Castile but Pedro I of
Castile and León inflicted a number of defeats on his namesake and
threatened to overrun his kingdom. Luckily for the Aragonese king,
France was an ally. The French king Charles V and the Pope joined
forces to pay for an army of French mercenaries to invade Castile and
put Enrique on the throne. Most of the mercenaries, with no war to
fight, had been passing the time ravaging France, so Charles V was
pleased to see them employed elsewhere. Early in March 1366 they
marched into Castile. Among their number were three English captains, Sir Hugh Calveley, Sir Thomas Dagworth and William Elmham,
who had ignored King Edward III's command forbidding Englishmen
to attack Castilian subjects. By the end of March Enrique had what
he wanted. He had been crowned in Burgos, King of Castile and León.

How could Pedro I hope to succeed against an army backed by
France? The only way he could hope to retrieve his kingdom now was

by finding external support himself. But where from? He did not have to think too hard. In Europe there lived a celebrated knight who had led his men against French armies with vastly superior numbers, and won! He was the quintessence of chivalry, a man who delighted in extravagant tournaments, falconry, hunting, fine clothes and jewels. Pedro would contact him and ask him for help. He would call in Edward, the Black Prince.

The Black Prince

KING EDWARD III'S eldest son, Edward, was born at the royal palace in Woodstock on 15 June 1330. Like his father, the young Edward showed little interest in books and learning. He wanted to be a knight. By 1336 he had attended his first tournament and by 1338 he was the proud owner of a full set of armour and a tent. With so many Edwards in the family at the time, it is good that he came to be known by another name, on account of the colour of his armour.

There was going to be plenty of opportunity to use his knightly skills. When he was just six, England and France embarked on what would come to be known as the Hundred Years' War. The trouble went back to 1066, when William the Conqueror won the Battle of Hastings. Although he became King William I of England, he was still the Duke of Normandy and a vassal of the French king. When the English king Henry II married Eleanor, Duchess of Aquitaine, another huge part of France, that bordering the Pyrenees and the Bay of Biscay in the south-west, came under the jurisdiction of the English monarch, but it was still under the ultimate authority of the King of France. The arrangement did not work well. Residents of English areas with a grievance would cause friction by going over the heads of their English masters to the authorities in Paris. Also, regardless of royal inheritances, the French monarchs wanted the English out. Meanwhile the French caused trouble in Edward's back yard, supporting the Scots in their war with England. French antagonism of the English also extended to the disruption of her highly profitable foreign wool trade.

Edward III had a strategy that went beyond denying that he was a vassal of the French king – he claimed the French throne for himself. When Charles IV of France died in 1328, there had been no male heir. Charles's cousin, Philip of Valois, had ascended the throne but Edward, a nephew of Charles, could argue that he was the rightful heir.

From the age of twelve, Edward, Prince of Wales, accompanied his father on campaigns abroad. When just sixteen he distinguished himself in the thick of the fighting at the Battle of Crécy. The battle, fought on 26 August 1346, was the culmination of a six-week rampage through northern France by ten thousand men bent on pillage and destruction. For his part in the spectacular victory, the prince was awarded three ostrich plumes and the motto *ich dien* (I serve), still used by the Prince of Wales today. King Edward followed up this success with the taking of Calais, whose gates opened to the English on Saturday 4 August 1347. The port was to remain English for two hundred years.

The following year, the Black Death came to Europe. One of the first English victims was the prince's fourteen-year-old sister. After the victory at Crécy, Edward III had concluded a marriage alliance with Alfonso IV of Castile: his second daughter Joan was to marry Alfonso's eldest son Pedro. However, the young bride-to-be died of the plague at Bordeaux in 1348, en route for Spain, and the Castilians promptly ended their alliance with the English and allied with the French. They assembled a large naval force to raid the English coast and prey on boats sailing to and from England's possessions in France. In the summer of 1350 they attacked the Gascon wine fleet as it headed for England. Ten ships were lost. The Spanish, under Admiral Carlos de la Cerda, then felt they had done enough and prepared to return home while the weather was still favourable. Meanwhile King Edward and the prince prepared to put to sea from Winchelsea in East Sussex to confront them. On 29 August around fifty English ships sailed out to meet the forty-seven Spanish vessels. As the ships closed, the English archers unleashed their deadly shower of steel-pointed arrows. The English boats crashed into the much larger Spanish ships and grappled them: the soldiers stormed aboard for the bitter and brutal fight to the death on the decks. It was a good evening's work for Edward's army: they captured half of the Spanish fleet. However, it was not decisive. There were concerns over what the ships that got away would do when they passed the coast of Aquitaine on the way home.

The prince returned to the maintenance of his authority in Aquitaine. In 1356 he commanded the English forces at the Battle of Poitiers. It was his finest hour. His six to eight thousand men were outnumbered two to one by the French, but he had his archers. His men first occupied defensive positions in the vineyards and above the sunken lanes but, once the longbowmen had turned the sky black, the English knights and men at arms went on the attack. A bloody struggle ensued. Eventually the French fell back without their King John, who gave himself up in a field beside the River Miosson, well aware that the prince would demand an enormous ransom for his freedom.

In the years before he lost his kingdom Pedro I of Castile and León had considered how England might be used to counter French support for his enemies. As a result, an Anglo-Castilian alliance was signed at St Paul's Cathedral in June 1362, England agreeing to go to Pedro's aid in the event of Castile being invaded. In July 1366 Pedro journeyed to Capbreton in Aquitaine to ask the Black Prince to honour this commitment. The task could not have been easier. With Aquitaine sharing a border with Castile, the last thing Prince Edward wanted was the heightened security risk of a pro-French monarch on the Castillian throne. But the Black Prince did not come cheap. He demanded a vast sum of money and the Basque province of Vizcaya, including the port of Bilbao. Pedro agreed. He knew he was promising too much but he wanted Castile back at any price.

The year 1367 started well for the prince when, on 6 January, his wife Joan gave birth to their second son at Bordeaux. The infant, who would one day be king, was christened Richard. One of his godfathers, who was visiting the prince at the time, was Jaime IV, the claimant to the kingdom of Mallorca.

On 14 February the prince's army departed from Saint-Jean-Pied-du-Port on the Aquitaine side of the Pyrenees and climbed towards the Pass of Roncesvalles, which leads into Navarre. Pedro I had already bought King John of Navarre's support by promising him land and money. By the end of the month the eight-thousand-strong force was at King John's capital, Pamplona. The army marched on, west towards Vitoria in the province of Alava, a place where 446 years later the army of Wellington would also seek battle. Over the years the provincial borders within countries change. Alava is now part of the autonomous community of Euskadi – the Basque Country – but then it was part of Castile. The first Castilian town that the prince's army came to was Salvatierra. After a short fight it opened its gates.

After six days of rest the army marched the twenty miles to Vitoria where Enrique's army was also heading. The prince and his army were poised to attack but Enrique was not going to give them the pleasure of a pitched battle yet. His horsemen attacked the prince's foragers by day and English encampments by night. They plunged swords into sleeping men and captured the bemused and rudely awakened. The terrain favoured such guerrilla tactics and was poor for forage so the prince decided to lead his men south-east, back into Navarre. There they turned and took a south-westerly route back to Castile, which they entered at Logroño on 1 April. Today, Logrono's prosperity comes from the Rioja wine trade; six and a half centuries ago it was also important as a crossing place of the Ebro, where Navarre bordered Castile, and as a town on the Camino de Santiago, which a number of the prince's men would previously have trodden. Fifteen miles further west, on the far bank of the Rio Najerilla, Enrique waited in the town of Nájera. On Friday 2 April the prince advanced along the Camino de Santiago to Navarette while Enrique left the town and crossed the bridge to camp in the open fields where he would do battle.

The prince used the cover of darkness to move north-east of the enemy so that, on the morning of 3 April, Enrique was forced into emergency manoeuvres to meet the onslaught. Edward's very mixed force of English and Castilian knights, Navarese, Majorcan and Gascon troops, and of course English archers, moved against an equally mixed force which included the best Castilian troops and, of course, the French. As the English vanguard under John of Gaunt went in, a deadly cloud of arrows flew over their heads into Enrique's ranks. A bitter hand-to-hand struggle ensued in which men yelled, lances pierced, swords slashed, horses whinnied and the mutilated screamed. The prince reacted to Enrique's men forcing him back by ordering his two flanks forward. Enrique's flanks did not have the stomach for the fight; they withdrew, leaving all the prince's men to concentrate on the Castilian troops, who buckled under such pressure. Many of Enrique's men were slaughtered or captured as they fled back towards Nájera. Great numbers perished, drowned in the river, cut down in the struggle at the bridge and slaughtered in the carnage that descended on the town. Enrique himself got away, leaving five to six thousand dead and two thousand prisoners. That night, the prince celebrated in the great comfort of Enrique's camp.

The following Wednesday, 7 April, Pedro regained Burgos and his throne in the city where the most famous Catillian nobleman, El Cid, was entombed. The prince stayed at the monastery of Las Huelgas. The job done, he wished to collect his payment and get out. But he had only to look around him, at the poverty of the place, to realise he would be lucky to get what he wanted. The new and vulnerable government was in no position to demand its subjects hand over huge amounts of cash to the Prince of Wales, or that the Basque province of Vizcaya switch allegiance. The prince himself was winning no friends as his hungry men captured and damaged communities in search of provisions. As Pedro travelled through Castile, in a genuine but futile effort to gather the payment, the prince's army moved on to Valladolid and then to Medina del Campo, one of the foremost market towns of Europe, before heading back towards Navarre via Soria. The prince fell very ill with a type of dysentery; it was probably this which prompted him to head home in late August. He was reunited with his wife Joan and eldest son Edward in Bordeaux early in September.

The expedition had achieved its principle objective, but at great cost to the Black Prince who now had to deal with an unpaid army and a disgruntled Aquitaine public unwilling to finance his debts through higher taxes. He struggled to keep control as Charles V aggravated the situation all he could. In 1370 Edward destroyed the city of Limoges, which had risen against him. With his illness returning in ever worsening bouts he decided to return to England.

Enrique did not abandon his desire to rule Castile. Supported by Charles V, he returned with more French troops and, less than two years after the rout at Nájera, defeated Pedro at Montiel. The prince's slim hope that Pedro would settle his account evaporated when Enrique de Trastamare personally put his half-brother to the sword.

The Black Prince never fully recovered his health after his Spanish adventure, and died at Westminster in 1376. He was buried alongside his favourite saint, Thomas Beckett, in Canterbury Cathedral. His father was a king and his son Richard (II) was a king. Never attaining the throne probably did not trouble him as it did Don Juan de Bourbon, the present Spanish king's father. His great territorial responsibilities and prowess in battle meant that the people of western Europe saw him as a king in all but title.

CHAPTER 3

Catherine
England's Beloved Spanish Queen

And if a man shall take his brother's wife, it is an unclean thing: he hath
uncovered his brother's nakedness; they shall be childless.

Leviticus 20:21

Spain 1492

FOR OVER HALF a millennium the Spanish have marvelled at how
incredible a year 1492 was. No sooner had Christian Spain
wrested back its old Iberian world from the Moors than Christopher Columbus appeared at Court with dreams of a new American
world awaiting exploitation.

The last Moorish king of Granada retreated from the splendid
Alhambra as his mother scolded him for weeping like a woman over
that which he had not defended like a man. His sorrow was in sharp
contrast to the joy of King Ferdinand of Aragon and Queen Isabella
of Castile that January day as they rode through the gates of that
beautiful city with their five children. The youngest was six-year-old
Catherine. Fair-skinned, with auburn hair and blue-grey eyes, she
was not destined to spend her adult days in the warm Iberian sun,
but far north in a land more accustomed to damp, fog and short
winter days. The daughter of Spain's greatest royal couple would
marry a notorious English king. The magnificent splendour of her
origins would make her later treatment and her humble end all the
more pitiful.

Queen Isabella's fourth daughter Catherine was born at Alcalá de
Henares on 16 December 1485. The fact that Isabella's mother was
Catherine of Lancaster probably accounted for the fairness of them all;
it also meant that they could count Alfred the Great and Henry II
among their ancestors. Being the child of great and powerful rulers
had its advantages, but it also meant your parents could use you as a
pawn. Hardly out of childhood, you might be placed at some foreign

court, chosen not for your own happiness but for the political benefits it would bring your family.

England 1499

KING HENRY VII looked to Europe for suitable alliances for his sons
Arthur, Prince of Wales, and Henry, Duke of York. They needed to be
carefully chosen as Henry still felt vulnerable at home. He had won
his crown years earlier at Bosworth Field, defeating Richard of York,
but there were still adversaries at large whom he saw as a threat to
his position.

After negotiations in which the Spanish envoy rejected Henry's
demands for a greater dowry, it being seen as sufficient that Ferdinand and Isabella condescended to send their daughter to a lesser
court, the marriage of England's Prince Arthur and Spain's Princess
Catherine was arranged. On Whit Sunday 1499 the two thirteen-year-
olds were married by proxy at Bewdley Manor in Worcestershire. Two
years later Henry VII prepared for Catherine's arrival. He instructed
that all the ladies-in-waiting from Spain should be beautiful. The English ambassador clarified this for Queen Isabella's benefit: their beauty
would ensure that they attracted English husbands and remained in
England as company for her daughter. Delayed by tempestuous seas,
Catherine and her retinue finally arrived at Plymouth on 2 October
1501. A delighted Prince Arthur set eyes on his Spanish princess for
the first time at the Bishop of Bath's Palace in Dogmersfield.

It was a match that pleased the people of England, not least the
merchants who anticipated good trading opportunities offered by
peace with powerful Spain. King Ferdinand looked forward to enjoying new support on the European stage, while Henry VII would consolidate his position at home and raise his profile abroad. On Sunday
14 November 1501 the atmosphere in London was one of joy and optimism. The royal wedding spun its magic and moved everyone to a
sense of joy as they filled the streets to see the characters of this Tudor
fairy tale. After the Archbishop of Cantebury had married the two the
festivities began, but as the knights fought to unseat each other the
newly-wed Arthur struggled to keep up with the pace.

That night fifteen-year-old Arthur and sixteen-year-old Catherine
were publicly bedded down. Exactly what happened next was to be
become the subject of intense public speculation. Some were to argue
strongly that the couple simply fell asleep and that the marriage was
not consummated in the next five months. These same people would

later insist that there was no way Arthur could have lain so long with his beautiful princess without touching her.

On 2 April 1502 the fairy tale came to an abrupt end. Arthur, Prince of Wales, fell victim to the plague which had taken hold in the country around the couple's home at Ludlow Castle. The grief-stricken Princess Catherine, still only sixteen and married for just five months, was a widow. She mourned her husband, so tragically deprived of a bright, exciting future, and lamented that she was now alone in a land which, until then, had proudly looked on her as a future queen. The value of Ferdinand's pawn, carefully moved to the Tudor court, had been nullified by Arthur's dying breath.

Ferdinand and Isabella were shocked by the news but it did not take them long to decide what they should do. Still valuing a strong alliance with England – they were fighting the French at the time – they decided their daughter should marry Arthur's younger brother Henry, Duke of York. Henry was very different from his brother. He expended great energy in riding, playing tennis and dancing; he also displayed a sharp intellect and a keen talent for languages and music. There were potential obstacles, however. The Pope might not permit it, it being against the rules of the Church for a man to take his brother's wife. Even if the Pope were to allow the union, the people might not accept his dispensation if they believed a judgement on such a matter to be beyond his authority. The chances of re-establishing the alliance between Spain and England would therefore rest on the conviction that Catherine was still a virgin.

When Henry VII's wife, the beautiful and popular Queen Elizabeth, died a week after giving birth in February 1503, he thought about marrying Catherine himself. But Isabella preferred her daughter to take a husband with a long life ahead of him; she did not want Spanish influence prematurely curtailed yet again. Henry, who had been in no hurry to agree a marriage treaty for his son, finally did so in June 1503, persuaded by his reluctance to return Catherine's dowry of a hundred thousand crowns. The matter of the papal dispensation was taken care of by the dying Isabella, who cunningly published it against the Pope's instructions. Catherine's life was now back on track. No longer the abandoned princess or the unfortunate expense Henry VII had been reluctant to maintain, she was back where she had left off, in Ludlow, a future queen of England.

Whilst Queen Isabella had striven to secure the betrothal of her daughter before her life came to a close, her very death set off a train of events which meant that, for the second time, Catherine was to find herself alone. With Isabella's death, Castile passed to her weak daughter Juana. Juana's husband was Philip, son of the Flemish-based Holy Roman Emperor Maximillian. Under Maximillian's influence the Anglo-Spanish trade treaty which supported the livelihoods of so many English sailors and merchants, was cancelled. The Spanish action angered England. Prince Henry reacted by reconsidering his future marriage to a daughter of the offending nation. Citing concerns that an illegitimate marriage might undermine his future authority, and that, in any case, he had not been an adult when it was agreed, he asked that the treaty be invalidated. On 27 June 1505 the Privy Council did just that and Catherine's dreams faded once more.

King Philip and Castile's Queen Juana had not planned to visit England in January 1506 but in those days of sail an unpredictable wind could change an itinerary. Catherine's sister Juana and her husband had just left the Netherlands for Spain when the elements conspired to divert them to England's shores. Catherine's short family reunion at Windsor was marred by her observation that all was not well with her unhappy sister. Despite the diversion of the visit, things were equally unsatisfactory for Catherine. She was destitute. She had no income from Ferdinand and none from Henry.

After the visitors returned to Spain Ferdinand cunningly regained Castile by the mysterious death of Philip and imprisonment of Juana. Once more he had reason and time enough to think of Catherine. He made her his ambassadress.

Despite Prince Henry's rejection of Catherine, the two continued to frequent the same society. She had a great affection for the vivacious, handsome prince and Henry had a lot of time for his bother's widow. His father, less happy with the relationship, put a stop to it. While saddening Henry and Catherine, the ban probably did the long-term prospects of the relationship a power of good.

Henry VII was still casting about for a new wife. His thoughts turned to Juana, his unexpected visitor in January 1506. He remembered Catherine's sister's beauty, and the fact that Castile was hers. The new ambassadress communicated Henry's interest but Ferdinand would have nothing of it, insisting his daughter Juana was mad and unfit to remarry.

On 22 April 1509 Henry VII died at Richmond. His death was to have as great an effect on the fortunes of Catherine as the death of her first husband. But this time the effect was positive. Prince Henry and Catherine had started seeing each other again as King Henry grew weaker. The prince told her of his love for her and his wish that she should be his queen. The lonely princess, forced to scratch out an existence on no income, treated so poorly by so many around her, saw the tables turn dramatically.

Henry and Catherine were married in secret on 11 June 1509. On Midsummer's Day in St Pauls Cathedral, Catherine, dressed in virginal white satin and gold, was crowned queen alongside her new husband, King Henry VIII. The people rejoiced for the handsome couple. She had won their hearts the day she first arrived in the land. He also was well loved. Tall, strong, intelligent and sociable, he was the archetypal king. The loving couple had to wait only until the autumn for more good news: Catherine was pregnant. Henry particularly wanted a son to guarantee his succession; Catherine just wanted a healthy child to end suspicions that her alliance with Henry was illegitimate and would be punished by infertility. This view was not widely held but it bubbled beneath the surface until finally proved groundless.

On 31 January 1510 Catherine gave birth to a girl. Sadly, she was dead. The queen soon became pregnant again, but at a time when she needed Henry's support she discovered his attentions had wandered to a mistress, Lady Fitzwater. He was furious that she had found out, and the stress caused her to miscarry. The triple agonies of 1510 looked as if they could all be part of a bad dream when, on New Year's Day 1511, the king and queen had their prayers answered: they were blessed with the arrival of a boy. On 22 February, to his parents' utter despair, the baby died.

The root of the queen's problems, which would cloud the years, was her terrible misfortune in not providing Henry with a male heir. Henry's frustration on the domestic front was compounded by his failure on the world stage which, unfortunately for Catherine, was due largely to her father, King Ferdinand. Ferdinand never stopped to consider the embarrassment he caused his daughter as he repeatedly double-crossed her ambitious but naive husband. When Henry realised the Spanish king's duplicity he did not have to look far for another Spaniard to scold and berate.

On 7 June 1512 ten thousand English soldiers landed at the coastal town of Hondarribia, close to the French border in the Spanish Basque country. Ferdinand had promised to help Henry in a conquest of Guienne in south-west France but the Spanish troops never arrived as they were busy trying to add Navarre to Ferdinand's possessions. Indiscipline and illness afflicted the English army, which attacked villages before heading home with two thousand fewer than had arrived.

The following summer Henry made Catherine his regent and took an invasion force to France. While he was away Scotland's James IV raised a huge army. Catherine, a true daughter of Isabella, the victorious warrior queen of Castile, sent off an army which defeated the Scots in a hard-fought battle at Flodden Hill. Henry returned home exulting over the victory and his wife's handling of the affair. Then the old ghost reappeared. The couple's happiness was overturned by the birth of another dead son.

Henry proceeded with his plans to take part of France, with Ferdinand's help. However the Spanish king kept stalling. When pushed he said he needed more time, then soldiers, then money. Those surrounding Henry grew suspicious of Ferdinand's inactivity, a tide of opinion Catherine fought against as she strove to assure her husband that her father would keep to his promises. When the truth came out, Ferdinand's envoy Don Luis Caroz had to escape from the mob in the streets but there was no escape for the queen. While maintaining that an Anglo-Spanish alliance stood strong and that its fruit would be an imminent attack on France, Ferdinand had been negotiating with the enemy for marriage alliances and even a joint attack on some of Henry's possessions. Catherine bore the brunt of Henry's anger and finally realised that her faith in her father's integrity had been misplaced. He was a manipulative and dishonest man of great ambition. It would not pay her to defend him in future. It was clear he had never taken her well-being into account when blithely humiliating her inexperienced husband. Catherine's swing of loyalty angered Don Luis Caroz.

After making peace with France, Henry and his wife escorted his sister Princess Mary to Dover from where she departed for the land whose king she was to marry. Amongst her retinue was fourteen-year-old Anne Boleyn.

Already distressed by the loss of so many infants and the treacherous behaviour of her father, Catherine was further saddened by the continued adultery of her husband. Whilst another pregnancy offered the queen some hope, she had to tolerate Henry's well-known visits to Bessie Blount in Newhall, in Essex. She desperately hoped for a healthy child to draw Henry back to her. All the prayers the deeply devout queen could offer were to come to nothing. She was delivered of another boy who lived for only a short time. The old gossip about her being unable to bear a child because of the illegitimacy of her marriage surfaced again.

Perhaps it was because Catherine had suffered rejection and

abandonment that she had so much time for the poor and dispossessed of England. At this time the country's wool trade was prospering to the great detriment of the production of food. Enclosed plots for the rearing of sheep took over common land previously cultivated, depriving families of their only means of feeding themselves. Catherine was touched by their predicament and tried to help, contributing to charities and even passing on her art of lace-making. The people held her in great affection and dearly wished that she could produce the baby she so longed for and deserved. Theirs and Catherine's prayers were finally answered when on 18 February 1516 the gossips were muted and the succession strengthened by the birth of a healthy living child, Princess Mary.

Meanwhile, homelessness, unemployment and poverty were spreading. Amongst all the strife an ugly mob congregated and chose its scapegoat. On May Day 1517 foreigners and their businesses were attacked in a violent orgy of xenophobic rage. The authorities acted firmly, ordering hangings and imprisonment for members of the mob. Catherine, who had waited so long for a child, stepped in on behalf of the desparate mothers who were about to lose theirs. As they gratefully welomed her intervention, it was not lost on them that her compassion was never compromised by the fact that many of the victims had been of her own Spanish race.

The royal couple continued to try for more children. Catherine was the daughter of a strong, powerful and successful queen, so in her eyes the birth of their daughter Mary had guaranteed the succession. Henry's country, however, had never witnessed the successful reign of a queen; for him the birth of a son was still vital. On 18 November 1518, child number six, a girl, was born. A few hours later she was dead. The sorrow and despair of both parents mounted. It was tempered for Henry, but deepened for Catherine, seven months later when the king's mistress gave birth to a healthy boy. If God had not allowed her to bear Henry's son because she had been married to his brother, where was the justice in Henry's harlot being delivered of a healthy son? Catherine now suffered daily reminders of her failures as Henry Fitzroy was brought to court.

When Catherine had first arrived in England, her political status had been very high. She was the daughter of a powerful and respected king and queen. As Ferdinand's deeds lowered the prestige of Spain in the eyes of the English, increasingly Catherine's status came to depend on her personal standing in England. Then in 1519 the importance of her family connections increased when her nephew Charles

was elected Holy Roman Emperor. Ruling a large area of central northern Europe along with Spain and its possessions, there was not a ruler
who commanded more territory in the world. In late May he met
Henry at Dover Castle, going on to Cantebury to meet the queen.

With Bessie Blount married off and banished, Henry's attentions
moved to the daughter of his first mistress, now one of the queen's
ladies-in-waiting. Her name was Mary Boleyn. At the time her sister
Anne occupied a similar post at the French court.

In 1521 the French king sent an army south and seized Hondarribia
and Navarre, which had the effect of driving Spain and England
together. Henry's right-hand man, Cardinal Thomas Wolsey, sailed
for the Continent, where he agreed that England would declare war
on France. This was no ordinary alliance based on a future military
commitment. It stood out from similar agreements in that it was
bound by the understanding that King Henry and Queen Catherine's
daughter Mary would marry powerful Charles when she came of age.
Furthermore, should Henry not have a son, then the eldest male child
of Charles and Mary would one day be King of England. Queen
Catherine, who had been so disappointed when her daughter had
earlier been betrothed to the Dauphin of France, could not have hoped
for a better partner for Mary. A united England and Spain would
be pushing together instead of against each other. Charles visited
England again to plan the action against France and to celebrate his
betrothal to Mary.

During recent years the pace of progress in the arts, sciences and
other disciplines had started to quicken. There was a sea change in
European thought, some of which would manifest itself in local
reassessments of religious values. The queen supported the 'new learning', contributing to the founding of St Paul's School and the Royal
College of Physicians. She wanted to make sure that her daughter
would be ready to rule wisely and that her education would reflect the
progress of the time as well as her cosmopolitan background. Catherine and the Spanish scholar Juan Luis Vives put together an impressive programme. The young Mary was joined in her classes by the
fortunate children of other noblemen. Catherine contributed to a fast
stream of advanced education for some of the most important players
of the Elizabethan age. Although Henry adored his daughter Mary,
unlike Catherine he did not regard her as his heir to be prepared in
all disciplines for her great responsibilities ahead.

The alliance with Charles was too good to be true; it was not long
before it showed signs of cracking. Henry had invested troops and

money in Continental gains but only Charles had seemed to reap the benefits. The situation reminded many of the fruitless support given to the treacherous Ferdinand. Suspicion grew into short-sighted over-reaction as Wolsey expelled Charles's ambassador for reporting back on the Cardinal's negotiations for peace with France. The cutting of diplomatic ties disregarded the bigger picture, which included the marriage treaty. Wolsey's foolish action had been backed by Henry, but it incensed Catherine; it was soon to prove costly.

After scoring a terrific victory over the French King Francis at Pavia, Charles needed to liaise with Henry as he wanted money to pay his troops. Communication would have served Henry well as he was keen to have part of defeated France. However nothing was straightfor-ward: Henry was having trouble raising money and Charles was now drawn into a marriage with Isabella of Portugal, whose dowry was nearly three times that of Mary. The lack of a communication chan-nel crippled England's ambitions but suited Charles: he could delay settling his financial debts to England, he would not have to cooper-ate in making her uncomfortably powerful by procuring vast areas of France, and he could go ahead and collect the large dowry that mar-riage to Isabella brought. If Henry later protested, Charles could claim he had needed to pay his army, and because his ambassador had been expelled from England he had unfortunately needed to seek a solu-tion elsewhere. When an English delegation went to Spain, Charles demanded a loan, Mary's dowry, and that the young princess be sent to him. Even if Henry and Catherine had been able to satisfy the first two demands, the third was out of the question and Charles knew it. Henry had been outplayed again.

And again Catherine was to pay the price for the way her family had treated her husband. She and Henry ceased to live together as man and wife, so gone was the chance of her giving him a son. Although Catherine had provided an heir, it was clear that Henry was keeping his options open: he granted various titles to his illegitimate son Henry Fitzroy. The queen's life now entered a new phase: she would have to fight not only to defend her daughter's right to the suc-cession, but also her position as queen.

When two of Catherine's ladies-in-waiting were sent away by Wolsey for refusing his demands to spy on her, Catherine was glad to accept Anne Boleyn as a replacement, even though her elder sister was the king's current mistress. She was upset when Anne moved on again, after her ill-fated romance with Lord Henry Percy.

The King's Great Matter

HENRY ENCOUNTERED ANNE in the garden of her father's house at Hever in 1525. As he had been instrumental in preventing her union with the man she loved, she had little time for him. The king was not used to being treated indifferently and his interest was awakened by a woman hard to get. Little did he know the chase would last six long, frustrating years.

Henry started visiting Hever more often. If Anne was still lamenting the loss of Lord Henry Percy then others in her family, such as her father Sir Thomas, were more concerned with the future. Always on the look-out for routes to political gain, their thinking finally rubbed off on Anne and she realised the great potential of her situation. Queen Catherine, who had never coped well with the British climate, was suffering increasingly from poor health. Should the woman brought up under the Andalusian sun finally succumb to England's cold and damp, then Anne might be queen. Anne decided she would not yield to Henry's charms and fall into line as his mistress for little personal gain, as her mother and sister had done. She wanted more. If she was to give herself to him it would be in return for the greatest prize of all, and she did not mind how long she would have to wait.

Queen Catherine had been married to the king for seventeen years and now she was being pushed aside by a former lady-in-waiting to whom she had shown much compassion during the Lord Henry Percy affair. The usurper was sharing her husband's social life at court and joining him on hunting expeditions. Catherine realised that, despite her ill health, she would have to attend court more often. It was ironic that Anne's threat to Catherine's position was all the greater because she refused to become the king's mistress. He was now madly in love. He had to have her and, as she would allow him his way only if they were married, the only option open to him was to divorce Catherine.

Henry probably convinced himself that arranging a divorce would not be too difficult. It was not as if he was asking the Pope to set a precedent: dispensation had previously been granted in the cases of a number of royal marriages, including that of King Louis XII of France. Until then he had enjoyed good relations with the Vatican. On the domestic front Henry would leave the organisation to Wolsey. As for Catherine, she was such a devout Christian he foresaw little trouble in persuading her into a convent. However, Henry's optimism faded when his Council shied away from making a judgement on the matter, the public expressed indignation and Catherine demonstrated that she would not go quietly.

The simple fact was that Henry wanted a divorce because he desired a pretty, fit young bride who could provide him with an heir. However, such desires were not grounds for divorce; he was obliged to create a justification. It had suited him eighteen years before to support Catherine's assertion that her marriage to Arthur had never been consummated; now he turned around and professed his concern that he had been living in sin with his brother's wife. As everyone knew Henry's real reason for wanting a divorce, his argument lacked all credibility and integrity. The bishops ruled that Pope Julius II's original dispensation permitting Henry to marry his brother's widow remained valid.

On 6 May 1527 dramatic and violent events in Rome shocked the Christian world and ensured that, far away in England, the king would never obtain the papal dispensation he so craved. Unpaid by Charles, the imperial army was out of control. Attracted by the wealth of Rome, it sacked the city: its people and property were exposed to eight days of pillage, desecration, wounding, rape and death. Pope Clement was now terrified of upsetting Charles; facilitating the mistreatment of the Holy Roman Emperor's aunt was the last thing he was going to do.

Before Henry had had the audacity to confess his concerns to his wife and suggest she enter a convent, he could have spent little time considering the consequences of a divorce from her point of view. For such a deeply religious woman accepting that she had lived as a mistress for so many years and produced so many infants by a man whom it would have been a mortal sin to marry, would be condemning herself to everlasting damnation. The daughter of Queen Isabella and King Ferdinand could not and would not condemn her own soul, give up her legitimate place on the throne and make her daughter Mary a bastard with no hope of succeeding to the throne.

Henry realised he himself could never persuade his resolute wife to go willingly. On a matter of such profound importance, affecting not just her and her daughter's titles but also their spiritual welfare, she could be guided only by the Pope. If Henry wanted Catherine to change her mind, he had to sway the Vatican first.

In the absence of proper diplomatic channels, Diego Hurtado de Mendoza had been sent to England by Charles. Prevented from seeing Catherine, his spies provided him with information. He had earlier asked Charles to prepare the Pope for the divorce request he was to receive from the English court. Now he had no doubt of where

English public opinion stood, asserting that, were six or seven thousand soldiers to be put ashore in Cornwall to fight for Catherine's cause, they would soon be joined by forty thousand Englishmen. Rebellion had often been discussed, but Catherine dismissed offers of military help.

Henry sent his delegations to Rome, and the Pope procrastinated. Granting Henry's wishes would provoke Charles. His hands were tied. The only option open to him was to leave things as they were. Finally, he authorized the holding of a Legatine Court. Cardinal Wolsey would preside with an Italian cardinal to decide the king's Great Matter. Cardinal Lorenzo Campeggio was ordered to travel to England as slowly as possible; when he arrived he was to try to resolve the matter out of court and thus avoid the Vatican's having to take sides. If it came to a court decision, it would have to be referred to the Vatican before coming into force. The cardinal was of advanced years and in poor health. Accepting that his own death might not be far off, like Catherine he was unwilling to make a judgement which might condemn his soul to eternal damnation.

The cardinal arrived to the sight of crowds noisily protesting against Anne's replacing their beloved queen. Cardinal Wolsey made it clear to him what the judgement of the Legatine Court was expected to be, threatening that if Henry did not have his way Rome's authority over England would end.

Before the court sat, Catherine shot a broadside into Henry's case. She produced a document, supplementary to Julius II's original dispensation, which covered any omissions of the bull and thereby diminished Henry's claims that it had been deficient. An angry Henry sent for the original document, which was in Spain. Charles held on to it.

On 8 November 1528, in an attempt to consolidate support, Henry addressed an assembly of principal citizens at Bridewell Palace. He appealed to their indebtedness to him – they had all prospered during his reign – and impressed on them the dangers of a disputed succession. However, his speech was undermined by an assertion so outrageously hypocritical that one wonders whether he kept a straight face when delivering it: '... if I were to marry again I would choose her above all women. But, if it is determined in judgement that our marriage is against God's law, then shall I sorrow parting from so good a lady and loving companion.'

Cardinal Campeggio failed to get Henry to drop his divorce demands, or persuade Catherine to go quietly. Equally, he himself was not persuaded by the offer of a handsome bribe, the wealthy bishopric of Durham. The case was therefore placed before the Legatine Court; it summoned the king and queen of England for trial in the Great Hall of the Monastery of the Blackfriars on Monday 21 June 1529. It was most rare for the two highest citizens in the land to be in the dock in their own country. Catherine, who passed through cheering crowds when entering and leaving court, pleaded for justice as Henry's counsel sought to prove her marriage to Arthur had indeed been consummated. Sir Anthony Willoughby's testimony did all it could to degrade the queen's dignity. He avouched that, on the morning after the wedding, Arthur demanded ale to quench his thirst for he had 'been in Spain that night'.

After many had risked their futures to testify in defence of the queen, and the king's men had done all they could to undermine the legitimacy of the original papal bull, the court nervously awaited Cardinal Campeggio's verdict. However, he was not to send one side of the court into raptures of relief and elation and condemn the other to shock and dejection. The master of anticlimax declared that he would have to consult the Pope.

While all this was happening, Anne was becoming increasingly frustrated: if she was not to marry Henry she was wasting her best years. Her family, nevertheless, had been profiting nicely with new earldoms and other trappings. Henry chose to send Anne Boleyn's father to the coronation of Charles, hardly a choice to please the host. Sir Thomas Boleyn took with him the offer of a bribe, but Catherine's nephew was above selling his aunt. Charles in turn upset Henry by presenting Sir Thomas with a summons from the Pope for the king to attend the hearing of Catherine's appeal at the supreme court in Rome. Henry's answer was to announce to the Church that Rome no longer held authority. He was now 'The Protector and Supreme Head of the Church of England'.

In July 1531 the king, queen and Princess Mary were at Windsor. Anne was also there, and it was with her that Henry set off on a hunting trip early on the eleventh. Regretting that she had not been up to see him leave, Catherine wrote to him. He replied, cruelly berating her for causing him so much trouble and forbidding her to write to him again. Catherine was never to see her husband again. More than a year later, when the one man who still prevented the divorce, the Archbishop of Canterbury, passed away, Anne saw that she was now almost at the finishing line, that there was no turning back, and finally gave in to Henry.

The defeated Catherine still drew much strength from the people, whom she continued to visit. She knew that, whilst Anne might parade in palaces at Henry's side, the public still saw Catherine as their rightful queen.

On 25 January 1533 Henry and Anne Boleyn were married, his first marriage having been declared null and void. On 5 July 1533 an official proclamation stripped Catherine of her title. She had bitterly accepted the loss of her husband, home and jewels (collected one day so that Anne could wear them) but she refused to accept that she had not been married to Henry. She would never admit that she had lived in sin for twenty-four years.

After the considerable problems of the preceding six years Henry prayed that his pregnant wife would present him with a son. Ironically, Anne gave birth to a baby girl who was made Princess of Wales, her seventeen-year-old half-sister being demoted to Lady Mary. The new mother, in an act of great insensitivity, had the gall to send to Catherine for Mary's Spanish christening robe for the baby Elizabeth to wear. Not surprisingly the request was furiously turned down.

The king and Parliament then acted to formalise his new position as head of the Church and that of his daughter Princess Elizabeth as heir to the throne. A new terror now gripped the country as the authorities punished any who would not swear allegiance to the Oath of Supremacy or Act of Succession. Catherine was greatly distressed by this wider suffering which spiralled from her rift with Henry. Many disagreed with the Act of Succession but did not think it worth disputing: if people more powerful than they had decided Elizabeth should succeed Henry, then so be it. However, the Oath of Supremacy was a different matter: accepting that could adversely effect their spiritual well-being. By supporting the severance with Rome, they would be offending God. Like Catherine and Mary, they were not prepared to play along with the politics of this world if it would condemn them to eternal damnation in the next. Perhaps the most distinguished victim of conscience was the greatly respected and popular Sir Thomas More, who accepted the change in succession but not supremacy. Despite the pleas of a loving family, he went to his death by beheading on 6 July 1535. Back in Spain, Charles was appalled.

Catherine's depression grew as her ex-husband created martyrs throughout the land. Spiritually she might have preferred to join them, but even Henry understood that the people would never tolerate her martyrdom. Catherine was also distressed about her sickly daughter, whose doctor feared she was being slowly poisoned.

Callously Henry prohibited mother and daughter from seeing each other.

As 1535 drew to a close, Catherine grew weaker and weaker. Fortunately her last few days were made easier by the unexpected and unauthorised visit of her beloved friend Maria de Salinas, who had been with her when she had first journeyed to England over thirty-four years previously. During the intervening years Maria had married, but when her husband Lord Willoughby had died she had returned to Catherine's side. After being deprived of her title Catherine had been forced to move from Ampthill to Buckden and Henry had ordered that Maria de Salinas should not go with her. It was 7 January 1536 and, as Catherine lay dying in Kimbolton Castle, Maria wrote down her final moving words to Henry: 'For my part I pardon you everything. I commend unto you our daughter Mary, beseeching you to be a good father unto her ... Lastly I make this vow, that mine eyes desire you above all things.' She then doggedly signed it: Catherine, Queen of England.'

At 2 o'clock that afternoon the candle blew out. Anne celebrated, the people mourned and Henry wept for the loss of a woman whom he had once loved so very much. Despite his tears he was not sentimental enough to make gestures or concessions, dismissing suggestions of a state funeral at St Pauls on the grounds of expense and ordering her interrment in Peterborough Abbey as the princess dowager, widow of Arthur. He did not attend the ceremony on 29 January and prevented Mary from doing so. Seven years later her resting place became a cathedral. She lies beneath a flower-covered stone slab on the north side of the sanctuary. Above hang two standards, one bearing the royal arms of Henry VIII, the other the arms of Aragon, Castile and León with her own personal emblem, the pomegranate of Granada. On the opposite wall, a plaque from the town hall of her birthplace Alcalá de Henares commemorates its formal twinning with Peterborough, the final resting place of Catherine, England's beloved Spanish queen.

CHAPTER 4

Bloody Mary

30 ml of vodka, 125 ml of tomato juice, 2 dashes of Worcester sauce, a good squeeze of lemon juice, a dash of Tabasco sauce, salt and pepper to taste and a slice of lemon. Shake all the ingredients together with ice and strain into a tumbler or balloon wine glass. Add a sprig of mint or stick of celery to decorate.

Recipe for a Bloody Mary

The queen, being born of a Spanish mother, was always inclined towards that nation, scorning to the English, and boasting of her descent from Spain.

Venetian Ambassador to England, 1554

They [the English] loudly proclaim that they are going to be enslaved, for the queen is a Spanish woman at heart and thinks nothing of Englishmen, but only of Spaniards and bishops.

Imperial Ambassador to England, 1554

SHE WAS THE GRANDDAUGHTER of the warrior queen, Isabella of Castile and the daughter of Henry VIII's long-suffering Spanish queen, Catherine of Aragon; her first betrothed and principle adviser would be the Spanish king and Holy Roman Emperor, Charles V; she would marry a Spanish king, Philip II; she would pray in Spanish. She was Mary Tudor, born in the palace of Greenwich on Monday 18 February 1516.

Henry VIII had wanted a son but, as his wife Catherine seemed unlikely to bear more children, he had to concede that this child would be his heir, and as such she was raised. Mary grew up at a time when Spain was a European superpower. Her grandparents, Isabella and Ferdinand, had led the successful fight to wrest the country back from the Moors at the end of the previous century. Now King of Spain, Charles V, had a fantastically rich empire that included the Netherlands, Burgundy in France, much of South and Central America and parts of Italy. As Holy Roman Emperor he could also count Germany amongst his possessions.

Charles V did not look to marry one of the ladies of his rich empire; he looked to England and his four-year-old cousin, Mary. Henry could not have wished for a wealthier, more powerful suitor for his daughter, and responded favourably to Charles's offer. Late in the summer of 1522 Mary was betrothed to the emperor. Her future looked dazzling. Not only was she being raised as heir to the throne of England but now she would also be empress of half the known world. The two met when Charles visited Windsor. Realistically, it was unlikely they would ever marry. They would have to wait six years, until Mary came of age. Charles, a man in his mid-twenties, was sure to look elsewhere before then, be it for political or romantic reasons. Mary was not destined to marry Charles, but for the moment she could believe she would. One thing was certain: she would never forget him. Mary was just nine when Charles found a wife of suitable political connections and age in Princess Isabella of Portugal.

In that same year, 1525, Mary's future as heir to the English throne was threatened by a young boy three years her junior. In 1519, Henry VIII's mistress Bessie Blount had given Henry what his wife could not, a healthy son. With no legitimate male heir, Henry worried about the future of the Tudor dynasty. In English history there was no precedent of a successful queen. To produce her own heir his daughter Mary would have to marry but, at a time when no woman had ever handled the affairs of state in England, it was assumed that whoever she married would hold the reins of power. Mary's marrying an Englishman might provoke unrest amongst different factions in the land; some would feel jealous and threatened by the sudden elevation of one of their peers. On the other hand, marrying a foreigner would threaten the independence of the kingdom. Henry decided to keep his options open. To the horror of his wife and daughter he elevated his mistress's son to the titles of Earl of Nottingham and Duke of Richmond and sent the six-year-old Henry Fitzroy north with a large household. He was deemed to have precedence over Mary.

Before Mary had much time to resent her downgrading, she was made Princess of Wales, a title that suggested she was still heir to the throne. In those days, having the title meant actually moving to Wales and fulfilling a role of great importance. A royal presence and the council that accompanied it brought the independently minded dependent territory under English jurisdiction. Ludlow Castle was to be her home. It was near the border with England in case the traditional Welsh resistance to English authority should become a real physical threat, endangering the princess and her three-hundred-strong household. The council had a tough time imposing its authority. Crime was rife and the people resisted paying taxes to 'foreign' rulers. There might have been a rebellion had the court not packed up and returned to England after a year and a half. For Mary, it had been a valuable experience. Sitting in state and receiving visitors, she had learnt what it was like to be the head of a regal household.

Mary was eleven years old when her father declared his marriage to her mother unlawful. For Mary, the consequences were devastating: his rejection of the validity of his marriage meant that he was also rejecting her legitimacy and right of succession. At an impressionable age Mary was to endure her father's ill treatment of her mother. Most hurtful of all was the embarrassing public debate about whether her mother had actually had sex with Prince Arthur.

The ever-creative Henry meanwhile thought of another way to secure the succession, one repulsive to his wife and daughter: he applied for papal dispensation for his daughter Mary to marry his son Henry Fitzroy. It seemed to him a very tidy solution. He would not have to disinherit Mary if she would marry the one person in the realm who would not provoke factional strife. The Pope was amenable, relieved he would not have to grant the divorce from Catherine, but Henry himself dropped the proposal as his heart was set on marrying Anne Boleyn.

Mary's was an extremely distressing youth. Like her mother and the Spanish ladies-in-waiting she was a devout Catholic, believing that Lutheranism and the rejection of papal authority was worse than a plague. It adulterated society's spiritual and moral values and angered God, denying people the chance of eternal salvation. The Protestants threatened Mary personally. They supported her father's divorce on the grounds that the Pope should not have allowed Henry to marry his brother's widow. They believed certain rules in the Bible had been laid down by God and could not be overruled by a mortal in Rome. Mary already knew what she would do with these Protestants if she were in power: she would deal with them with the most effective tool that could be used against a plague – fire.

Her distress at witnessing her father turn against her mother was increased when fifteen-year-old Mary was forbidden to see Catherine. The queen had been banished from court to a residence called The More, in Hertfordshire. Mother and daughter kept in touch by letter. Henry loved his daughter but was distressed that she should have taken her mother's side. Keeping the two apart would punish their obstinacy and also reduce Catherine's influence which encouraged Mary's disloyalty. His actions were influenced by Anne. She was impatient to become queen and jealous of the affection Henry still showed

Mary. Anne saw Mary as a threat to her unborn children: doubtless she would dispute their right to the succession.

In April 1533 Henry wrote to his daughter with the news that he had married Anne. A second letter instructed her to cease correspondence with her mother. The Archbishop of Canterbury, Thomas Cranmer, annulled the king's marriage to Catherine the following month and, on the first day of June, Anne was crowned. Mary now felt she had lost any chance of succeeding to the throne of England – but, if she did, Cranmer would be among the first to burn.

Just three months after her coronation, Anne gave birth to the new heir to the throne. Disappointingly for Henry, it was another girl. Mary was ordered to hand over her jewels to her new half sister, Princess Elizabeth. She was also informed that she was no longer a princess. Mary stood firm and refused to relinquish her title; acquiescence would imply she accepted that her mother's marriage and her own birth were not legitimate. As a devout Christian, her conscience would not allow her to concede that she had been born in sin.

Henry was angered by the stubbornness of his daughter. How dare she, against his orders, self-style herself princess and heir to the throne? He reacted by dissolving her household and sending her to live as a maid of honour in Princess Elizabeth's household at Hatfield. The seventeen-year-old Mary was humiliated. Worse still, she feared for her life: there were time-honoured methods of silencing unwanted claimants to the throne. Meals looked unappetising when she fancied they contained poison. If Henry were to die, say in a hunting accident, Mary knew Anne would not think twice about having her killed. Mary protested her rights throughout her two and a half years in Elizabeth's household. On one occasion Anne offered to reconcile Mary to her father on condition she acknowledge Anne's status as queen. Mary replied that she knew of no other queen in England save her mother, but that she would be happy to accept help from the king's mistress were it to be volunteered.

Mary was nineteen when her beloved mother died at Kimbolton. Her death was the more tragic for the two having been denied visits or correspondence right until the end. However, after this devastating start to 1536, Mary's fortunes began an upward surge. Anne's marriage to Henry was built on shaky foundations which now began to fracture. Like the predecessor whose position she had usurped, Anne had failed to produce a son. In May she was arrested on charges of adultery and plotting to kill the king. Her fall from grace was total. In a matter of days she was tried, condemned and beheaded. Anne's marriage to Henry was annulled the day before she lost her head, so her daughter Elizabeth became illegitimate. A couple of months later Henry's only son, Henry Fitzroy, Duke of Richmond, died. Mary was suddenly once again heir to the throne, after a break of just over three years.

The king's new wife Jane Seymour was keen to see a reconciliation between Henry and his first-born, believing a harmonisation of affairs would have a positive effect on the country as a whole. Henry was prepared to welcome Mary back to court on two conditions: that she reject the supremacy of Rome and that she accept her mother's marriage had been illegal. Mary was close to being back in favour but she was reluctant to compromise principles her mother had defended to her dying day. However, after threats and intimidation from privy councillors, Mary gave in. She was of no use to anyone as another traitor, to be executed for defying the Act of Supremacy. So she signed. Verbally she assured her father that her change of heart was sincere but in a letter to Charles she maintained that her signature against the articles meant nothing as it had been written under duress.

In 1536, Mary's twentieth year, the dissolution of the monasteries began. Their fortunes went one way as hers went the other: her chamber within the royal household was re-established. Then, the following year, came an event that again stole away Mary's prospects of ascending the throne. At long last a wife of Henry VIII presented him with a healthy baby boy. Weakened by the strain of childbirth, Jane Seymour did not live to enjoy the great favour that the delighted father would have shown her. Mary accepted that her half-brother and godson, Edward, was now heir.

Over the next few years Mary's chamber remained stable against a background of changing stepmothers. She did not get on with all of them. Catherine Howard's close family links with the Boleyns did not endear her to Mary, and it did not help that she was five years Mary's junior. Mary however returned to court after Catherine's execution for infidelity and enjoyed Henry's favour as she fulfilled the role of hostess during entertainments arranged to help Henry find a new wife. Her standing was enhanced by the Anglo-Imperial treaty by which her cousin Charles and her father became allies against the French.

In July 1543 Henry married his sixth wife, Catherine Parr, who welcomed Mary into her household where the two shared a close and affectionate friendship. In December 1546, realising he did not have long to live, Henry made his will. The line of succession was set as

Edward and his heirs, followed by any son of Catherine Parr, and then Mary. Believing it to be a real possibility that Mary might one day ascend the throne, Henry commanded that she could do so only if the Privy Council approved her marriage.

Henry VIII died in January 1547 and nine-year-old Edward became king. As he was too young to govern, that task fell to sixteen councillors. They embarked on a programme of political and religious reforms which spelled trouble for Mary. The crunch came in March 1549 when the Act of Uniformity outlawed the mass and ruled that the new service based on the Book of Common Prayer be used throughout the land. A series of revolts broke out, though not all the rebels shared the same cause. Some protested against the imposition of the new service; others demonstrated against an urgent social and economic issue, the enclosure of common land. The revolts were put down by an army that included Spanish mercenaries. Mary was more difficult to deal with. She believed that, as a minor, Edward could not possibly rule on such fundamental matters as religion. She would only respect his will, whatever it turned out to be, when he came of age. This disobedience presented the Council with a dilemma. It could not tolerate Mary's stand as she was flagrantly breaking the law and providing inspiration for anyone else that chose to. As a potential rallying point for opposition, she was a threat to state security. However they could not deal with her too harshly: her cousin Charles was the most powerful man in Europe and Mary herself was just a heartbeat away from ascending the throne and having the power to punish her adversaries.

The Council had sent Mary away from court to live in the country where she could not personally influence her young brother, with whom she had always had a close relationship. They tried by letter to cajole her into conformity. This having failed, they summoned her senior servants and instructed them to put pressure on her. This also met with an uncompromising response. They conceded that Mary could continue to hear mass, but only privately in her own bedchamber. She showed her contempt for this compromise by providing mass to any outsiders who visited her. To the Council, Mary was 'the conduit by which the rats of Rome might creep into their stronghold'. She realised that their patience with her was wearing thin. Perhaps the time had come to escape.

In late June 1550 four warships and four smaller boats of the imperial fleet arrived off the Essex coast on the pretext of looking for pirates. They had come to collect Mary. The plan was for her to slip aboard a corn boat as it was unloading at Maldon, near her Woodham Walter residence. This would take her downstream to the waiting ships. Early on 2 July the imperial agent Jehan Dubois arrived at Maldon, expecting to collect his charge. Instead he met the controller of Mary's household, Robert Rochester, who bombarded him with reasons why the escape should be aborted. The Council had ordered the roads to be watched; there were spies in the household; escape was not necessary after all. Dubois must have been perplexed. The escape plan was in response to Mary's cries for help. He had put his own life in danger to escort her. The two men travelled to Woodham Walter to see if Mary was ready to leave. They found her unprepared, remonstrating that she needed a couple more days to pack and make ready. The delay was too dangerous for Dubois. He was forced to abort his mission and depart.

Over the next three years considerable pressure was put on Mary to desist from celebrating mass. She was especially distressed when her thirteen-year-old bother rebuked her by letter and in public for breaking the law. To him her offence was the greater because of the privileged position she held in the kingdom. On the other hand the Emperor demanded, through his ambassador, that his cousin should not be harassed for her religion. To put the matter in perspective for the Emperor, the English ambassador to Brussels asked that he be allowed to celebrate the English service at his home. The request was regarded as impudent in the extreme. To Charles, his cousin's wish to practise the true religion in a heretical land bore no relation to Sir Thomas Chamberlain's suggestion that he practise heresy in a land where the true faith reigned supreme.

Fifteen-year-old Edward's death from tuberculosis was a slow one. It gave his Lord Protector, the Duke of Northumberland, plenty of time to consider the prospect that Princess Mary, with whom his Council had quarrelled for so long, would soon be queen. It was a painful thought; she was sure to punish them. If they did not lose their heads, they would face imprisonment and lose their titles and estates. The land they had gained when the monasteries had been dissolved would surely have to be returned. Papists and foreigners would run the country. It was well known that Mary took advice from the emperor more readily than from any Englishman. And who would she marry? The duke started to treat Mary with more respect, sharing information on affairs of state with her, but he would need to do more than that to protect his power and keep the country Protestant. The dying king had no wish for the country to return to Rome, so he agreed to the duke's plan, which was to make a will stipulating that on his death the crown should pass not to Mary but to the little-known Jane Grey.

The granddaughter of Henry VIII's sister Mary, Jane Grey was fourth in line to the throne after Mary, Elizabeth and her mother, Frances Grey. The crown should not be willed to Frances because she was too old to bear a son; and it should not be willed to the Protestant Elizabeth because Elizabeth was not married to one of the Lord Protector's relatives. Jane Grey was the wife of his fifth son, Guildford Dudley.

Shortly before Edward died, the Council summoned Mary to his bedside. She was not so gullible as to walk into their trap, withdrawing instead to her residence of Kenninghall in Norfolk. She was there when her brother died on 6 July 1553. Four days later Jane, who was just sixteen, was proclaimed Queen of England.

The rising was spontaneous. Despite Edward's will, the people firmly believed Mary to be their rightful queen. Heartened by this support, and duty-bound to deliver England to the true faith, Mary did not look to escape abroad from almost certain death under Jane's regime, but made a stand. She proclaimed herself queen. Many Protestants rallied to Mary's cause, their loyalty to the true crown eclipsing religious differences. Expecting a fight, Mary and her growing army moved to Framlingham Castle in Suffolk. The Duke of Northumberland led an army of three thousand cavalry and infantry and thirty cannon north, to crush the revolt. He need not have bothered. He had totally misread the situation. Thousands were arriving daily at Framlingham to support Mary. Town after town was declaring for her, as did the crews of seven ships patrolling off Yarmouth, charged with preventing her flight to the Continent. It dawned on Northumberland that the tide of public opinion was resolutely against him; he even discerned discontent amongst his own Spanish mercenaries. Then many miles back down the road, behind his back, the Council decided Jane's nine-day reign was over. Mary was at last Queen of England.

On the third day of August 1553 cheering crowds gave a joyous welcome to their sovereign as she entered London. Three weeks later, at the Tower of London, Northumberland lost his head.

Mary was crowned at Westminster Abbey on 1 October 1551. Before the year was out, Parliament had annulled her parents' divorce, restored the mass and outlawed Protestant services. On the Continent, Charles V was overjoyed with his cousin's elevation, and not just for her sake. If she would marry his twenty-six-year-old widower son

Philip then the balance of power in Europe would tip against France, in his favour. Mary shied away from marriage due to a strong aversion to sex. This stemmed partly from her reaction to the sordid public debate and trial which had considered whether her mother had consummated her marriage to Prince Arthur. However, Mary was conscious that, should she not produce an heir, she would probably be succeeded by her Protestant half-sister Elizabeth. And so it was that Mary came to marry a Spaniard who one year came to England to be its titular king and another year sent his great Armada to destroy it.

The direct consequence of Mary's decision to marry Philip was a rebellion that almost cost her the throne. In an age when there was a real possibility of invasion and occupation by foreign powers, when English merchants and sailors suffered much abuse abroad, it is not surprising that England was a very xenophobic nation. Spaniards were particularly loathed for the barbaric Inquisition. During Henry VIII's reign the Spanish government, determined to keep Protestants from its shores, ruled that any ship entering a Spanish harbour could be searched and, if any heretical book was found, the crew could be tried by an Inquisition tribunal. Henry protested and Charles, keen then to get along with England, revoked the ruling. One of many stories that reached England during Edward's reign was of the appalling torture and death of a Bristol man at the hands of the Inquisition in Portugal. William Gardiner had both his hands cut off; to prolong the agony of his burning, instead of being tied to a stake he was hoisted over the flames on a rope, then repeatedly raised and lowered. Eventually the rope burnt through and he fell into the flames.

In January 1554 Sir Thomas Wyatt gathered a force of several thousand rebels in Kent. Their aim was to march on London, remove Mary and replace her with Elizabeth. The Council rushed to raise a defence force as the queen had no army to call upon. In a stirring speech at Guildhall, Mary declared that her first and most important marriage was to the realm. It would take precedence over her marriage to Philip, which had been accepted by the Council. The people were impressed and denied the rebels access through the gates. With London Bridge blocked, Wyatt crossed at Kingston and approached the city from the west on 7 February. The fighting was limited and before long the rebellion collapsed. Heads had to roll; in the end over one hundred did, including that of Lady Jane Grey. Mary had previously decided to spare her but now her attitude to rebels had hardened.

Philip, the only son of Charles V, had been born in Valladolid in 1527. At the age of sixteen he had married the Infanta Maria of

Portugal, a liaison requiring papal dispensation as the two were cousins twice over. The bride's mother was a sister of the groom's father and the bride's father was a brother of the groom's mother. Maria died eighteen months later giving birth to a boy, Don Carlos.

In the name of family duty Prince Philip of Spain, with nine thousand nobles and servants aboard one hundred and twenty-five ships, set sail for England on Friday 13 July 1554. A week later he stepped ashore at a rain-soaked Southampton. He did not plan to stay long. He would get married and, shortly after, make his excuses and join his father in the Netherlands. He met Mary for the first time at Winchester the following Monday. For him she was a sorry sight compared to Dona Ana de Osorio, the mistress of ten years whom he had left behind. But Mary was delighted with her prince. When they parted, Philip pleased his hosts by bidding them good night in English. It was unfortunate that, for a man who wished to be seen as King of England, 'Good night, my lords all' were the only English words he is ever recorded as uttering. The next day the couple learnt that Philip was not just a prince but also a king, his father having granted him the kingdom of Naples. On the day of the wedding Mary kept the bridegroom waiting half an hour before they were married in Winchester Cathedral. Ironically by later standards, the bride wore black and her bridegroom white.

There were strict marriage conditions. Philip could support Mary in her duties but was to play no part in the government of the kingdom. He was not crowned. In the event of Mary's death, he would have no claim to the throne. He could not place his own men in English offices and certainly could not involve the country in the wider struggles of his father's Empire. He was to receive no financial support; all his money was to come from abroad.

That autumn Mary rejoiced in her finest hour. After twenty years of schism, Parliament reversed Henry VIII's Act and restored the supremacy of the Pope over the Church of England. The queen had another reason to be delighted: she was convinced she had conceived an heir.

With reconciliation with Rome on the statute books, the time had come to sterilise the land of the plague of Protestant heresy. Before the year was out, Parliament brought back a law by which heretics could be burnt to death for not embracing Roman Catholicism. Almost immediately after attaining her finest hour Bloody Mary began to ensure her future notoriety.

The persecution began with vengeance in February 1555, when

Bible translator John Rogers was burnt at the stake at Smithfield. Five days later at Gloucester the fire, slowed by the greenness of the reeds, took forty-five minutes to consume the Bishop of Worcester. Mary might have assumed that she was consolidating the place of the Roman Catholic Church in England, but far from it. Those flames were searing resentment against English and Irish Catholics into the population that would last hundreds of years. John Foxe, a Protestant priest, escaped abroad to finish his book on martyrs since Roman times. He now had a new chapter to add and he could write from personal experience: many of his friends and associates were being persecuted. In the book he claimed that Protestants had supported Mary at Framlingham after she had promised to uphold their religion. Renard, the imperial ambassador, understood the harm that was being done and advised her and Philip to stop the executions. For once Mary ignored imperial advice. Her husband, however, ordered his chaplain to preach against the burnings in order to disassociate himself and other Spaniards from them, although, judging from his behaviour later in his life, he would not have been averse to burning English Protestants.

The executions were utterly repugnant to the population, including Catholics, who feared reprisals under the next Protestant monarch. The responsibility for all the suffering lay firmly at Mary's door. She was the advocate of the shortsighted policy, and she could have halted it at any time. She did not. Two hundred and eighty-three suffered an agonising death. Many more were bullied into taking mass. The burning that probably gave Mary most satisfaction was that of Thomas Cranmer, the Archbishop of Canterbury who had annulled her parents' marriage. He recanted his Protestant views after being sentenced to death, hoping for mercy. Mary was unimpressed by his change of heart and ordered that the execution proceed. Cranmer then withdrew his recantation, apologising to the people for his weakness.

Mary and Philip were greatly embarrassed by many violent incidents between their Spanish and English subjects. The English hated the lackeys of a man they feared had designs on the English throne. The Spanish despised the foul-mouthed, beer-swilling, overcharging islanders with their ugly, badly dressed women and no fear of God. There were mass brawls in which people were killed, one involving over five hundred English and Spanish. People of both nationalities were hanged for robbing and murdering each other.

The distressed Mary would not hear of her beloved husband's leaving for the Low Countries before their child was born. In late April

1555 she retired to the privacy of her apartments and prepared to give birth early in May. The expected delivery date slipped to June: for once in her life Mary prayed that pain should begin. June passed without the silence of the apartments being broken by the piercing cry of a new-born. The cot stood empty. News of a safe delivery was so eagerly awaited in England and on the Continent that, on more than one occasion, false rumours triggered premature celebrations. Charles V delighted in the dream of a grandson who would be heir to the throne of England. July passed by and the humiliated queen and her physicians had to admit that she was not pregnant and never had been. The abdominal swelling was probably a symptom of a medical condition such as ovarian dropsy. There was bitter disappointment all round, not least for Phillip who had been unnecessarily delayed. He now prepared to leave, to assume the responsibilities in the Netherlands that his father wished him to undertake. At Greenwich, on 29 August, a very unhappy Mary said goodbye to her beloved husband, not knowing when she would see him again.

Mary took solace in evenings spent writing letters to Phillip. His brief and formal replies were excuses for delaying his return. His reasons were genuine, his father having handed over to him the Netherlands, Castile, Aragon and the Indies. If tempted to head for his Spanish kingdoms, he did not do so for two reasons. Firstly, war in the Netherlands was inevitable; secondly, he wished to remain close to England, a country which, as titular king, he would revisit when necessary.

Philip used his wife's desperation for his return to ask for something he had not pressed for when in England – a coronation. When Mary had been expected to bear them an heir the matter had been less important. He now demanded a share in the government of the kingdom to justify his presence. Parliament rejected this demand out of hand and Mary, without a lever, was reduced to simply begging for his return. She was distressed by stories that her twenty-eight-year-old husband was making up for time lost in England with a colourful social life including liaisons with other women. At the French court, King Henri II predicted that Philip would attempt to dissolve his marriage. In April, Mary sent Lord Paget to speak to Philip but his mission was to no avail. She appealed to the emperor, writing of her 'unspeakable sadness' at the absence of his son from her side. It is doubtful whether he ever received the letter; having handed over the reins of power, he had returned to Spain. If Philip wanted to keep Mary on his side, he was playing a dangerous game. His contemptuous absence could have turned her deep love for him into hatred and bitterness. This seemed to be happening when she ordered the removal of his portrait from the council chamber. Then, due to events far away in Italy, Philip saw a use for England and decided to return.

In May 1555 a sworn enemy of Spain had become Pope. Pope Paul IV loved Italy and for him memories of the Spanish taking Naples and sacking Rome were bitter. He held a particular grudge against Philip, who had tried to block and then reverse his election to the seat of the apostolic see. Spain and France, rivals for Flanders and Italy, were enjoying a truce when his holiness decided to stir things up to the detriment of the Spanish. In response, Philip ordered the Duke of Alba to invade the Papal States. The truce with France was over; Philip, short of finance, had suddenly to deal with two French armies, one facing the borders of the Netherlands, the other heading towards Italy.

The quest for military and financial support sent Philip back to his wife's arms in March 1557. She was overjoyed with their reunion though saddened that it should have been precipitated by her husband's disagreement with the Pope. It would have been more diplomatic for Philip to have left at home the woman rumoured to be his current mistress, the Duchess of Lorraine.

The Council was vehemently opposed to involvement in a foreign war. What had England to gain from joining a dispute between Spain and France over territory in the Low Countries and Italy? Besides, England could not afford it. The harvest of 1554 had been meagre, and it was yet worse the following year. It was to be three in a row when in 1556 a heatwave and drought damaged the yield. The malnourished populace needed food, not war; the merchant community opposed a conflict that would damage their livelihoods and endanger their lives on visits to the Continent.

Mary realised that if the Council was not persuaded she could say goodbye to her husband for ever. She summoned council members to appear before her individually. Threatened with the loss of their estates and positions, one by one they fell in line. Then two French ships appeared off Scarborough with a small force led by an English traitor, Thomas Stafford. They landed and took the castle, having easily overcome its tiny garrison, but within a week the invaders were prisoners. The raid, which was construed as French-sponsored provocation, reduced the opposition to war with France: Mary and Philip had got their way. The aggression was so convenient to the royal cause that it is tempting to see it as conspiracy. England declared war on France.

Mary was happy again as Philip stayed in England to oversee preparations for naval and land forces. In later years, when his treasure
ships were being boarded by English seaman, his towns and colonies
raided by English sea dogs and his Armada opposed by the naval firepower of perfidious Albion, Philip might well have felt it ironic that
he should have played such a positive part in making England a strong
maritime nation. Mary once more bade her husband farewell at Dover
on 6 July. The following day an English herald stood before Henri II
in the French court at Rheims and read him a declaration of war.
Mary's beloved husband had gone for ever, but she was about to lose
far more than Philip. He was set to strike a greater blow to England
as its titular king than he would ever do as its sworn enemy and King
of Spain.

Between the Netherlands and Paris there was but one place of
strength, the town of St Quentin in the valley of the River Somme. It
was there that Philip's commander-in-chief, the Duke of Savoy,
amassed troops in August 1557. On 10 August they took the fort and
destroyed the French army that had come to relieve it. The next day
Philip arrived with a contingent of eight thousand troops from England. They had missed the battle but joined the siege of the town,
which fell just over two weeks later.

The name St Quentin now made French blood run cold. It was one
of the most complete defeats they had ever suffered. Many French soldiers had perished in the Somme in the rush for the fortress and as
many as ten thousand were killed or wounded in battle. The town's
women had been raped and, before St Quentin could be completely
pillaged, it had been set alight. Philip was to build a magnificent
monastery outside Madrid and dedicate it to the victory. King Henri
II could not easily strike back at the Empire so he turned on their
collaborator, England. France would make the islanders regret their
part in this. Mary would pay for the 'unjust quarrel' she had picked
with France to please her husband. On the menu was Calais, a small,
poorly defended English enclave on the Normandy coast.

The French had long hankered after Calais. It had been English for
more than two hundred years. Philip had visited the town on his way
back to England earlier in the year; his warning to the Council about
its inadequate defences and his offer to reinforce the garrison with
Spanish troops had been brushed aside.

The Duke of Guise was back from Italy, where Philip's Viceroy in
Naples, the Duke of Alba, had frustrated his attempts to assist the
papal forces. He needed a victory. As his forces invaded the English

territory outside Calais on the last day of 1557, the garrison commander, the Earl of Wentworth, sent an urgent appeal to Philip for assistance from the Spanish army less than twenty miles away. The call was never answered. Calais fell on 7 January 1558. With the capture soon after of Guines, another fortress in the Marches of Calais, England lost its foothold on the Continent. It was a bitter blow for the Council and for English pride. Mary was distraught. She was later to declare that, when she was dead and opened up, they would find Calais lying in her heart. She tried to blame the hapless Earl of Wentworth but the people knew better: responsibility for England's humiliation lay firmly with her Spanish husband.

Mary was pregnant with Philip's child, or so she thought. She had delayed the announcement to make sure of the pregnancy this time. Philip was delighted. The baby was due in March. The expectant mother made a will, lest she not survive the birth. It was her second phantom pregnancy. Suffering from a fatal dropsy, Mary's health deteriorated, aggravated by severe melancholy. She was depressed not just by her false pregnancy and the loss of Calais but also by her husband's absence, the failure of the burnings to eradicate heresy, the outrage they caused and the growing likelihood that she would be succeeded by Anne Boleyn's daughter, her Protestant half-sister Elizabeth. Well before Mary was gone, she was humiliated by the attention the Spanish were giving her sister. Philip even considered marrying Elizabeth on his wife's death, to maintain his position. Meanwhile, far away in a monastery in Spain, her father-in-law and lifetime confidant Charles V passed away.

Early in the morning of 17 November 1558 the fires at the feet of the Protestant martyrs blew out. The killer queen was dead. That night new fires were lit: bonfires to celebrate the ascension of a new queen. In a letter to his sister, Philip admitted feeling a 'reasonable regret for her death'. Mary was buried in Westminster Abbey on 14 December. Shortly afterwards, her favourite lady-in-waiting Jane Dormer married Philip's ambassador in England, the Count of Feria. They moved to Spain, where their household entertained Catholic refugees from England.

Mary had come to the throne by popular demand. Had there been opinion polls in 1553 they would doubtless have shown her to be the most popular incoming monarch ever. The nation felt for a woman who had grown up being persecuted by her own father and separated from her mother. But five years of tyranny and swimming against the tide, and the bad luck of three terrible harvests, combined to sweep away her popularity. Seventeenth-century Protestants were to call her Bloody Mary. Before then her half-sister Elizabeth was to ensure that her name held wicked connotations in the consciousness of the nation. The moral of the story is that, if you are to treat your successor shabbily, do not do it by halves. Do not harass, imprison or try to disinherit her; one day, when you are gone, she will write your history.

CHAPTER 5

Pirates

Thence we sailed against the Spaniard
With his hordes of plate and gold
Which he wrung with cruel tortures
From Indian folk of old,
Likewise the merchant captains
With hearts as hard as stone
Who flogged men and keelhauled them
And starved them to the bone.

Charles Kingsley, 'The Last Buccaneer'

The Spaniards wondered much at the sickness of our
people, until they knew the strength of their drinks,
but then wondered more that they were not all dead.

Anon

NEVER IN THE FIELD of human history was so much given to so
few by one who did not even own what he was giving. In 1493
a generous Pope Alexander VI granted South America to Spain
and Portugal in gratitude for their Catholic faith. This pope, Rodrigo
Borgia, was himself Spanish. The following year his papal bull was
enshrined in the Treaty of Tordesillas. Settlers duly arrived in the New
World and in 1510 started cultivating sugar cane, using aboriginal
labour. As demand for such workers increased, their numbers were
decimated by another European introduction – illnesses against which
they had no immunity.

The colonists had more land than they could dream of but they
could not make it pay without hands to work it. And so they looked
to Africa, importing Negro slaves. In 1518 the first slave trade licences
were issued: with so much demand it was going to be a lucrative trade.
Eager to keep economic gain to themselves, the Iberian nations
prohibited foreign slave traffickers from trading in areas under their
sovereignty. Such restriction inevitably led to smuggling. English
seaman John Hawkins bought Negro slaves in West Africa and sailed
to the West Indies where he sold them to colonists so desperate for
workers that they were indifferent to the nationality of the supplier.

The Spanish, angered by the violation of their monopoly, attempted to clamp down on what they saw as unacceptable contraband trade. When John Lovell arrived at Rio de la Hacha in Columbia in May 1567, Captain-General Miguel de Castellanos refused him permission to trade. Much of Lovell's human cargo was in poor shape; he had little option but to land ninety-two Negroes and leave.

The following year John Hawkins took another squadron to Rio de la Hacha. On board the advance vessel was Francis Drake. On 4 June 1568 Miguel de Castellanos replied to Drake's request for water by opening fire and forcing his withdrawal. Five days later two hundred of Hawkins' men landed a mile from the town, which they invaded after defeating a Spanish force. Treasure was collected, houses torched and slaves off-loaded. The message was clear: English seamen came to trade peacefully but, if prevented from doing so, they would stop at nothing to realise the profits they and their investors expected. They accepted Spain's conquest of South America but not the trade restrictions.

Hawkins continued west, to Santa Marta. Its governor agreed to trade after a mock battle, staged to give the impression that he had resisted the English. Here one hundred and ten Negroes were sold. The English were less fortunate at Cartagena, which resisted a bombardment; they had no choice but to sail away. But the weather intervened, forcing the English back into contact with the Spanish. This was to go down in history as the first battle fought by English-speaking people in the New World. Afterwards many English were to conclude that, as the Spanish were determined to frustrate free trade, it was as well to drop any pretence of engaging in it. If the governor of each coastal town was to refuse permission to trade, prompting landing, storming and pillaging, this course might just as well be pursued from the start.

The ships were tossed and battered by a hurricane that lasted eight days. Too damaged to undertake the long journey home, they headed for San Juan de Ulua in Mexico to effect repairs. Coincidentally that port was expecting the annual treasure fleet from Seville; on sighting Hawkins' ships with false colours they assumed it had arrived. The dignitaries who went to meet their visitors were astounded at their true identity. The English made it clear they sought only to carry out repairs and would leave once these had been completed. Two days later the real Spanish fleet arrived. Aboard was New Spain's new viceroy, Martin Enriquez, come to restore the rule of the Spanish Crown following a challenge by Martin Cortes, the son of Hernan Cortes who had first conquered Mexico for Spain. He was in no mood to deal with other threats to Spanish authority. The Spanish fleet was short of victuals and on a dangerous shore, so when the English stipulated that they could enter the port only if Hawkins' squadron was left to finish its repairs in peace and then allowed to leave, Enriquez hastily paid lip-service to the demand. However he was enraged at criminal foreign heretics dictating terms on Spanish territory and ordered the attack once the fleets were moored side by side. Guns erupted and a battle raged for six hours. Hawkins aboard the *Minion* and Drake on the *Judith* escaped, leaving behind ships, comrades and about £200,000 in treasure. The duplicity at San Juan de Ulua raised the stakes. English seamen felt they had tried to play fair and been rebutted. Peaceful commerce was not possible: Spain's actions had legitimised their piracy. Anyway, if they were to rob Spain of treasures they would not be taking them from the legitimate owner, they would be mugging a mugger.

The great attraction of piracy for the seamen was gold and the power it brought. Much of it was in the form of treasure plundered from the spectacular Aztec and Inca empires. To add to this, hugely rich silver mines had been discovered in Bolivia and production from these rose dramatically as new methods of extraction were developed. Mule trains carrying riches across land and ships taking them to Spain became irresistible targets. Taking treasure was facilitated by poor defences in the New World. Spain had a dilemma. If she shipped out arms her people in the New World would be able to defend Spanish treasure, but the arms might equally be used by rebels like Martin Cortes.

The risks were high, but many merchant seamen viewed piracy as an attractive alternative to eking out an honest living. It meant an end to hard, ill-paid labour in poor working conditions and a chance of adventure and great profit, using skills they already had. It meant escaping from a rigid hierarchy into a community of equals. For many the choice was between poverty and piracy. Slave labour had narrowed the opportunities for many a white man; some were reduced to robbing simply to survive. In times of peace there was an upturn in piracy as large numbers of seamen found honest employment impossible to come by.

Many expeditions which set forth to plunder were directly and indirectly sponsored by the monarch. The budgets of Henry VIII and Elizabeth I were insufficient to finance a national navy, though they needed one to protect their territories. The solution lay in a simple deal. The monarch would allow privateers to attack and seize the vessels of hostile nations provided they would come to the nation's defence when required. This private navy became an attractive investment for many, not least the monarch. This was an important factor in the rapid growth of piracy.

The history of British piracy is long and complex. Thousands of incidents were perpetrated by thousands of characters, but a couple of individuals stand out from the crowd. One was an Englishman who had so many hoping to join his expeditions that he put the press gangs out of business. The other was a Welshman who gave his name to a brand of rum.

Sir Francis Drake

FRANCIS DRAKE was born in Tavistock in Devon around 1540. His childhood was disturbed by his family's flight to Kent during a Catholic rebellion in 1549. In Kent, against a background of Mary's marriage to the King of Spain, her persecution of heretics and Wyatt's rebellion, Drake's father eked out a precarious existence for his family as a Protestant preacher. Later Drake was to dedicate his life to fighting the two forces which had brought fear and resentment to his youth: Spain and Rome. Fuel would always be thrown on the fire that burnt within him by his knowledge of how so many of his compatriots were suffering at the hands of the Spanish Inquisition.

After serving his apprenticeship on a coasting bark which carried freight across the North Sea and English Channel, Drake moved to Plymouth, where he fell in with William and John Hawkins. In 1564 he served as purser on a trading voyage to north-east Spain. He saw his first pirate action in 1566 when he travelled with that ill-fated expedition of John Lovell which ended in abandoning ninety-two slaves near Rio de la Hacha. He next shared in the débâcle at San Juan de Ulua.

Anglo-Spanish relations deteriorated mainly as a result of unrest in the Netherlands, for which the Spanish blamed the English. Cross-Channel trade was suspended and England grew wary of the ruthless Spanish army's close proximity. The temperature rose further when, in November 1568, five ships carrying the pay for the Spanish army had their cargoes impounded when they docked at Plymouth and Southampton to shelter from poor weather. Two months later, after a gruelling voyage, Drake arrived back from San Juan de Ulua.

In 1570 Drake left Plymouth with the *Swan* and the *Dragon* to become the first known Englishman to make a successful raid in the West Indies. Little is known of this voyage which Drake later described as principally a reconnaissance. The following year his second incursion caused havoc on the Spanish Main. His men captured and plundered three Spanish frigates, one of which was carrying the king's correspondence for Peru and Panama. He preyed on merchant ships, seizing the merchandise from about sixteen, and at Venta Cruces his men took goods straight from the wharf. It was an expedition that warmed the hearts of his backers and alarmed the Spanish, not least their king. Drake returned with £66,000. He had achieved notoriety but felt he had a long way to go before he could feel satisfied that the Spanish treachery at San Juan de Ulua had been avenged.

Nombre de Dios (meaning Name of God) was a small town on the Caribbean coast of Panama. It was here that newly mined gold and silver was stored before being loaded onto the treasure fleet transporting it to Europe. And it was there that Drake headed when he left Plymouth with the *Swan* and *Pasco* in May 1572. In late July he arrived and launched an attack on the 'Treasure House of the World' at dead of night. He and his men stole ashore, seized a battery and entered the town. Shots were fired, bells were rung; most of the inhabitants fled. Drake was injured but he and his companions failed to appreciate how badly, and how much blood he was losing. His men forced their way into the governor's house and gazed upon an enormous pile of silver bars. If there was so much treasure here, what would the quayside treasure house contain? Admiring such riches was to be the highlight of their night's endeavour, however. After a great thunderstorm delayed their progress to the waterfront, the expedition ended in failure. Drake collapsed from loss of blood and the treasure house was found to be empty, its contents having gone east six weeks before.

After taking several ships Drake looked again to the main treasure route. Fearing his return the Spanish had strengthened Nombre de Dios so he needed to seize the treasure before it was taken there, on its passage across the isthmus from Panama City. He made contact with cimaroons, slaves who had escaped from their Spanish masters to the hills. They would be useful as scouts and were only too glad to harm their former masters. On 11 February 1573 Francis Drake climbed a tree and viewed the Pacific Ocean for the first time. The Spanish were masters there. The Pacific towns and shipping had no reason to fear him. Later he would sail into the 'peaceful ocean' and change all that. He climbed down and addressed himself to the business in hand, ambushing the treasure train. A premature move on the mule train by one of the seamen warned those following and £35,000 worth of treasure escaped Drake's grasp as it was sent back down the track to safety. Their cover blown, Drake's party hurried back to the Caribbean where they took Venta Cruces. It proved hardly worth the fight.

In late March Drake met a Huguenot privateer called Guillaume le Testu. The two led a joint attack on a treasure convoy whose guard must have assumed the long trek through the jungle had been successfully accomplished, so near to Nombre de Dios was it when the ambush came. The assault was a success. A large quantity of gold was carried down to the sea. Back at sea they took another ship, on which they found more gold. They arrived home in April 1573 with some £30,000 in riches, but without realising that the political climate in England had changed. Spain was no longer the enemy it had been when the *Swan* and *Pasco* left Plymouth. Guarding his freedom and his haul of treasure, Drake lay low. Soon Spanish successes in the Netherlands and the presence of their 'International Brigade' in Ireland meant that Anglo-Spanish hostility was rekindled. Drake once again had a licence to plunder.

When he next ventured out to avenge his and his queen's injuries on Spain he headed for the ocean he had spied from the top of a Panamanian tree nearly five years before. He had attacked ships in the Caribbean, he had tried to seize treasure on the waterfront, he had successfully seized it as it was being transported across land from the Pacific to the Caribbean coast; now he would seize it in the Pacific before it arrived at Panama City. It was a simple strategy: follow the supply chain back to where it is least protected.

Late in the summer of 1578 Drake's *Golden Hind* completed its successful passage through the Strait of Magellan and started travelling north up the coast of Chile. On 5 December he arrived at Valparaiso, the port for Santiago, capital of Chile. As the *Golden Hind* approached a ship carrying a large quantity of gold its crew had not an inkling that they were in any danger. Pleased to see the arriving visitors, they drummed a welcome. Completely unprepared, they put up no defence: their ship became the prize of men who later landed to strip the town church of its silver.

Five hundred miles further north was the Peruvian (now Chilean) settlement of Arica. Drake had high hopes of this place. It was from here that silver from the great mines at Potosi was put aboard ships for the journey to Panama City. But the first town on the treasure route proved a disappointment, yielding only a small quantity of silver from two boats.

The crew of the *Golden Hind* had come a huge distance with a view to gaining great riches, assisted by the element of surprise and a total lack of local defences. They were therefore disturbed now to find that warnings of their presence were preceding them. At Chule in Peru soldiers stood ready to defend the bullion as locals jeered at Drake and his men from the waterfront. His best chance now lay in surprising a ship at sea. Further up the coast he seized a vessel whose captain told him of a ship that had recently left Calloa, the port for Lima, the capital of Peru, bound for Panama City. It was carrying a great cargo of silver. The chase was on. If caught, the *Nuestra Señora de la Concepción* would *make* the voyage. It was to be better than that. She was also to *make* the Bank of England and help establish London as the centre of world commerce.

During the chase Drake took time off to raid the port of Paita in Peru and, on leaving, seize two ships, one of which carried eighty pounds of gold and some silver. On 1 March *Nuestra Señora* was sighted. The *Golden Hind* caught up, under cover of darkness; the following morning she went alongside. A burst of artillery, a volley of musketry and the English boarding party took control of the greatest prize of all. It took six days to transfer a haul which included eighty pounds of gold and twenty-six tons of silver.

Continuing north, Drake's men assaulted two other ships and, between 13 and 16 April, plundered one final coastal settlement, Guatalco in Guatemala. There was silver to be had and, more importantly, plenty of food and drink, for they were about to go home the long way. Whichever way they chose would have been dangerous. Going south round the tip of South America would have meant facing hugely dangerous seas and the likelihood of running into Spanish patrols. Heading west meant crossing the largest ocean in the world and hazarding the uncharted waters of the orient. Many of the crew must have felt the odds on getting their fabulous cargo home were not good. West they went, away from Spanish avengers and the cruel seas of Cape Horn. Nearly a year and a half later, on Monday 27 September 1580, they arrived back at Plymouth. But why were people not at work; why were church bells ringing? The ship's log had been meticulously kept – surely no mistake had been made? No mistake, just an oversight: they had crossed the international date line. It was in fact still Sunday 26 September.

The Spanish ambassador Mendoza complained angrily to Queen

Elizabeth, demanding restitution of the treasure to Spain. He might have had a more sympathetic ear had Spanish troops not landed in Ireland to support a rising against the English the year before. Queen Elizabeth was fascinated by Drake's account of the voyage and, as an investor, delighted with her return of £300,000. Spain might have lost some treasure but there was plenty more in South America. The richest and most powerful nation in the world had gained Portugal and was taking control of the troublesome Netherlands. The queen's contempt for Mendoza's petitions was made plain on 4 April 1581 when she bestowed a knighthood upon Drake, visiting him on the *Golden Hind* at Deptford. Anglo-Spanish relations went from bad to worse. English moves to restore the Portuguese monarch incensed Spain and Spanish complicity in the Throckmorton Plot to assassinate Queen Elizabeth enraged England. In response to continued activity by English pirates in the New World, Philip II ordered the arrest of all English ships in Iberian ports. The queen responded by unleashing her most dangerous sea dog, Sir Francis Drake, first to rescue, then to damage.

On 14 September 1585 Drake's fleet of more than thirty vessels left Plymouth. Arriving at the mouth of the Vigo River in north-west Spain, he sent a message to the governor at Bayona demanding to know why English ships had been impounded. Eager to placate such a large force, Don Pedro Bermudez assured him that they had now all been released. The fleet moved up-river to threaten Vigo as a thousand-strong defence force gathered on the shore. Drake and Bermudez rowed to meet each other. It was agreed that the fleet would leave peacefully on condition the crews could first gather provisions in town. The arrangement held and Drake's fleet headed for the open sea, leaving their hosts humiliated and impotent but nonetheless grateful that their towns had not suffered the miserable fate of others visited by Drake.

Sailing south, they visited what are now the Spanish Cape Verde Islands. These locals were not as cooperative as Bermudez had been. Ransom demands were ignored, the inhabitants fled and a captured English boy was beheaded and gutted. Drake retaliated by destroying the capital, Santiago, along with Porto Praya and Santo Domingo. The fleet then sailed for the West Indies in search of richer pickings.

On New Year's Day 1586 Santo Domingo, capital of Hispaniola (later the Dominican Republic and Haiti) and Philip II's most important town in the Caribbean, fell to a surprise attack by Drake's men, who had capitalised on the vulnerability of its landward defences. As there was little loot, the next best option was to hold the town to ransom. The inhabitants could have their homes back if they cooperated; they could see them destroyed if they did not. Drake sent a Negro servant to the Spaniards with a flag of truce; he was horrified to see him return mortally wounded. Two Dominican friars were promptly strung up and the Spanish avoided Drake's threat of hanging of two prisoners a day only by themselves hanging the messenger's murderer. A month later, after more than £11,000 had been paid, Drake departed.

Eighteen years before, Cartagena had been the last place attacked before the ships of Hawkins' expedition had been battered by the storm that forced them into San Juan de Ulua. That time it had resisted the bombardment. It was the richest city on the Spanish Main and Drake fancied another attempt on it. On the night of 9 and 10 February one thousand of his men approached along the beach. After limited fighting, which claimed the lives of twenty-eight of Drake's men, Cartagena fell. A ransom of £50,000 was paid, but not before many houses had been destroyed. Drake's men considered keeping Cartagena but decided against it due to the terrible fever there.

The fleet moved on. The trail of destruction was lengthened by an attack on the Spanish settlement of Saint Augustine in Florida. Drake arrived back in Plymouth on 28 July 1586. The expedition's profits of £65,000 were exceeded many times by Philip II's losses. Drake's largely unobstructed passage had made Spain's financiers nervous. How could they be sure she could honour their loans when her wealth was so poorly protected? Suddenly, thanks to Sir Francis Drake, the King of Spain's credit collapsed.

It was to be England's intervention in the Netherlands that finally persuaded Philip II to invade England. The story of his 'Invincible Armada' is covered in the next chapter. Drake would be in the English Channel to meet it but before that he first harried Iberian ports to try to prevent its assembly. From the Spanish point of view these acts were as piratical as ever, but to the English he was now legitimately defending the realm, fulfilling his obligation to his queen who earlier, unable to afford her own navy, had granted him a privateer's licence.

Drake went south with two thousand two hundred men aboard twenty-four ships, arriving off Cadiz on 19 April 1587. No flags flew from the English masts as they entered the outer harbour and the Spaniards were slow to identify their uninvited guests. When the English flags were run up the onslaught began, provoking great panic. On the sixty Spanish vessels, there were not enough crew to hoist the sails, not enough time to raise the anchors and not enough ammunition to mount a defence. Ships which failed to escape the mêlée were abandoned, plundered, torched and sunk. The following day Drake entered the inner harbour and burnt a 1,500-ton galleon belonging to the Armada's Commander, the Marques de Santa Cruz. Later that day the wind enabled Drake's departure. A humiliated Cadiz was left to reflect on how effortlessly the hated English had sailed into their midst to capture and destroy some thirty ships and a vast amount of stores. It was said later that Drake had 'singed the King of Spain's beard' but Philip probably felt he been struck a heavy blow across the face, and punched in the stomach as well.

Sagres is close to the most south-westerly tip of Portugal, Cape St Vincent, on the Algarve coast. A fortnight after terrorising Cadiz, eight hundred of Drake's men landed there and attacked the castle perched on the cliffs. High and thick though its walls were, they could not save it and the garrison surrendered when the attackers set fire to the gates. Drake's men went on to take the fortified monastery of St Vincent, another fort and a village, which they plundered as the fleet scoured the bays and cleared them of all boats.

Having struck several blows in defence of the realm, Drake now doubled the expedition's success by making a huge profit. He found the *San Felipe* in the Azores, where he had gone after failing to lure the Armada's commander, Santa Cruz, out of Lisbon for a fight. The property of King Philip, its vast cargo, which included bullion, jewels, china and silk, had a value of over £100,000. This wealth was badly needed in England. Although the Armada had been delayed for a year, its arrival had now been ensured and extensive preparations were needed to meet it.

*

ON 28 AUGUST 1595 an expedition commissioned to raid the King of Spain's Caribbean possessions left Plymouth. Amongst the two and a half thousand men who travelled aboard the twenty-seven ships were the country's two greatest seamen, neither of whom would ever see England again.

Drake and Hawkins had received news of a lone galleon of the Mexican silver fleet, laden with bullion, which had put back to Puerto Rico for repairs. But this time the Spanish were prepared. They sent five fast frigates to collect the treasure, captured an English ship, assessed the fleet's strength and took early warning to Puerto Rico. The English arrived on 12 November 1595, and there the ageing

Sir John Hawkins passed away, his death casting a shadow across the whole expedition. Puerto Rico's defensive preparations proved sufficient and Drake's men went in search of easier prizes elsewhere.

Twenty-seven years before, gunfire had repulsed Drake from the town of Rio de la Hacha and that time Hawkins had punished the locals' lack of cooperation by razing the town a few days later. Drake now returned to do the same himself. His men invaded and managed to seize most of the valuables. Then, with the ransom negotiations going nowhere, the town of 'Axe River' went up in flames.

Twenty-three years after a leg wound, a thunderstorm and an empty warehouse had spoilt his first visit, Drake came again to Nombre de Dios. From there Sir Thomas Baskerville led eight hundred men across the isthmus towards Panama. Three days later and halfway there the way was blocked by a fort garrisoned by one hundred and twenty Spaniards. Unable to break through, and with casualties mounting, Baskerville decided to turn back. Nombre de Dios was sacked and they sailed away. Short of options, they were back in the area three weeks later; why is not clear. In his cabin on the *Defiance* Sir Francis Drake lay dangerously ill with dysentery. Knowing he had only hours to live, he struggled into his armour so he could die like a soldier, which is what he did in the early hours of 28 January 1596. He was buried at sea off Nombre de Dios. Puerto Bello was destroyed in his honour.

Not surprisingly, news of Drake's death brought joy to Spain and her colonies. It also inspired a vengeful epic poem by Lope de Vega. *La Dragontea* was published in 1598. It was a history in verse of Sir Francis Drake's last voyage, in which England's hero is described as the very incarnation of the devil. Drake's death was described with relish:

> With that he died; his frozen tongue was stilled.
> The staring pupils flickered now no more;
> The livid mouth, cold with the chill of death,
> Spat out the stubborn soul; out from the breast
> Into the deep, eternal mouth of Hell.

… but the poem nevertheless betrayed the author's immense admiration for 'the dragon':

> His eyelids, raised, released the light of dawn;
> His snorting breath lit up the heavens with fire;
> His mouth sent tongues of flame into the sky;
> His nostrils poured out black and smoking clouds.
> Armoured in glittering scales of greenish black,

His steely sides remained impregnable
To all the darts, and all the spears of Spain,
While he heaped gold, and gold, on glittering gold.

Nearly three hundred years later, in 1895, Sir Henry Newbolt poetically conveyed the supposed dying words of one of England's greatest in 'Drake's Drum':

Take my drum to England, hang it by the shore;
Strike it when your powder's running low.
If the dons sight Devon, I'll quit the port of Heaven
And drum them up the Channel as we drummed them long ago.

Captain Henry Morgan

THE FOLLOWING CENTURY the main threat to Spanish colonies came from the buccaneers, men based in the Caribbean who from time to time united for organised raids on predominantly Spanish ships and settlements. Considering the havoc and terror they inflicted, their own organisation was surprisingly civilised. Their councils made democratic decisions on such matters as targets, the division of prizes and compensation in the case of injury. In between raids many of them lived in the British colony of Jamaica.

The ascent of Oliver Cromwell as Lord Protector of England in 1647 brought the renewed backing of the English state for attacks on Spanish possessions. In 1654 Cromwell ordered Admiral Penn and General Venables to take a fleet and army to wrest Hispaniola from the Spaniards but the force of thirty-eight ships and seven thousand soldiers failed to break the spirited Spanish resistance. Unable to return home empty-handed, the force turned to the then Spanish colony of Jamaica, where a small Spanish force was easily overcome. From then on Jamaica's capital Port Royal became a den of iniquity inhabited by many of the Caribbean's most ruthless rogues, including the most notorious of them all, Henry Morgan.

Henry Morgan was born in Monmouth, in Wales, around 1635. He sailed with Penn and Venables and, in the years that followed the taking of Jamaica, began to distinguish himself in raids on Central America. Following successful assaults on Villahermosa in Mexico and Gran Granada in Nicaragua, and after the execution of Morgan's senior Edward Mansfield by the Spanish, Morgan took control of the buccaneers. With the endorsement of the Governor of Jamaica, in 1668 he set off for Havana in Cuba with twelve ships and seven hundred men. Hearing that this objective was too well defended, he changed course for another Cuban target, Puerto del Principe, which soon capitulated and was duly plundered and burnt.

The place where Morgan really made his name, and earned heroic status back in Jamaica, was Puerto Bello. The third largest city in the New World, it had by this time replaced Nombre de Dios as the main treasure port. With three forts to protect it, an element of surprise was essential. In the middle of a July night in 1668, twenty-three canoes carrying Morgan and five hundred men slipped on to the beach three miles from the city. The five manning the look-out post that night must have been petrified when they saw the menacing hordes approach but they did their duty and opened fire, so warning Puerto Bello.

The first two forts soon fell but the defence of Santiago Castle was more stubborn. This was of great concern to the buccaneers as the more time they spent on its reduction, the longer the population had to hide their valuables. Morgan figured that the defenders would cease their fire, or at least reduce it, if he used captured priests, friars and nuns as a human shield. These servants of the Church were forced to advance ahead of the buccaneers towards the fort, place ladders against the walls and start climbing up. Unluckily for them the governor of Puerto Bello valued their holy lives less than the security of the city. Nevertheless the castle soon capitulated and the invaders began a fifteen-day orgy of pillage, rape, torture, murder and drunkenness. Torture and pillage went hand in hand as many inhabitants fiercely guarded their hidden valuables. Morgan wrote to the president of Panama demanding a ransom in return for not burning the city. Negotiations followed Don Agustin's initial rejection of the demand and soon mule trains were winding their way from Panama to Puerto Bello carrying the cash. Small wonder that Henry Morgan was acclaimed a hero when his ships arrived back in Jamaica: they carried half a million pieces of eight, mountains of plundered goods and three hundred slaves. For Port Royal it was boom time. The orgy of drunkenness and debauchery begun in Puerto Bello was to last a long time.

When the money ran out, the buccaneers needed to look for the next Puerto Bello. Morgan held council aboard his flagship *HMS Oxford* in January 1669 to decide where the assembled ten ships and eight hundred men should head next. It was decided that the treasure port of Cartagena should have that dubious honour. That night a boisterous party aboard *HMS Oxford* saw much drunkenness and firing of guns. One of the shots ignited the magazine and *HMS Oxford* was ripped apart by a terrible explosion. Three hundred and fifty men were killed. Amazingly, Henry Morgan was among the ten survivors. The buccaneers from the other ships searched for bodies, not to land and bury them but to strip them of valuables.

Despite the loss of their flagship, the expedition proceeded, but in view of the reduced head-count it was decided not to attempt Cartagena. They sailed instead for Maracaibo in Venezuela. Here general panic ensued when the population learnt of the approach of the buccaneer fleet. Many headed inland with as much as they could carry. The pirates landed and made easy work of the place, always prepared to twist tourniquets around inhabitant's heads or apply red-hot irons if they were slow to lead them to the best loot. The next stop was Gibraltar in Venezuela, which Morgan's men surprised by approaching from an unexpected direction, through a mangrove swamp. The need to satisfy the buccaneers' insatiable greed again resulted in the sadistic abuse of its population. Returning to their ships, low tide delayed their withdrawal; by the time the tide was high their way was blocked by three Spanish warships. Against this threat Morgan launched a captured Cuban merchant ship loaded with explosives. It sailed alongside the largest Spanish ship, the 412-ton *Magdalena*. A massive explosion on the former set fire to the latter and the buccaneers slipped away in the chaos.

Back in Port Royal one of Morgan's grateful backers, Governor Sir Thomas Modyford, rewarded him with a plantation. The Spanish complained bitterly to London, which in turn reprimanded Jamaica, ordering all attacks on Spanish settlements and shipping to cease forthwith. But when English boats en route for Jamaica were attacked and news came that Mariana, queen mother and regent of Spain, had declared war against the English in the Indies, Admiral Morgan was commissioned to attack Spanish possessions on land and at sea. He gratefully took up the challenge and went to join his buccaneers.

Panama was the pivotal point for commerce between the Atlantic and the Pacific. This flourishing trade included luxurious and exotic items such as pearls, porcelain, spices and perfumes. From Spain came manufactured goods and the fine wines of Jerez. Even more important, it was the main treasure port on the Pacific coast of central America for gold and silver from the south. The people were fashionable and proud of their city, built in a colonial baroque style. It was an episcopal see and had a high court. There were beautiful palaces, stylish homes and wealthy churches full of art treasures.

Morgan was now planning to bring terror to its streets as he planned the greatest expedition of his career.

Late in 1670, Morgan set sail with nearly forty ships and two thousand buccaneers. He proposed to surprise Panama by taking it from the landward side. Having taken the Fort of San Lorenzo at the mouth of the River Chagres, his men moved upstream in canoes. After seven days they landed and began a gruelling nine-day trek through the jungle. They were soon in poor condition, having brought with them little food, assuming they could take it from villages en route. But news of their progress preceded them; forewarned farmers burnt and hid their provisions. Just before a combination of hunger, insects, fever and bad weather could arrest their progress, the bell tower of Panama Cathedral was sighted.

On the plain outside Panama City a Spanish defence force of two thousand one hundred infantrymen and six hundred cavalry assembled to meet them. The buccaneers held their ground and managed to repel the cavalry and infantry charges. They were less daunted by the two thousand head of cattle forced to stampede in their direction. With these oxen shooed away, and the military having fled back to the city, the buccaneers advanced to take their prize. This expedition was destined to be remembered not for the value of its booty but for its destruction of a fine city. Much of the treasure had already left by sea; most of the inhabitants had fled with their valuables. What was left the Spanish preferred to destroy rather than see it fall into the hands of the approaching rogues. All the wooden buildings were set alight and the ammunition store was blown up. Morgan's men faced little resistance entering the city; their real challenge was the race against time to secure the valuables before the whole place was consumed by fire. It was a desperate race that angered the men whose expectations had been so high but were now going up in smoke before their eyes. For a month they searched the ruined city and its surrounds, torturing prisoners to discover hidden money. Such was the ruin of one-hundred-and-fifty-year-old Panama that, when it came to be rebuilt, not enough was left standing to justify rebuilding in the same place. They started anew several miles away. The plunder of £30,000 was a large sum only until divided among two thousand claimants. Back at Fort San Lorenzo tensions over the fair division of the spoils boiled over. Morgan took advantage of the chaos to slip away, leaving many of his fellow buccaneers without a share.

Jamaica again hailed the return of its hero and main source of foreign exchange. London had to be more diplomatic. Despite the

Queen of Spain's declaration of war, there had officially been peace between England and Spain, and it was necessary to be seen to act against citizens infringing this. Modyford and Morgan were recalled to London. The governor faced a token and comfortable incarceration in the Tower of London for a couple of years; Morgan was free to mix with high society. Eighty-three years before, Queen Elizabeth had knighted a pirate of whom the Spaniards had complained bitterly. History now repeated itself as King Charles II followed suit. Back in Jamaica, the new governor was worried by piracy and the threat of the French. Who better to send as the new lieutenant governor than Sir Henry Morgan. He was to be responsible for despatching justice to the pirates.

Sir Henry was not the most successful of civil servants. In 1683 he was suspended from office for abuse of power and drunken disorder. He died on 25 August 1688 , his health declining due to heavy drinking. Jamaica honoured the passing of her great citizen with a state funeral. On 7 June 1692 three terrific earthquakes and a tidal wave destroyed Port Royal. The tomb of the great buccaneer was never seen again. For many Spaniards, this was proof that there was such a thing as divine retribution after all.

CHAPTER 6

Philip's Annus Horibilis

I know I have the body of a weak and feeble woman, but I have the heart
and stomach of a king, and of a king of England too, and think foul scorn
that Parma, or Spain, or any prince of Europe should dare invade the
borders of my realm ...

Queen Elizabeth I, Tilbury, 1588

IT WAS THE SUMMER of 1588 and, in England, the common
people went about their daily lives with considerable unease. An
invasion force sent by the most powerful nation in the world was
sailing towards their coasts. Aboard were gallows and instruments of
torture to be used on civilians, or so the preacher and the man at the
inn assured them. There was an atmosphere of great foreboding. The
coasts were sealed off, but what good was that? Everyone knew that,
once they had landed, England's little army would be unable to stop
the cruel Spanish veterans who had cut down Protestants with such
efficiency just across the water in the Netherlands.

So why was King Philip II of Spain attempting what William the
Conqueror had effected in 1066, what Napoleon and Hitler would plan
in 1804 and 1940? Firstly, there was his desire to serve God by restoring papal authority in England. As the most powerful man on earth,
Philip believed it his divine duty to deliver the island people back to
the Catholic faith. Secondly, he was already involved in an expensive
northern European war. His large army in the then Spanish Netherlands, defending the authority that he had inherited from his father,
should have finished the job by now but every time it looked as if the
Dutch rebels might finally be too weakened to fight on, they would
rise again, boosted by funds, arms and troops from England. It became
clear that the only way of defeating the rebels was to attack their
foreign supporters. Thirdly, Spain simply had to act against the piracy
that was depleting its revenue from the New World. England's
seamen had no respect for Spain and Portugal's monopoly of New
World trade, as claimed in the Treaty of Tordesillas of 1494. At first
English merchants had traded peacefully, but when the Spanish used
force to prevent this, the stakes were raised. Spain's violent defence

of its illegitimate monopoly was an excuse for the English to plunder at land and sea. In 1586 no silver from mines in Peru and Mexico made it back to Spain. It sickened Philip that the activities of John Hawkins were not simply the acts of an English subject out of control but those of a man with the backing of Queen Elizabeth herself. Fourthly, a catalogue of events since the attack on John Hawkins' fleet in 1567 had sent Anglo-Spanish relations spiralling lower and lower so that, by 1585, the two countries were involved in an undeclared war. Philip had supported the slaughter of a Protestant community in Florida, refused to accept an English ambassador because he was a Protestant, embargoed all English ships and property in Spain and the Netherlands, financed the Irish rebels, supported plots to overthrow Elizabeth and annexed Portugal. In turn Elizabeth, had impounded Spanish treasure arriving in Plymouth aboard Spanish ships fleeing from French privateers, embargoed Spanish property in England, prohibited trade with the Spanish Netherlands, commissioned an attack on the Spanish fishing fleet and, as already mentioned, supported the privateers and the Dutch rebels.

As described in the previous chapter, in September 1585 Sir Francis Drake sailed to Vigo in Galicia to demand to know from the governor why English ships had been impounded. Having been assured that all had been released, Drake left peacefully only on condition his men were allowed to gather provisions in the town. On their own territory the Spanish were made to feel grateful though being robbed – at least their town had not been wrecked. It was a humiliation and provocation that a seething King Philip could not let pass. England would have to be taught a lesson.

Alonzo de Bazan, Marques de Santa Cruz, had commanded the victorious Spanish navy which crushed a French fleet in the Azores in 1583. He had long lobbied his king to support him in following up this earlier success with an invasion of England. Philip now consulted him on the best way of doing it. Santa Cruz thought of some numbers and probably doubled them. His plan was for a huge amphibious invasion force of five hundred and ninety-six ships and seventy-two thousand men. Spain's most distinguished general, the Duke of Parma, who was fighting in the Netherlands, suggested that thirty thousand of his troops be shipped across the Channel, protected by twenty-five warships, and put ashore in Kent or Essex. On the advice of Bernardino de Escalante, who had sailed to England with Philip in 1554, the two plans were combined. A Spanish fleet under Santa Cruz was to secure the straits of Dover, making it safe for Parma to ferry his 'Army of

Flanders' across. The army was then to march on London as the fleet sailed round the corner into the Thames estuary. The year chosen for the 'Enterprise of England' was 1587.

The Armada would consist of one hundred and thirty ships carrying two thousand four hundred and thirty-one guns, seven thousand seamen and nineteen thousand troops. Vessels were requisitioned not just from Spain but from as far afield as the Baltic and Venice. When the captains of the Dundee trader *St Andrew* and the English ship *Charity* had sailed for Malaga and Gibraltar respectively, they could not have dreamt that, the next time their ships approached the British Isles, they would do so as renamed components of the Spanish Armada. Food also had to be requisitioned. One of those responsible was Miguel de Cervantes, a veteran of the great naval Battle of Lepanto in 1571, when the Spanish had defeated the Turks. Requisitioning was his duty but what he really wanted to do was write. In 1605 he would publish *Don Quixote* and claim his place as Spain's greatest literary genius. (He died on 23 April 1616, seemingly on the same day as William Shakespeare but actually a week later because Spain and Britain used different calendars at the time.)

Ironically, the English navy that awaited the Spanish Armada was much the stronger for Philip's input. As titular King of England, married to Mary, he had persuaded the Privy Council to invest in naval defence. One of the ships laid down was the *Philip and Mary*. Not surprisingly, despite the belief that it was bad luck to rename a ship, it became the *Nonpareil*. The Armada was big but it has been generally forgotten that the English fleet, with a hundred and ninety-seven ships to call on, was bigger. Numbers apart, how did the two fleets compare?

Spanish and English naval tactics were totally different. This was reflected in the design of their ships. The more traditional Spanish aimed to take over enemy ships by closing in on them, firing one broadside to shock the personnel, and grappling. Troops would then storm aboard for hand-to-hand combat on deck. English tactics, considered cowardly by the Spanish, were to keep a distance and skilfully use long-range guns to bombard the crowded decks until the enemy retreated, surrendered, sank or were sufficiently weakened to make boarding safe. Side by side the towering Spanish ships looked far more intimidating. These floating fortresses were built with high decks so that their more numerous troops could fire down onto the enemy and board easily. English ships stood low in the water, built to manoeuvre easily and quickly to take advantage of their greater firepower. English cannon were designed for rapid reloading. Once in place, expert gunners could fire at three times the rate of the Spanish.

According to Queen Elizabeth's commander-in-chief, they were the best soldiers in Christendom; according to another senior English commander, no army surpassed them in order and discipline. Unfortunately they were not describing their own army but that of the enemy. The Duke of Parma allotted half his army, a total of twenty-seven thousand men, to the invasion. He had several hundred barges made, requisitioned others and had new canals built to enable them to reach Dunkirk and Nieuport. He sought to boost his forces further with thirty Scottish merchant vessels. To facilitate their hijacking, he sent a large consignment of gold to Catholic leaders in Scotland. The gold arrived but the ships did not.

England did not have much of an army when the crisis loomed. Most soldiers were poorly trained amateurs, called up as late as possible so as to save the militia unnecessary expense. People were reluctant to pay extra taxes for something that might never happen. The few professional soldiers that there were earned little respect; there were not yet any proud regimental histories. It was just another poorly paid job with the added drawback of extreme danger. In command of the English army was the Earl of Leicester, a veteran of the unsuccessful 1584 Netherlands campaign. He found the burden of leadership altogether too stressful.

Besides the English and Spanish navies and armies, there was another player whose intervention could prove critical. Justin of Nassau was the illegitimate son of the assassinated leader of the Dutch Protestants and rebels, William of Orange. In 1588 his thirty vessels patrolled the Dutch coast, ready to blow Parma's barges out of the water should they dare to venture out.

As the day that the Armada would sail for England came nearer, Drake was despatched by Queen Elizabeth to make a pre-emptive strike at Cadiz. He succeeded in singeing the King of Spain's beard, as described in the previous chapter, before going on to Sagres on the south-westerly tip of Portugal, where he captured some fifty supply ships, including a number carrying wood for the Armada's water barrels. Before heading home he captured a treasure ship in the Azores. Philip heard the news and fell seriously ill. Parma thought it prudent to drop the whole enterprise. The net result of Drake's expedition was to buy England a whole year to prepare for the coming of the Armada. It is true that Philip had health problems before the Cadiz raid but this was a particularly stressful time for the sixty-year-old king, working flat out on details and strategies.

In late June 1587 the Spanish council of war decided that Santa Cruz and his fleet should put to sea to protect the incoming treasure fleet. Eighty-six ships waited off Lisbon so that, as soon as Santa Cruz returned, they could set sail for England. By the time the last ship came in, however, it was October, too late in the year for an attack. It would have to be the following year.

Early in 1588, as the day for the sailing of the Armada approached, the expedition suffered a huge setback. Spain's finest admiral, Alonzo de Bazan, Marques de Santa Cruz, the sixty-two-year-old commander-in-chief of the fleet who for years had dreamt of invading England, died from typhus in Lisbon. To achieve a great objective you must believe in your ability to do so: Santa Cruz had been the great believer. As he laboured to make the fleet ready he could imagine it blasting, grappling and seizing English ships in the Channel, on the way to its rendezvous with Parma. Unfortunately for Spain, the man that Philip chose to replace him had little confidence in the expedition. He would far rather have stayed at home. There was general shock when this premier nobleman of Spain, Don Alonzo de Guzman, Duke of Medina Sidonia, was chosen, felt not least by himself. He immediately put pen to paper in an attempt to persuade Philip to pick someone else. He protested poor health, limited experience of the sea, proneness to sea-sickness and lack of spare wealth due to debts. He had little under-standing of navigation or warfare at sea; he was not acquainted with any naval officers. The king admired the man's modesty and persisted; the unfortunate duke was obliged to obey. Philip admired his prac-ticality and administrative strengths, and knew that as a member of one of Spain's oldest aristocratic families he commanded great author-ity. Two councillors ensured that the king never received Medina Sidonia's next letter, describing the Armada enterprise as flawed and doomed to failure.

Elizabeth's choice of commander-in-chief was also decided on breeding and not fighting record. Lord Charles Howard of Effingham took charge. His 'loose cannon' Sir Francis Drake was his second-in-command.

Philip was a very religious man, pious to the point of obsession. In 1588 the keeper of 7,422 religious relics assured Medina Sidonia, '…the cause being the cause of God, you cannot fail'. The year before he had countered Parma's reservations with the argument that, as the enterprise was for His cause, God was sure to send good weather.

Medina Sidonia's sailing orders echoed his master's sentiments: 'From the highest to the lowest, you are to understand the object of our expedition, which is to recover countries to the Church now oppressed by the enemies of the true faith. All personal quarrels are to be suspended, and I charge you, one and all, to abstain from profane oaths.'

Half the Spanish ships had religious names, saints' names like *San Juan* (St John) and *San Pedro* (St Peter), or names such as *Espirutu Santo* (Holy Spirit) and *La Trinidad* (The Trinity). On the English side were names like *Revenge, Triumph* and *Tiger*. Armada sailors were forbidden to do anything to offend God, be it swearing, feuding, gambling or womanising. One hundred and eighty priests and friars travelled with them to keep them from straying. At daybreak and sunset the ships' boys would sing the 'Salve' and 'Ave Maria'.

Medina Sidonia soon proved himself as an organiser. The fleet was ready just weeks after his appointment. On 30 May 1588 the Invincible Armada set sail from Lisbon, for the next two weeks making painfully slow progress against uncompromising winds up the coast of Portugal. The duke had insisted that the fleet stick together, so the speed was that of the slowest hulk. As the first casks of meat, fish and biscuits were opened the men grimaced and threw many straight overboard. Possibly Drake's seizure of those barrel staves had started the rot. Dirty old casks had had to be used, spoiling the food. But the casks had also been filled too early and the hot Lisbon sun had not helped. Fouling of the water in inadequate casks was also a problem with so many thirsty rowers and animals aboard.

On 19 June the flagship *San Martin* entered the harbour of La Coruña with a view to landing the sick and taking on fresh supplies. Out at sea a great gale scattered the Armada. Most of the ships, many damaged and with a large number of sick on board, came in over the next few days, but a week later thirty-five were still missing. A desperate Medina Sidonia fired off an extremely negative letter to the king, appealing for him to call the enterprise off, using every argument he could think of. If Spain lost its fleet it would lose Portugal and the Indies as well. He even suggested that the unseasonably bad weather could be divine intervention.

As the Armada re-victualed in La Coruña, the English fleet awaited a northerly wind to take them south to Spain to attack the Armada on its own coast. The weather they wanted came. On 17 July they headed south but a hundred miles from their target the wind changed; they were forced home. That same wind brought the Armada out. All its ships had by then returned. It had taken on fresh food and water; the sick had recovered. The Armada set sail for England for the second time on 21 July, hoping for good summer weather this time.

Progress across the Bay of Biscay was desperately slow. But for the hulks, they might have been out of the area when the next storm blew up and scattered forty vessels. For most ships it is safer to ride out a storm at sea than head for harbour and run the risk of being smashed against the rocks. The masters of the vulnerable galleys, however, favoured the shelter of the coast. These boats, whose design had been ideal for centuries of Mediterranean warfare, headed for France. The slaves at the oars knew that hitting the rocks could either kill them or free them. The galley *Bazana* was wrecked as it attempted to enter Bayonne. Those on the galley *Diana* saw the chance to mutiny. One of those galley slaves, who fled when it ran ashore, was a Welshman, David Gwynn, who successfully made it to England. None of the four galleys rejoined the Armada; neither did the 768-ton *Santa Ana* which limped into La Hogue minus its main mast.

Before the rest of the ships had rejoined the fleet, it was spotted some way south-west of the Scilly Isles by Captain Thomas Fleming of the *Golden Hind*. Everyone knows what Sir Francis Drake was doing when, on Friday 29 July, Fleming rushed up with his news – he was enjoying a game of bowls; a game, we are told, he was unwilling to interrupt for the sake of a mighty Armada approaching English shores. There was time to finish the game and defeat the Spaniards as well. The fact is that Drake knew the tide and wind were not conducive to setting sail immediately.

That day the men of the Armada stared across the sea at the out-line of the English coast. They crossed themselves and prayed. They could see palls of smoke from beacons alerting the whole country to the fact that the Armada, so long talked about and feared, had finally arrived. Late on Saturday night, 30 July, four Falmouth fishermen had the shock of their lives. They were captured by a Spanish pinnace and taken to the flagship. Terrified, they revealed that the English fleet had already sailed out of Plymouth.

Medina Sidonia now knew more about the English movements than those of Parma. He was extremely worried that he had not heard from the general. He needed confirmation that Parma was ready. He could then sweep up the Channel to the rendezvous, secure the crossing and leave before the weather worstened. Any delay could bring conflict with the English fleet. It was a communications night-mare. He knew that his messages to Parma were taking a week to be delivered; any replies would take another week to come back. He might wait around for a fortnight only to receive word that Parma's army had been ready two weeks before.

On the morning of Sunday 31 July the two fleets were in full sight of each other not far from Plymouth. Many Englishmen must have exclaimed to one another, 'Look, the Dagos are flying our flag!' for emblazoned on each sail was a huge red cross. Had the person ordering the decoration not realised that, more than just a simple religious device, the red cross was the flag of England and Saint George? Perhaps it was deliberate: psychological warfare is as old as war itself. 'Dago' was a term of contempt for Latins derived from the Spanish name for James, Diego, that sailors and merchants must have heard on their visits to Spanish ports.

An English pinnace, *Disdain*, sailed towards the Armada, which was sailing east in the shape of a crescent, its battle formation. The single shot that it fired before turning back informed the men of the Armada that the English were not prepared simply to steward them peacefully up the Channel. They were ready to fight. From the outset the English demonstrated that they did not intend to stick to traditional tactics of sea warfare. 'Que demonios hacen?' (What the hell are they doing?) the Spaniards must have exclaimed as sixty English vessels sailed towards the crescent in single file. In turn they fired off a broadside, then peeled away. This long-range gunfire did not inflict great damage or injury but, in the skirmishes that developed, Juan de Recalde's *San Juan* turned to face Drake's *Revenge* and received a severe battering. Another large ship, the *Gran Grin*, also took a hiding. As some of the Armada turned into the wind to assist the two isolated ships, Lord Howard led his fleet away. He would wait for another forty ships to join his fleet before he really got down to business.

Was the Armada responsible for its own bad luck? Whilst sailing towards the *San Juan* to provide assistance, the *Nuestra Señora del Rosario*, commanded by Pedro de Valdes, crashed into another ship and then, with its steering handicapped, into yet another. Things deteriorated further as the foremast fell onto the main mast. The heavily armed *San Salvador*, carrying the Armada's paymaster general and a fortune in money, was rocked by a massive explosion in its powder magazine. Two hundred men, more than half the crew, were killed in the blast rumoured to have been the deliberate action of a German gunner who had quarrelled with the captain. The fire was extinguished and presumably much of the money taken off before the ship was abandoned by the rest of the Armada with fifty of the most horribly injured still on board. To the chagrin of Pedro de Valdes, his ship was also abandoned; the duke feared that an attempt to save it would have risked the safety of the whole Armada. Pedro had a member of his own family to blame: his cousin Diego was the duke's principle adviser.

The Armada continued east past Prawle Point and across Lyme Bay towards Portland. That night, the responsibility of leading the English fleet was given to Drake. A lantern on the *Revenge* enabled the other ships to follow in the dark and, very importantly, stay together. But Drake's mind was elsewhere: out there, drifting helplessly, was a rich prize waiting to be taken. He had dedicated his life to taking Spanish prizes, it was how he had made his fortune; he could not bring himself to ignore this one just because he was meant to be leading the fleet. He extinguished the light and disappeared into the night. Unable to see any light, most of the ships pulled up but Lord Howard's *Ark Royal*, the *White Bear* and the *Mary Rose* sailed on. The next morning, Monday 1 August, the four hundred and sixty-four men on the *Rosario* saw that they had company. Don Pedro soon accepted that his 1,150-ton, 46-gun ship, with its barrels of powder and chests of treasure, was lost. The shame of surrender was ameliorated only by the fact that he was surrendering to Drake himself. The ship was taken to Torbay by the *Roebuck*; Pedro de Valdes was granted the pleasure of watching the rest of the campaign from the *Revenge*.

That same morning, the men of the *Ark Royal*, *White Bear* and *Mary Rose* also awoke to find they had company – the Armada. Luckily for Lord Howard, his three ships were able to slip away. Medina Sidonia was more interested in reorganising his ships and effecting repairs than getting involved in another battle. The English fleet did not fully regroup until that Monday evening. Drake's action infuriated some of the English commanders: he had risked their ships' safety, given the enemy a whole day to progress in peace and taken treasure that might otherwise have been shared by them. On Tuesday morning the fleets faced each other off Portland Bay.

The English fleet split into four groups. Lord Howard and Sir John Hawkins (on *Victory*) sailed their groups directly at the Armada. Drake led his out to sea; Sir Martin Frobisher's headed towards the shore to prevent the Armada from entering Weymouth Bay. His 1,100-ton *Triumph* was huge by English standards; only Lord Sheffield's 1,000-ton *White Bear* came anywhere near it. The flagship *Ark Royal* was 800 tons and Drake's *Revenge* just 500. The Armada had seven ships over a thousand tons, including Martin de Bertendona's *Regazona* which

weighed in at 1,294. But in the game the English were playing, size
was not important – it was all about firepower. The *Regazona* might
have been two-and-a-half times the size of the *Revenge* but she had
only thirty guns to Drake's forty.

The Spanish thought that their time had come. Frobisher's ships
were between them and the shore, cut off from the rest of the English fleet. The lack of wind, which prevented the English from escaping, did not worry the Spanish: they had galleasses to row towards
the enemy across a sea that was then almost perfectly calm. The four
galleasses, *San Lorenzo, Zuniga, Girona* and *Napolitana* were from Naples
and commanded by Don Hugo de Moncada. Each was powered by a
combination of the wind and three hundred oarsman. It was their
high compliment of guns that distinguished them from galleys. The
cannon from other Armada ships roared as they closed in on their
quarry. The men of the Armada willed them to get alongside the English ships, grapple them and send their troops aboard. The banks of
oars drove the galleasses closer, closer; they were almost there ... Then,
just as they were preparing to grapple, a current swept them away.
They tried again, urged on by troops desperate to avenge the battering of the *San Juan*, the loss of the *Rosario*, Cadiz, piracy ... the list was
long. Another galleass closed in. Behind, other Armada ships were lin-
ing up. The biggest ship in the English navy would be theirs before
lunch. The next galleass was almost there. Spectators held their
breath. Nearly, nearly ... But then, as the current again took hold, no
amount of frenzied rowing could keep them in position. It was agonising to watch, not least for Medina Sidonia, who made his feelings
known to Don Hugo. The galleasses came round again, with the same
result. After an hour and a half, to the frustration of the Spanish, the
changing wind blew in five English ships which forced the galleasses
to retire to the Armada.

Had the Spanish been defeated by bad luck again? No, the English
seamen had been using local knowledge. There was always a period
of calm in the morning between the time when the breeze came from
the land and when it came from the sea. They also knew about the
Portland Race, the fast-flowing current in the area. While the Spanish thought they had the upper hand, they were actually being
rounded up from all sides like a flock of sheep. Now, crushed together,
they made a perfect target for fast-firing English guns. With the wind
in their favour, Howard's group went for the centre. Their guns blazed
at the first ship they came to, the vice-flagship *San Juan*. The *Rata Santa
Maria Encoronada* went to her assistance. When Medina Sidonia's *San*

Martin approached she immediately drew the attention of Howard's group who, for more than an hour, filed past firing broadside after broadside into her and other Armada ships that came to join the fray. There was no escape out to sea: Drake's group was attacking from that direction.

Despite the ferocity of the twelve-hour battle and the huge expenditure of English powder and shot, the Armada sustained limited damage. It resumed its eastward course towards the Isle of Wight. Little did the Spaniards know the following English were fretting for lack of ammunition.

The following day, Wednesday 3 August, both fleets reorganised forces. The English took delivery of badly needed ammunition, including what was on the *Rosario*. There was some action when the English bombarded the isolated *Gran Grifon*. The *San Martin* and *San Juan* became involved but the English declined to widen it into a general battle. At dawn on Thursday 4, the English saw that the galleon *San Luis* and the merchantman *Duquesa Santa Ana* had fallen behind the Armada and were close to Sir John Hawkins' group. As thirty English ships closed in for the kill, three galleasses and a galleon, the *Rata Encoronada*, raced to rescue the Spanish ships. The galleasses came under fire from the *Ark Royal* and *Lion* and sustained substantial damage, but the *Duquesa* was saved. The English strategy was similar to that of two days before: the fleet formed an enveloping half moon with Frobisher pushing forward near the shore, Howard steering towards the centre and Drake and Hawkins pressing in from a seaward direction. Inshore, the *Triumph* led an attack on the *San Martin*. So close did she come that the crews of the Spanish ships believed they might finally get to grapple, encouraged by the fact that the *Triumph*, in tow, was moving awkwardly. They believed the largest ship in the English navy to be disabled and that, two days after the frustration off Portland, their troops would flood her decks. It seemed unlikely that a lucky wind and current would come to Frobisher's rescue a second time. But Frobisher knew what he was doing: as the Spanish closed in the *Triumph* sailed swiftly away and half a dozen ships under Howard headed towards Medina Sidonia's *San Martin* and began a furious fight. Drake and Hawkins were not idle: they sought to unbalance and confuse the Armada with a furious assault from the south. Hassled by gunfire, winds and currents, the Armada had no option but to sail straight past the Isle of Wight, under whose cliffs it had hoped to shelter until word came from Parma.

If the Spanish were concerned that their progress was too fast, the

English were equally anxious that, despite five hours of fighting that day, and their previous efforts, the Armada proved largely impregnable and unstoppable. Howard used the honours system to reward effort and maintain morale. Two commanders arose from the deck of the *Ark Royal*. One was, in the eyes of the Spanish, England's second most notorious pirate – Sir John Hawkins. The other was the commander of the great ship they had almost grappled – Sir Martin Frobisher. The Armada drifted on through the rest of Thursday and Friday; on Saturday afternoon it anchored off Calais. The governor of the French port welcomed this commercial opportunity. Sunday trading flourished; the price of vegetables doubtless rose that day. However, the governor frowned at the parking arrangements and informed his guests of his concern that they were drawn up on a very hazardous part of the coast. The Armada had had to stop here: to go on would have risked being carried past the rendezvous point. Medina Sidonia's heart must have leapt when his secretary Arceo brought word from Parma, but sunk again at the news that Parma would not be ready for a fortnight.

Aware of their own problems so much more than those of their adversary, each fleet lacked confidence and feared what the other might do next. The English worried that invasion could begin at any moment – they had to act without delay. On that Sunday evening Lord Howard, Sir Francis Drake, Sir John Hawkins and Sir Martin Frobisher met aboard the *Ark Royal*. They were joined by Lord Henry Seymour, who until then had been guarding the straits of Dover. With the arrival of his squadron, the English fleet exceeded one hundred and forty ships. The commanders discussed how to dislodge the enemy, how to cause such havoc that they would run aground or sail past the rendezvous point in confusion. It was decided to use the favourable tide and westerly wind to send in the *fire-ships*.

Eight fire-ships were prepared. Pitch was slapped all over them so that they might catch fire quickly and burn fiercely, and the cannon were loaded. At midnight crews sailed them towards the Armada before setting them alight and rowing back to the English fleet. Two were intercepted by Spanish pinnaces under Captain Antonio Serrano and towed away. This was extremely brave when one considers that the Spanish probably assumed they were actually huge floating mines of the kind used against the Spanish in the Dutch Wars. In 1584 Parma, having already captured most of the Flemish towns, had endeavoured to add Antwerp to his conquests. The great trading city is located in the heart of the country, at the head of a great estuary that stretches forty miles from the sea. Parma's engineers had cut off this vital sea link by building a huge bridge from bank to bank. It was half a mile long and very well defended. In April 1585 the Dutch rebels had commissioned an Italian engineer, Frederico Giambelli, to design floating bombs to destroy the bridge. One of the vessels ran into the bridge and exploded with such ferocity that eight hundred Spaniards were killed. Who was to say that the vessels heading towards them now were not the latest versions of Giambelli's 'Antwerp hell-burners'? The six that had not been towed away drifted closer, belching flames, shot and smoke. Panic ensued and the Spanish ships either cut or dumped their anchor cables. At last the tight, impregnable unit was breaking up. Stopping its progress was now a Spanish problem: without anchors there was little they could do to stand against the strong currents.

One ship that did not go far was Don Hugo de Moncada's galleass *San Lorenzo*. Having broken her rudder in a collision during the panic, she ran aground. The following morning, Monday 8 August, Lord Howard repeated Drake's folly of exactly one week before: he concentrated on this one beleaguered ship instead of leading his fleet straight into an attack on the disorganised and vulnerable Armada. The men he despatched to take her fought with the occupants in the first hand-to-hand struggle of the campaign. Although the Spanish had favoured such combat they did not win, most of the soldiers having escaped to the *Rata Encoronada* when she first got into difficulties. In the fighting Don Hugo de Moncada was shot in the head. As the English plundered their prize a party sent by the governor of Calais arrived to claim the *San Lorenzo* as theirs on the grounds that it was beached on the French coast. Lieutenant Thomson met them reluctantly but civilly and they reached agreement: the French would have the ship and guns, the English everything else. However, upon leaving, out of sight of Thomson, they were robbed and violently ejected. The common sailor who had seen around fifty of his compatriots killed and wounded in the taking of the *San Lorenzo* did not care for treating with these greedy French spectators. The French responded by opening fire from the shore, which brought the plundering to an end and claimed more English casualties. The distraction of the *San Lorenzo* gave the Armada time to regroup for battle.

As most of the Spanish ships crawled away from the Dunkirk banks into deeper water, their flagship bravely stood west of them and took the battering from the ships of Drake, Hawkins and Frobisher. The English had an extra squadron this time, that of Lord Seymour. His men had missed the previous actions so wasted little time now smashing into the Armada. The English hoped to drive the Spanish onto the banks: if they could not force the whole fleet aground, then they could pick off individual ships and batter them into submission. The Armada refused to be drawn into a general engagement; it continued up the coast in a tight group. Nonetheless the exchange of shot was greater than in any other sea battle. The ferocious Battle of Gravelines raged for nine hours, from nine in the morning until six in the evening. It was a bitter struggle; there were real casualties this time – more than one thousand dead. Many Spanish troops waiting on deck for grappling and hand-to-hand combat were savagely mown down and decks were awash with their blood. The English decks were almost deserted. There were no troops for cannon fodder. Below deck the guns roared; many times the shot went straight through the hulls of Spanish ships. Sails, rigging and masts were destroyed, rendering the Spanish ships even more awkward to handle. The nimbleness of the English vessels enabled them to sail in, fire a broadside, turn head on to minimise the size of target they offered, then turn again and deliver another broadside. The 665-ton *Maria Juan* was sunk, taking a hundred and fifty men with her, while Don Francisco de Toledo's 800-ton *San Felipe* and Don Diego Pimentel's 750-ton *San Mateo* were forced to run aground.

As the Armada sailed past the rendezvous point, to which it would struggle to return, no elated sense of victory gripped the English. The Armada was still more or less intact. If it came back, how would they stop it? No amount of pretty sailing and skilled gunnery could save them when ammunition was virtually exhausted.

Incredibly, as the Battle of Gravelines had been raging, the Duke of Parma had been embarking his troops. He later claimed that they would have been in a position to sail that night had the Armada arrived. Was this just a late bid to show Philip that he had done his utmost to follow the invasion plan through?

By the following day, Tuesday 9, the Spanish must have suspected that their enterprise was not after all blessed by the Almighty. They looked up at their sails filled by a north-west wind and down at the Zeeland banks coming nearer and nearer. If they could turn away from the banks into the wind they would run into the English fleet. They were not ready for another fight so soon. They were not to know the English had little to throw at them: they thought they were doomed. Despair was everywhere. Alonzo de Bazan, Marques de Santa Cruz, would have been turning over and over in his grave. Then sails fluttered as the wind veered to the south-west. A wave of relief swept through the Armada as it eased away from the banks into deeper water without the English attacking. Maybe God was with them after all! Perhaps he had been testing them and would now be with them all the way to a glorious victory.

That evening, a council of war aboard the *San Martin* debated whether to go back and try again to rendezvous with Parma, or whether to sail for Spain. If flight was shameful then risking Spain's fleet in further action was irresponsible. The following day Medina Sidonia announced that they were going home – the long way, round the top of Scotland and down past Ireland. It would be a long voyage, with barely enough food and water for the men, let alone the animals. A part of the North Sea became a sea of horses as they and the mules were thrown overboard, still alive. The poor animals that had been terrified by the roar of cannon and the slamming of shot into the ships met a terrible end as they finally gave up the struggle to keep their heads above water. Why had they not been kept and slaughtered for food?

The duke was still determined that the Armada stick together as a unit. It was not yet a case of every man for himself, get back to Spain as fast as your ship can carry you. Don Cristobal de Avila's prize for getting ahead of the pack in his ship the *Santa Barbara* was to swing by the neck from the yard-arm.

What had gone wrong? Why had the Enterprise of England failed? It was simple: the plan was fundamentally flawed. It was never feasible for the Armada to unite with Parma's vulnerable troop carriers given the poor communications of the day, the currents, the weather, the hostile attentions of the English and Dutch fleets, and the lack of a suitable port for the union. Basically, it was a stupid idea and Philip, who had been well aware of the risks, had only himself to blame for his blind faith. When it all went horribly wrong, it went the way Medina Sidonia and Parma had expected it to. Of course there were other factors too. The English had imposed their style of naval warfare, using swift, manoeuvrable ships and skilled gunnery, and it cannot be denied that the Spanish were particularly unlucky with the unseasonably bad weather of the summer of '88. Many of their ships were suitable only for the calmer waters of the Mediterranean. Driving rain, strong winds and rough seas made sailing them extremely difficult. Another piece of bad luck had been the death of their inspirational leader, Santa Cruz.

While the Spanish knew the game was over, the English were still suspicious of their next move. They could not believe that, having come so far with a great Armada and nineteen thousand troops, the Spanish would simply disappear over the horizon, never to be seen again. Surely the proud, brave Spaniards would not contemplate retreat without achieveing something? Even without Parma they could still land their own troops on the east coast of England. Maybe they would re-victual and repair in Norway or Denmark and attempt another union with Parma. Perhaps Parma might cross the straits without the Armada. Lord Howard was angry that the Armada remained a threat because his fleet lacked the ammunition to deliver the final blow.

More than a week after the Armada started to sail north, accompanied by her thirteen-hundred-strong bodyguard, Queen Elizabeth set off for her army's camp at Tilbury. Dressed in white and mounted on a large white horse, she paraded among her twenty thousand troops, then addressed them:

I am come amongst you as you see, at this time, not for my recreation and disport, but being resolved, in the midst and heat of battle, to live or die amongst you all, and all to lay down for my God and for my kingdom and for my people, my honour and my blood even in the dust. I know I have the body of a weak and feeble woman, but I have the heart and stomach of a king, and of a King of England too, and think foul scorn that Parma, or Spain, or any prince of Europe should dare invade the borders of my realm...

Loud cheers filled the air; patriotic men hoped the Spaniards would land right then so they could march into battle in defence of their beloved queen and country. It is ironic that one of the greatest rallying speeches of all time was made to an army that did not have to fire a shot or thrust a sword. Just two days later, on 18 August, nearly two thirds of the troops were relieved of their duties. It is unclear why the camp should have been at Tilbury. The Romans did not land in the area, neither did the Normans; why should the Spanish? Parma's halfhearted objective was eighty miles away, at Margate in Kent.

The English fleet did not follow the Spaniards far. They had long given up the chase when fishermen sighted the Armada south-east of the Shetlands, about the time the queen made her great speech. It may have been August but the weather was rough: men shivered in the fog as the cold wind and water penetrated their creaking, leaky ships.

If you plotted a dot for each Armada wreck and joined them up you would have a very accurate outline of the north and west coasts of Ireland. It was there that twenty-six ships and their crews met a violent end. If the men did not die as their vessels were smashed against the rocks then they were plunged into icy seas. If they did not drown in the surf some must have struggled onto the beach. If not stripped and slaughtered by scavenging locals they would have headed inland. If not then hunted down and slain by English soldiers a few might have made it back to Spain. If they did, they would have deserved some glory. Their incredible tales to half-believing audiences at some inn in a Basque fishing village would have described 'how I went to hell and back'.

Despite Medina Sidonia's order to stay together, bad weather and the deteriorating state of many of the ships and their crews did not allow it. By the beginning of September many of the weakened, hungry, thirsty and cold crews began to lose the battle to keep their ships afloat and on course. The hulks *Barca de Amburg*, *Gran Grifon* and *Castillo Negro* had not been built to weather such heavy seas. Before the *Barca de Amburg* went down on the first day of September, all her crew managed to escape to the *Gran Grifon* and *Trinidad Valencera*, but they had escaped only to temporary safety: both of these ships were doomed to hit the rocks or run aground. The *Castillo Negro* disappeared without trace with all hands on board. The *Gran Grifon*, which had taken a battering when isolated off Dorset back on 3 August, ran aground off Fair Isle on 27 September. Today one of her guns can be seen in the museum in Lerwick in the Shetland Islands. Some say that the inspiration for the colourful Shetland sweaters came from the clothes worn by the Spanish who escaped from the ship before she broke up.

Meagre and spoiled rations caused growing numbers to be added to the sick lists as gales, driving rain and fog continued to impede progress. Some ships gave Ireland a wide berth, others entered the hazardous, uncharted waters of the emerald coast. Some ships did benefit from local knowledge as off the Shetlands five Scottish fishing boats and their crews had been captured. One can imagine the distress of the Scotsmen at finding themselves aboard the filthy, leaking Spanish ships, among the sick and dying.

On 14 September Don Alonso de Luzon's grand Venetian ship, the 1,100-ton Mediterranean war machine *Trinidad Valencera*, smashed into the rocks in Kinnagoe Bay, County Donegal, on the north coast of Ulster. Seeking sanctuary amongst their Catholic brothers, Don Alonso shepherded the four hundred and fifty survivors towards the castle of a local bishop. Nearby they met with English troops, supported by a greater number of Irish regulars, and tried to negotiate for a ship and safe passage. But the English feared that soon thousands of desperate, vengeful Spaniards could be coming up the beaches, mixing with locals and triggering a rebellion. Major Kelly demanded that the Spanish surrender. Don Alonso refused. The English and Irish attacked, bringing the hungry Spaniards back to the negotiating table. This time Don Alonso agreed to surrender; his men laid down their arms. But the English and Irish did not have the resources to steward prisoners of war *and* patrol the coast for new arrivals. Nineteen thousand Spanish troops could be on their way, troops who regarded the English as heretics, who had declared war on them and set out to invade their land and subjugate their people. These were not innocent shipwreck survivors but an enemy army that, if allowed to organise itself, would constitute an overwhelming threat. Extermination was the policy of Queen Elizabeth's Lord Deputy of Ireland, Sir William Fytzwylliam. All the best English troops were in the Netherlands, leaving him with just two thousand men. The only way he could ensure that his garrison kept control was to order the death of all survivors. He did not even want them to spare the 'better sort' for ransom; there were an awful lot of 'better sort' aboard the Armada, they could soon add up to a threat. The following day the English and Irish set about the slaughter. Three hundred fell to the lesion of the musket ball, the jab of the bayonet, the thrust of the pike, the stroke of the sword; a hundred and fifty escaped to the bishop's castle: many of these did eventually see Spain again. As for Don Alonso, he was kept prisoner in London for three years, praying for the day sufficient ransom was delivered to secure his release. Today many articles from the ship he left behind can be seen in the Ulster Museum. In the end the policy of extermination did not account for more than eleven hundred Spanish lives.

The men of the *Barca de Amburg* were not the only ones to escape from one vessel only to come to grief in the next. On 22 September the 820-ton Genoan-built *Rata Santa Maria Encoronada*, commanded by a second Don Alonso, Don Alonso de Leiva, ran aground in Blacksod Bay, County Mayo. After a long march round the huge bay, the men boarded the *Duquesa Santa Ana*. The crowded ship set sail for Scotland but got only as far as Loughros More Bay in County Donegal before also running aground. After another long march most of the men joined the *Girona* in Killibegs Harbour. Don Alonso de Leiva's third ship, which sailed north with sixteen hundred on board, hit the rocks near the Giant's Causeway off Country Antrim. Only nine survived.

They did not include Don Alonso. Again, many articles from this ship are in the Ulster Museum.

Some Spaniards did manage to land, take on water and get away again. Juan Martinez de Recalde, in the 1,050-ton *San Juan*, entered Blaskett Sound on the south-west coast of Ireland with the assistance of one of the captured Scottish fisherman. Followed in by Marcos de Aramburu's 750-ton *San Juan Bautista*, they spent three days taking on badly needed fresh water. The English watched them but did not dare to intervene due to inferiority of numbers. They were briefly joined in the sound by Fernando Horra's smaller ship of the same name, *San Juan Bautista*, and Don Pedro de Pacheco's 945-ton *Santa Maria de la Rosa*, but both of these vessels promptly sank. Six other Spanish ships entered port in the Shannon and managed to get away again.

The great storm of 20 September accelerated the demise of many ships and their crews. The arrival of the ships was a rare opportunity for the locals to obtain gold, silver, weapons and clothes. The sailors and soldiers still had on them all the money they were paid at La Coruña. It was a bonanza which came all at once; the local people had to move fast to get as much as possible while they had the chance. Hundreds participated in the grabbing frenzy as exhausted, famished, disorientated, half-drowned and largely unarmed men struggling ashore were immediately set upon, punched, bludgeoned, knifed or axed and stripped of everything they had. The worst of the killing beaches was Streedagh Strand in Sligo where five miles of sand was strewn with over a thousand corpses.

One man who did manage to struggle up the beach to the relative safety of a field was Captain Francisco de Cuellar from the 530-ton *San Pedro*. His is an extraordinary tale of brushes with death and narrow escapes. Like Don Cristobal de Avila, Captain de Cuellar had made the mistake of allowing his ship to get ahead of the pack in the North Sea. He was sentenced to death by Medina Sidonia but spared by judge advocate Martin de Aranda. The fleet would get the message from just one body, Don Cristobal's, swinging from the yard-arm. It was his first lucky escape. He was moved to Aranda's 728-ton *Lavia*, which later ran aground off Streedagh Strand. Two hundred yards from the beach, the captain faced a dilemma. He could not stay aboard – it was only a matter of time before the waves would beat her to matchwood – but he could not swim, and even if he could make it ashore he could see how two hundred Irishmen there were treating his compatriots. In the end he plunged into the surf and clung to some wreckage. He attained the shore, but only after suffering a wounding blow to the legs from another piece of wreckage. The bloody legs might have helped; miraculously Cuellar crawled to the dunes without being clubbed or stripped. A terrified, speechless and naked survivor joined him. That night two men approached them, one with an axe, and they feared the worst. The axe swung – but to cut rushes which were laid upon them as protection from the elements. They were not enough: Cuellar's silent companion died beside him that night. Next morning Cuellar headed inland and found a monastery. There were no sympathetic monks waiting to feed and clothe him, just twelve of his compatriots hanging from the rafters of the desecrated chapel. Desperate for food, he returned to the beach where crows and wolves now feasted. There he was stabbed in the leg and robbed, but at least he found some food. Later he was beaten up again and narrowly failed to catch up with an Armada ship collecting survivors. This was lucky: it soon went down with all hands on board. Protected by a local clan chief, Cuellar managed to lie low for the next few months. He then headed north to Dunluce. It was now 1589. He must have thought the game was up when, while visiting some local girls, he encountered two English soldiers. Fortunately their attention was on the girls so he managed to escape. With the help of the Bishop of Derry he boarded a boat to Scotland and, six months later, one of several ships heading for Flanders. Justin of Nassau was waiting and launched an attack, which claimed many lives. Cuellar's ship ran aground but, for the second time, he managed to reach the shore on a piece of wood, and lived to write an account of his year on the run.

One Armada hospital ship, the 581-ton Baltic hulk *San Pedro El Mayor*, did a full circle of the British Isles before going down off Hope Cove in south Devon. The survivors were spared; they did not represent a threat. Parma eventually bought back those without rank for £10 each. Wrecks were a valuable source of timber for building and parts of this ill-fated ship holds up the roof of the Thurlestone Inn not far from Hope.

So, what of the men who had sailed or marched on the victorious side? When they picked up their wages, did they find a little extra in there from a grateful nation? Were they shown such lasting gratitude that they would in future not hesitate to leave their trade routes, harvests and forges to run out a cannon or pick up a musket in defence of Queen Elizabeth and the realm? Unfortunately not. Much illness had broken out in the unsanitary wooden boats. When men were landed there was no provision for looking after them; even the fit struggled to survive for they had not been paid. Lord Howard was livid with the Lord Treasurer. Heroes of the campaign died in pain, in poverty and without dignity, forced to beg for scraps from passers-by offended by the stench. Half of the men aboard the Armada ships may never have seen Spain again, but half of the English armed forces also never saw Christmas again.

By the middle of August the news that the Spanish nation waited to hear arrived in Madrid – *the Armada had won a magnificent victory over the English fleet*. Fifteen English ships lay at the bottom of the sea, others had been captured and a frightened Drake had fled. The news came from Spain's ambassador in Paris, Don Bernardino de Mendoza. King Philip was hopeful but unconvinced; he wrote to Medina Sidonia for confirmation. Mendoza kept on sending good news about the victorious Battle of Newcastle and Drake's capture. Even at the end of September he reported the capture of the English and Scottish fishing fleets – and what fine weather they were enjoying! When the truth came out he must have struggled to get anyone to believe him on any subject ever again.

Mateo Vazquez was private secretary and chaplain to King Philip and was no doubt proud at having attained such a privileged position. For many years he had enjoyed unsealing letters and passing on good news of economic and territorial gains to his employer. His job had its downside of sharing bad news with the king but he could never have contemplated having to tell him that the Armada was no more. He could not bring himself to utter the words and instead forwarded a letter to his master on the subject. Philip was mortified and prayed it was not true. Two and a half weeks later Medina Sidonia's messenger, Don Balthasar de Zuniga, arrived in Madrid. It was true. Remnants of the Armada were coming home in a terrible state. Could the king make provision for the reception of so many sick, hungry and exhausted men?

On 21 September, the day after the great gale had claimed three of his ships off Ireland, Medina Sidonia arrived at Santander with just eight of them. At the same time twenty-seven more arrived at other ports in northern Spain. Eventually a total of about seventy made it home. Disease and starvation had killed one hundred and eighty men aboard the *San Martin*. The duke himself had been very ill and had to be carried the length of Spain to Cadiz. Before he went south he wrote to the king to report on the catastrophe that had befallen them. Unbelievably, his account was followed to Madrid by more good news from Mendoza. Miguel de Oquendo, commander of the squadron of Guipuzcoa, landed at San Sebastián. He refused to see his wife and children but locked himself away to die alone of the shame and misery of running from the enemy only to be battered by the elements in places he should not have been. Juan Martinez de Recalde, the Armada's deputy commander, felt the same; he died just two days after reaching La Coruña. Philip ordered food, clothes and medicine to be despatched to the ports of La Coruña and Santander. He also made provision for the many left widowed and orphaned by the campaign.

Queen Elizabeth attended a thanksgiving service in St Paul's Cathedral on 4 December. She had much to be thankful for. Her throne was safe. England had successfully seen off an invasion force sent by the most powerful nation in the world, which had been severely weakened as a result. The defeat of the Spanish Armada meant that Britannia, and no longer España, ruled the waves.

King Philip was left to private prayers and grief for the seventy ships and eleven thousand men lost. He aged visibly as all around him the nation mourned. It was a shattering blow to Spain's self-confidence, and it was not a self-contained defeat. Without a fleet to protect them, the Spanish colonies and treasure ships would be even more vulnerable; the Dutch rebels would grow even more troublesome. The decline of imperial Spain had begun with Philip's *annus horibilis*.

CHAPTER 7

After the Armada
Cornwall and Cadiz

They shall land upon the rock of Merlin,
Who shall burn Paul, Penzance, and Newlyn.

Merlin the Wizard

Out of a fired ship, which, by no way
But drowning, could be rescued from the flame,
Some men leaped forth, and ever as they came
Near the foe's ships, did by their shot decay;
So all were lost, which in the ship were found,
They in the sea being burnt, they in the burnt ship drowned.

'A Burnt Ship', John Donne (1572-1631)

The Spanish Raid on Cornwall

IRONICALLY, WHILE THE DESTRUCTION of the Armada guaranteed that a full-scale Spanish invasion of England would not be attempted again, it increased the likelihood of small-scale incursions. Just seven years after those one hundred and thirty ships swept up the Channel and threatened to land thousands of troops, a much smaller number of Spanish soldiers rampaged through three Cornish communities, torching buildings, looting property and killing civilians that got in their way. The English authorities effected a cover-up; were it not for Richard Carew's account in the Survey of Cornwall in 1602, Captain Carlos de Amezola's report to the Spanish king might have been put down to wishful thinking.

Eight miles from Land's End, facing Mount's Bay on the east side of the Penwith Peninsula and at the bottom of a steep valley is the old fishing village of Mousehole. Less than half a mile inland, on the hill, is the tiny village of Paul. Just over a mile north of Mousehole, along the coast, is Cornwall's busiest fishing port, Newlyn. In 1595 Mousehole was doing rather well; it was in fact larger and more prosperous than either Newlyn or Penzance. Besides fishing and farming, there was the trade and transport of cloth, tin and stone through the harbour. There were two markets a week and two annual fairs. Some merchants lived in two-storey granite houses with glass windows and slate roofs but most people lived in cottages with earth floors, walls of a clay, straw and rubble compound, wooden shutters for windows and thatched roofs – ideal for a marauding Spaniard with a torch in his hand.

In 1588 the weather and the opportunities for escape that 'accidentally' running ashore offered slave crews had meant that none of the four galleys that had set out from Spain had made it to the Channel. Now, in July 1595, four were in the Blavet estuary, a Spanish-held enclave on the south coast of Brittany. Their commander, Captain Carlos de Amezola, planned a commando-style raid on Cornwall. It had several objectives. Firstly, there was a religious aim: prompting a rebellion to restore the Catholic faith to England. It was over half a century since Cornishmen had risen against the replacement of the Catholic mass by the Protestant service but the captain and his principal chaplain, the black-robed Friar Domingo Martinez of the Order of St Dominic, still hoped that there were many who would rise again. Secondly, there was intelligence to be gathered: on the state of English harbours, lest Spain send another armada; on the intended destination of the expedition Drake and Hawkins were preparing; and on the military movements of England and her allies. Thirdly, there was the attraction of property, much of which had been seized from Spanish ships by English privateers and landed at Mousehole, the first place it could be turned into cash. The Spanish were particularly keen to recover the valuable cargo of one of their great East Indiamen. The goods had been stored in warehouses at Pernambuco in Brazil after the ship hit a shoal. The port was then raided by the English under Admiral John Lancaster, who would only just have arrived home – so the Mousehole warehouses might still contain the goods. Fourthly, it was simply a chance to do some damage to the land of pirates and heretics.

Captain Carlos would not guide his ships into Mount's Bay ignorant of currents, shoals and rocks, neither would Captain Don León lead his troops ashore unaware of the best landing places or the lie of the land beyond – for with them sailed a traitor, an English renegade captain named Richard Burley. One of the few Englishmen who had sailed with the Armada seven years before, he knew King Philip personally.

On 25 July 1595 the residents of Mousehole, who had been concerned by recent reports of Spanish galleys off St Ives, Padstow and St Keverne near Falmouth, awoke to the shocking sight of four Spanish galleys in the bay. Their worst fears were realised as over two hundred men armed with muskets and pikes stormed ashore. As Mousehole burned, Squire Jenkyn Keigwin was slain defending his house, a fine building that still stands. That only two other inhabitants were to die during a raid by so many heavily armed men demonstrates that the locals saw resistance as futile and concentrated on getting away. The troops must have been under orders to minimise the killing; it was a rising that Friar Domingo Martinez really wanted. The dead squire's house was spared the torch but not the local parish church at Paul. As residents fled further round Mount's Bay, Sir Francis Goldolphin of Penzance, a deputy Lord Lieutenant of Cornwall responsible for mustering local militia, tried to take charge. He summoned troops in the area and sent to Sir Francis Drake and Sir John Hawkins at Plymouth requesting their help but also warning them lest these four ships be part of a much larger force. The Spaniards returned to their ships and sailed to Newlyn where four hundred of their number landed. From the top of the hill there they observed what meagre defences stood in their way. They had time to celebrate mass. After burning Newlyn they marched towards Penzance, barely a mile away, as their ships fired on Godolphin's little defensive force of less than a hundred. It dissolved as the Spanish 'Pirates at Penzance' entered the town and set about torching it before returning to their ships. They spared the chapel of St Mary: Richard Burley told them mass had previously been celebrated there.

It had been so easy that next day they doubtless wanted to land again but they observed the growing Cornish forces assembling near Marazion and St Michael's Mount. Bullets and arrows forced them away from the shore. Knowing the bay to be a potential trap, their enthusiasm for another raid must have begun to wane. Two days after they arrived, and before English ships arriving from the Lizard and Plymouth could corner them, a fresh north-westerly wind filled their sails and bore them swiftly away.

The Cornish were left to bury three of their number – Jenkyn Keigwin, James of Newlyn and Teek Cornall – and rebuild their communities. Mousehole lost its importance as merchants turned to the less exposed ports of Newlyn and Penzance. The raid greatly concerned Queen Elizabeth and her secretary of state Lord Burghley who acted to ensure that defences were improved – and of course to suppress the bad news.

The Anglo-Dutch Raid on Cadiz

IN APRIL THE FOLLOWING YEAR, thirty-eight years after Philip, as
titular King of England, was blamed for the English loss of Calais, his
forces based in the Spanish Netherlands captured the port for Spain.
With their presence in Blavet, Calais and the Netherlands, Spain now
had a dangerous grip on the Channel. England was also wary of the
Spanish potential to land in Ireland and foment a rebellion there that
could lead to invasion from the west. Without delay, England needed
to hit out at Spain and reduce the threat she posed. Fortunately she
had an ally even more desperate to reduce the Spanish threat – the
Dutch. An Anglo-Dutch Armada was assembled. It sailed for Spain at
a time when Spanish morale had just received a massive boost: news
of the deaths of Drake and Hawkins. For the English it was important
to show Spain that, although Drake was gone, they still had the ability, the men and the confidence to sail into Spanish ports, capture their
ships, raid their warehouses and pillage their homes.

The enormous fleet that sailed from Plymouth early in June 1596
consisted of a hundred and twenty-eight ships, a fifth of them Dutch.
On board were six thousand soldiers. The command was shared
between Charles, Lord Howard of Effingham and Robert Devereux,
Earl of Essex. The Rear Admiral of the fleet was Sir Walter Raleigh.
A gentleman passenger who sailed with the fleet was to distinguish
himself as resident war poet. He was John Donne, the son of a
London merchant. He had studied at both Oxford and Cambridge, and
probably travelled in Spain before returning to England to read law.
He was encouraged by the fact that one of the expedition leaders,
Essex, was a lover of the arts; Donne hoped he might provide patron-
age for his work in the future.

As it sailed south the fleet was careful to remain out of sight of land,
not an easy task two centuries before the genius John Harrison finally
solved the problem of accurately calculating longitude. After two and
a half weeks they approached their objective – Cadiz, chosen for its
great wealth and importance, the richness of the prizes likely to be
moored there and the possible ease of seizing and holding the port.
On Sunday 20 June its citizens awoke to the terrifying sight of the
fleet in the bay. That day the winds were strong and the sea rough.
The raiders bided their time. They chose not to land until the following day. The citizens that did not flee waited anxiously.

Early next day the Anglo-Dutch fleet attacked the Spanish fleet that was made up of just twenty-one warships, nineteen galleys and forty merchantmen. Predictably it was a rout with carnage on the decks and great numbers drowning after jumping for their lives. Admiral Don Diego de Sotomayor and Vice Admiral Don Juan de Alcega preferred to burn the *San Phlippo* and *San Tomas* rather than see them taken and their example was followed by many other captains. The poet Donne was aghast at what he saw, recording the horror in 'The Burnt Ship'. With the best ships burning there was no hope for the rest. The Spanish lost fifty-seven ships in total by fire and capture.

The Dutch and the English both later claimed to be the first to land. Whoever it was, the Spanish put up a fight despite overwhelming odds. The allied troops faced resistance as they approached the walls of Cadiz and, once over them, had virtually to fight from house to house as shot flew from rooftops, doors and windows. The castle did not surrender until the next day. The allies suffered two hundred killed and wounded. The population braced themselves for the violence of the army but little happened: Essex had ruled against it, an extremely civilised gesture which impressed Philip II. It would, however, not have been popular among the troops. If a town did not surrender and they risked their lives to take it they felt entitled to treat it as they pleased – that was their incentive. Soldiers still thought that way two centuries later when they stormed French-held Spanish strongholds in the Peninsular War.

Outside Cadiz, troops had been busy securing the strait that led to the mainland. Their losses were as high as those in the town due to an outbreak of drunken disorder which left many isolated and vulnerable to the hovering enemy.

Amazingly, the invaders were able to stay for two weeks. Despite this undermining of the king's credit no army came hurtling down the road from Seville to punish the invaders. They had time to discuss the idea of keeping Cadiz permanently (they decided against it), bury Sir John Wingfield, commander of one of the nine regiments, in the cathedral, exchange prisoners and systematically ransack the town. On Sunday 4 July the order went out to re-embark. Men weighed down with loot struggled up the gangplanks as Cadiz began to burn. An exchange of prisoners saved many English from the brutality of Spanish dungeons and galleys but unfortunately those taken from Drake's last expedition arrived too late to benefit.

On the way home the fleet put into Faro in Portugal, at that time under Spanish rule. Pickings were scant compared with those in Cadiz, the inhabitants having fled with most of their possessions. However,

Essex did collect some rather fine books from the bishop's library which he later presented to Sir Thomas Bodley for the library he was assembling at Oxford University. After a foray inland, Faro was fired and the forces re-embarked.

Unfavourable winds prevented the fleet from sailing to the Azores and an absence of enemy ships made entering La Coruña pointless, so home they sailed. Lord Howard and Sir Walter were the first to arrive, docking in Plymouth on Friday 6 August. Business was soon brisk in Bristol, Plymouth, Southampton and London as more ships came in and booty was carried ashore.

Without doubt the expedition was successful. At a time when Spanish morale was riding high, because of satisfaction with their grip on the English Channel and the deaths of Drake and Hawkins, the success of the Anglo-Dutch Armada was very demoralising. It proved the English still had the confidence and ability to take Spanish ports. The previous year's raid on Cornwall had been avenged. Queen Elizabeth did not herself see it as a great success, however: her one interest was in a financial return on her investment. The expedition had covered her £50,000 outlay but there were no huge profits. The Spanish treasure house had contained only 44,000 ducats, most of the money having been successfully hidden under graves and in the church vaults.

Twenty-three-year-old John Donne's career blossomed after his return, though not through the patronage of Essex, who was beheaded for trying to foment a rebellion in 1601. John Donne is considered by many to have written the greatest love poetry in the English language. He is also noted for his religious verse and sermons. In 1623 he wrote 'Devotions upon Emergent Occasions' which includes the famous lines:

No man is an Iland, intire of it selfe; every man is a peece of the Continent, a part of the maine; if a Clod bee washed away by the Sea, Europe is the lesse, as well as if a Promontorie were, as well if a Mannor of the friends or of thine owne were; any mans death diminishes me, because I am involved in Mankinde; And therefore never send to know for whom the bell tolls; It tolls for thee.

More than three hundred years later the American writer Ernest Hemingway drew his inspiration for the title of his classic novel on the Spanish Civil War, *For Whom the Bell Tolls*, from this passage.

CHAPTER 8

The War of
the Spanish Succession

The word's gone out, and now they spread the main
With swelling sails, and swelling hopes, for Spain:
To double vengeance pressed where'er they come,
Resolved to pay the haughty Spaniard home:
Resolved in future conduct to atone
For all our past mistakes, and all their own.
New life springs up in every English face,
And fits them all for glorious things apace:
The booty some excites, and some the cause;
But more the hope to gain their lost applause.
Eager their sullied honour to restore,
Some anger whets, some pride and vengeance more.

From 'The Spanish Descent' by Daniel Defoe, 1702

P OOR, MALFORMED KING CHARLES II of Spain had been physically and mentally ill virtually all of his life. The cause was
incest: the Spanish royal family had been inbred for years, its
family tree a mass of twisted, intermingling branches. Cousins, uncles
and nieces became husbands and wives. Try to follow this chaotic succession if you can. When Charles V abdicated in 1555, he bequeathed
Spain, the Netherlands and the Indies to his son Philip and the Holy
Roman Empire, a shifting complex of lands in western and central
Europe, to his brother Ferdinand. The imperial crown was in theory
elective; in practice it was hereditary within the Hapsburg dynasty of
Austria. Ferdinand's son Maximillan married within the family, taking his cousin, Philip's sister Maria, as his wife. They had a daughter,
Anne of Austria (later the great-grandmother of semi-imbecile Charles
II of Spain and Louis XIV of France). She married her uncle, Philip II
of Spain, and in 1578 gave birth to a son who was named after his
father. Philip IV married his niece and it was their son who grew up
to be King Charles. Nature steps in to prevent such malformed
inbreeds from producing ever more grotesque and sickly offspring:
incest results in infertility. Charles's inability to produce an heir was

not just a personal embarrassment and inconvenience to Spain, it was of great concern to the whole of Europe where a delicate balance of power could easily be upset.

The Britlish worried that the next Spanish monarch could be from the French Bourbon royal family: the resulting Franco-Spanish empire would threaten Britlish trade everywhere from the West Indies to the eastern Mediterranean. With Spanish possessions in the Netherlands, Italy and the New World under its control, Bourbon power would be formidable. Britain's navy would be hard pressed to defend British merchantmen as France would control almost every strategic location including Gibraltar, the Balearics and Sicily. Worse still, wealth from Spain's profitable New World trade would mean that over time the empire would grow ever stronger. The French were equally worried. If the next Spanish monarch was from the Austrian Hapsburg royal family the resulting empire could dominate Europe as it had in the previous century under Charles V. Britain was less concerned about such an alliance as Austria had no navy.

With so much at stake, while the Spanish king still lived Britain and France negotiated for a share in Spain's outlying possessions on his death. In 1695 Charles II had declared the Electoral Prince of Bavaria to be his heir. Assuming this accession, Britain and France had secretly signed a partition treaty, but the young prince's death soon nullified it. A second treaty was then concluded, based on Charles, Archduke of Austria, being heir. This treaty also had to be torn up as, under Bourbon pressure, Charles II willed his throne to the Duke of Anjou. This was dangerous for Britain. The duke's grandfather was no less than the Sun King, Louis XIV of France. Britain, Holland and the Empire would need to be naively optimistic to believe that King Louis would not interfere in his grandson's affairs.

When Charles died on 31 October 1700, Britain, Holland and the Empire's worst fears were realised. King Louis quickly took control. He declared that the Pyrenees no longer existed as a border; he despatched his grandson, the new King Philip V of Spain, to Madrid and dealt with Spain's possessions in the Netherlands and Italy himself.

International trade, the lifestream of Britain's economy, was under threat. France could close the straits of Gibraltar at any time. As the problem was still hypothetical, however, how could King William persuade the British Parliament to go to war? He did not need to: King Louis did the persuading for him. When William's predecessor, the dethroned Stuart king, James II, died in exile in September 1701, the French king recognised James's son as the new King of England, Scotland and Ireland. Controlling Spain's Mediterranean and Caribbean ports was one thing, honoring a pretender to the British throne was quite another. Reeling from this insult, the British Parliament and people threw their support behind their country's joining a 'Grand Alliance' against France. When William died in March 1702 his successor Queen Anne took up the mantle, joining the allies in a declaration of war – this was to be the *War of the Spanish Succession.*

The plan was for the emperor to take on the French in Italy and for the English and Dutch to open theatres of war in the Netherlands and on the Spanish coast. The Spanish people would have to be persuaded to accept the Austrian monarchy in place of the French. Cadiz was targeted. Not only was it Spain's principle naval base but it was also the entry point for riches from the Indies, much of which now ended up in France.

One hundred and sixty ships under the command of Sir George Rooke sailed from Spithead on 12 July 1702. Amongst the many transport vessels were thirty British and twenty Dutch warships. On board was a land force of ten thousand British soldiers under the Duke of Ormond, and four thousand Dutch. The objective was to seize Cadiz. If it was too well defended, they could take Vigo, Pontevedra or La Coruña on the way home. Cadiz, situated on an island connected to the mainland by a causeway, had a fortress defended by a garrison of nine regiments of foot and one thousand horse. When the fleet arrived on 23 July, the Duke of Ormond was all for striking while the iron was hot; Rooke was altogether more cautious, preferring to take a few outlying settlements first and gather intelligence before making the attempt on Cadiz. Unfortunately the admiral got his way.

At daybreak on 26 July twelve hundred troops went ashore. Resistance was limited. The following day the mayor of Rota surrendered his small town and castle. The troops had not come to capture towns for their own nations but to claim them for the House of Austria. Accordingly the Duke of Ormond issued a proclamation in the name of Queen Anne but the Anglo-Dutch troops that plundered dwellings and churches in El Puerto de Santa María a few days later did nothing but damage to the cause of Charles III. The soldiers' drunken conduct was not discouraged by the fact that Lieutenant-General Sir Henry Bellasis, second-in-command of the whole army, joined in.

On 2 August the fortress of Santa Catalina surrendered. The Duke of Ormond then concentrated his efforts on capturing a fort on a promontory north of Cadiz; if he succeeded, it had been agreed that

Rooke would enter the Bay of Cadiz and attack the French ships, but these designs were scuppered when the enemy sank three merchant ships across the mouth of the harbour. A few days later Ormond abandoned his mud-filled trenches; the enterprise was going nowhere. The Bourbon King of Spain's beard had not been singed, merely tickled. Rooke advocated a bombardment of Cadiz from the sea but the ocean swell made accuracy difficult. Besides, the damage and injury caused by such an attack would not have sent its residents rushing to support the allied cause. The troops re-embarked.

A deputation from the Austrian party in Madrid and Toledo was keen for the army to spend the winter in some other Spanish port. Ormond agreed but Rooke and his admirals preferred to return home: other landings were too risky and, with winter coming, provisions were insufficient. On 29 August the fleet sailed for England.

Back in Britain, government Ministers' minds turned to a convoy of New World treasure ships known to be on its way to Spain or France, escorted by French ships under the command of Rear-Admiral Chateau-Renaud. The Ministers acted by despatching a fleet under Admiral Sir Cloudesly Shovel to capture the convoy and its bounty. Meanwhile, officers of a detachment of Rooke's returning fleet, which had stopped at Lagos to take on water, chanced on the information that the treasure fleet had reached Vigo. Literally it was a golden opportunity to redeem the failure of Cadiz. On 22 September they arrived off the Galician port.

On either side of the harbour entrance was a battery; with forty guns, the one to the south had twice the firepower of its opposite number. It was decided that it needed to be taken before the ships could burst through the boom of chains and masts that straddled the mouth of the inner harbour. Two thousand five hundred troops landed and did the job at the expense of eighty-six of their number. The flagship *Torbay* then penetrated the boom, followed in by four English and three Dutch warships. In the mêlée the *Torbay* lost sixty men, burnt or drowned as it was grappled by a French fire-ship. Despite Chateau-Renaud's desperate orders to scuttle his fleet, fourteen of the twenty-five ships were taken by the attackers intact. The prize was indeed a very big one. The value of the plunder was estimated at £1m.

Daniel Defoe told the story in his poem 'The Spanish Descent':

> The mists clear up, and now the scout decries
> The subject of their hopes and victories:

The wished for fleets embayed, in harbour lie,
Unfit to fight, and more unfit to fly.
Triumphant joy throughout the navy flies,
Echoed from shore to shore with terror and surprise.
Strange power of noise! which at one simple sound
At once shall some encourage, some confound.
    In vain the lion tangled in the snare
With anguish roars, and rends the trembling air:
'Tis vain to struggle with Almighty Fate;
Vain and impossible, the weak debate.
The mighty boom, the forts, resist in vain.
The guns with fruitless force in noise complain.
See how the troops intrepidly fall on!
Wish for more foes, and think they fly too soon.
With eager fury to their forts pursue,
And think the odds of four to one too few.
The land's first conquered and the prize attends;
Fate beckons in the fleet to back their friends:
Despair succeeds, they struggle now too late,
And soon submit to their prevailing fate:
Courage is madness when occasion's past,
Death's the securest refuge, and the last.
    And now the rolling flames come threat'ning on,
And mighty streams of melted gold run down.
The flaming ore down to its centre makes,
To form new mines beneath the oozy lakes.
    Here a galleon with spicy drugs inflamed,
In odoriferous folds of sulphur streamed.
The gods of old no such oblations knew,
Their spices weak, and their perfumes but few.
The frighted Spaniards from their treasure fly,
Loath to forsake their wealth, but loath to die.
    Here a vast carrack flies while none pursue,
Bulged on the shore by her distracted crew:
There like a mighty mountain she appears,
And groans beneath the golden weight she bears.
Conquest perverts the property of friend,
And makes men ruin what they can't defend:
Some blow their treasures up into the air
With all the wild excesses of despair.
    And now the victory's completely gained;
No ships to conquer now, no foes remained.
The mighty spoils exceed whate'er was known
That vanquished ever lost, or victor won:
So great, if Fame shall future times remind,
They'll think she lies, and labels all mankind.

Cloudesley Shovel's fleet then arrived and Rooke and Ormond left him to mop up; they headed for the joyous reception awaiting them in Portsmouth. It was not a pleasant homecoming for Lieutenant-General Sir Henry Bellasis, however; he was court-martialed and thrown out of the army for his part in the pillage at El Puerto de Santa María.

The following May Portugal joined the Grand Alliance, which subsequently proclaimed Charles, Archduke of Austria, King Charles III of Spain. On his way from Vienna to the peninsula, Charles dropped in to see the queen at Windsor, eventually arriving in Lisbon in March 1704. The allies had planned to enthrone him in Madrid after a land invasion by the Portuguese army but such was the sorry condition of Portugal's military machine that it was decided instead to concentrate on attacking Spanish coastal fortresses such as Barcelona.

The fleet of forty-nine English and Dutch warships and other vessels commanded by Admiral Sir George Rooke arrived off Barcelona on 29 May 1704. Aboard were two thousand three hundred and seventy troops under the command of Prince George of Hesse Damstadt. He was a local hero. Seven years before he had commanded the Catalans within the fortress of Barcelona as they struggled for fifty-five days to resist a French siege. He hoped that his arrival, backed up by a show of strength, would prompt a popular rising for Charles III. However, the governor of Barcelona acted quickly, arresting Austrian supporters before a rising could begin. In response, the prince landed sixteen hundred marines. As a show of strength it was unconvincing. The desired rising still failed to materialise and the force re-embarked two days later.

After sailing the Mediterranean for a few weeks Rooke's fleet arrived off Lagos in Portugal and was joined by Sir Cloudesley Shovel's fleet. With seventy-two ships and thirty thousand men it was now a force to be reckoned with, but Rooke still insisted on more troops before Cadiz could be attempted again. His caution was beginning to irritate King Charles and Prince George. Fortunately for them, he liked the next idea.

The capture of Gibraltar was immensely significant: it was Charles III's first Spanish foothold. True, it was only two square miles of Spain, leaving a hundred and ninety thousand more to go, but the value of the Rock lay not in its land area but in the fact that it provided a gateway to the country for Charles, an access point that would allow the allies to play to their strengths and use naval power to support and supply a push into Spain. It would also enable its master to dominate entry to the Mediterranean. It was probably the most strategically important place of all time. It would be successfully defended, and Britain would later conveniently forget that she had actually captured it with the Dutch for 'Hapsburg Spain', and she would hold on to it. This has meant that while the War of the Spanish Succession has largely faded from public consciousness, part of its legacy – the Rock and its community – never has done. Gibraltar continues to play a part in modern British history to this day. The capture and the defence of the Rock are covered in the next chapter.

*

THE FRENCH FLEET under the Lord High Admiral of France, the Comte de Toulouse, was searching for Rooke who had stayed in the area to protect the Rock against a counter-attack. The allied fleet consisted of fifty-three warships, six frigates, seven fire-ships and two bomb vessels carrying 3,614 guns and 22,543 men. The sides were very evenly balanced, the French counting on just two fewer warships, the same number of frigates, one less fire-ship and just thirty-seven fewer guns. However, they did have the advantage of twenty-eight large galleys. Rooke regrettably had recently permitted four warships to go off on convoy protection duties and another six to return to Holland to collect recruits.

At mid-morning on Sunday 24 August the fleets closed near Malaga. The first shot came from Vice Admiral Sir John Leake's flag-ship, the Prince George. It was a bitter struggle in which the opposing fleets bombarded each other all day. When the fighting ceased at about 7 o'clock, not one ship had been sunk, though many had been reduced from proud wooden castles to splintered wrecks. No advantage was gained by either side. Nine allied ships had been forced to withdraw as their ammunition ran out. The human cost was high. The allied decks were covered in the blood of 787 dead and 1,931 wounded; the French casualty figure exceeded three thousand.

*

WHILE ALL THIS ACTIVITY was occurring on the coast, there was also some limited action on land. Louis XIV had sent an Englishman, an illegitimate son of the dethroned King James II, James Fitzjames, Duke of Berwick, to command the French and Spanish Bourbon army in the Peninsula. In Portugal, six and a half thousand British troops under the command of the hot-tempered Duke of Schomberg and Leinster awaited orders. They were part of the twenty-one-thousand-strong allied army. It was decided that they should be sent to reinforce Portuguese fortresses close to the Spanish border. Stanhope's regiment went to Portalegre, Stewart's to Castel Vide and the rest of the British to Elvas.

In the Spanish province of Extremadura, several miles from the border, a magnificent Roman bridge spans the gorge of the River Tagus at Alcántara. On 3 May Philip V joined Berwick there and the next day their army, which outnumbered the allies by seven thousand, invaded Portugal and began to seize fortress after fortress. Soon Berwick arrived at Portalegre; not long after his guns had opened up the dejected Portuguese within surrendered the place complete with Stanhope's troops. The British suffered a second reverse as the Bourbon army, swollen with four thousand Spanish reinforcements, laid siege to Castel Vide. Stewart's regiment under Lieutenant-Colonel Hussey was determined to hold the castle but his Portuguese comrades were less committed; as Hussey negotiated with Berwick outside, inside the castle the Portuguese were throwing his gunpowder down the well. Hussey had no choice but to surrender.

The invaders did not have it all their own way, however. The elderly Portuguese Marquis das Minas succeeded in forcing a large part of the Bourbon army back towards Spain and he recaptured the Portuguese fortress of Monsanto. It was the oppressively hot July weather that finally forced the entire invading Bourbon army back over the border. Berwick then displeased his superiors by refusing to take his army south to join the siege of Gibraltar, believeing that frontier defences could not spare such a loss of personnel. The allies went on the offensive with the aim of sacking the Spanish border town of Ciudad Rodrigo but Berwick put up a stout defence and the enterprise fizzled out.

While James, Duke of Berwick commanded the Franco-Spanish army in the peninsula, Henry de Massue de Ruvigny commanded the British. It was not a time for identifying sides by the commander's name. James and Henry's circumstances mirrored each other. The former had given up his estates and fled to France on the deposition of Catholic King James; Henry, a French Protestant, had fled with nothing to England when persecution of the Huguenots had begun again. Both were determined to fight for the causes of their adopted homes. Henry distinguished himself in Ireland, for which he was made Earl of Galway. In 1704 the fifty-six-year-old Earl was enjoing retirement in rural Hampshire when the call came to lead an army into Spain.

Seventeen thousand allied troops assembled in Portugal to invade the hot, dry Spanish province of Extremadura. Besides twelve thousand Portuguese and two thousand three hundred Dutch troops, their number included Galway's British contingent of two hundred cavalry, two and a half thousand infantry and some small artillery. In late April 1705 they crossed into Spain and laid siege to the border fortress town of Valencia de Alcántara. The Spanish infantry were busy elsewhere, trying to win back Gibraltar, and the town fell on 8 May. The next stop was Albuquerque. That fell on 20 May.

After the initial successes, things got much tougher when the French commander in Spain, Marshal de Tesse, arrived from Gibraltar. A break from the sweltering summer heat was followed by an allied attack on the fortress of Badajoz. The siege guns opened fire on 11 October and the garrison of fifteen hundred French and five hundred Spanish replied with their own deadly fire. The man who had been trying to enjoy his retirement in Hampshire was among the casualties: his right hand was shattered and later had to be amputated with part of his lower arm. As the breach in the walls of Badajoz grew big enough for an assault to be mounted, Marshal de Tesse arrived with four thousand foot and five thousand cavalry. After engagements with the new arrivals the allies abandoned the siege and headed back to Portugal.

The British and French were to meet again at Badajoz a hundred years later. In between their many battles, the officers of the opposing sides treated one another with a great deal of civility and respect. Such was the case when the French allowed Galway to go to the town of Olivenza for treatment; they even provided their best surgeons.

*

QUEEN ANNE'S GOVERNMENT elected to send another expedition against the Spanish coast in 1705, hoping it would trigger a rising by the Catalans who were ready to support the Austrian cause. This could divert French attention away from allied operations in Extremadura. The fleet under Sir Cloudesley Shovel, consisting of fifty-two British and fourteen Dutch warships, along with eleven bomb vessels, set sail from Lisbon in late July. Aboard was a land force of six and a half thousand men under the command of Charles, Earl of Peterborough. The peer's appointment was a political one. He was not really a soldier, though in his younger years he had briefly been one without seeing active service. Also on board were a five-hundred-strong Catalan force, and King Charles himself.

On 3 August King Charles enjoyed his first public appearance as a Spanish king on Spanish territory when he landed in state at Gibraltar and was received as the lawful sovereign. Two days later, with another three thousand two hundred fighting men on board, the ships sailed again, arriving on 11 August in Altea Bay on the east coast, not far north of Benidorm. Crowds of well-wishers on shore demonstrated that they were in friendly territory. A land force was despatched to take the fortress at Denia and after this had peacefully surrendered the fleet continued up the coast. Prince George of Hesse Damstadt went ahead to Mataró, north of Barcelona, where he found proof that the Catalan people were ready to rise: a deputation representing the sausage-making town of Vic came to demonstrate their loyalty to Charles.

On 22 August the joyous citizens of Barcelona welcomed their new king. They would have assumed that, having bravely declared for Charles, it would be but a short time before the 9,670 soldiers and twenty-four thousand seamen with their three and a half thousand guns would make hasty work of reducing the four-thousand-strong garrison. They were wrong. They had not reckoned with the Earl of Peterborough, determined not to spoil his record of never seeing active service. He complained that the garrison was too large, and no doubt reinforcements would be sent from Madrid; Barcelona was too close to France; the ground was too boggy for trenches; the expeditionary force was needed in Italy to assist the Duke of Savoy. A real soldier would not have shown such disobedience to orders. After two weeks, Peterborough agreed a compromise with the frustrated king and prince: his force would not leave Spain but it would also not take Barcelona; it would march south to València and prepare for a march on Madrid in the spring. If the men were angry at leaving a fight, their feelings were nothing compared to those of King Charles and the betrayed Catalan people.

The prince, however, was not finished with Barcelona. He devised a scheme for its reduction. Just south of the city is the mountain of Montjuïc, upon which now stands the Olympic stadium. At its summit is a stout fort. People familiar with it may assume that it had been the city's main defence, but in 1705 this was not the case. The town itself, with its huge walls, was the fortress. Montjuïc was but a small, incidental fort of little value, garrisoned by no more than two hundred Neapolitans under the command of Lientenant-General de Caracioli. The prince decided to persuade Peterborough that, at the very least, he should take this little fort before leaving, knowing that if they did the obvious next step would be to capitalise on the success and make an attempt on the town. Peterborough was beginning to understand the ridicule he would face if he returned home with nothing. He agreed to the enterprise.

On Sunday 13 September four hundred British and Irish grenadiers marched on what they were told was a gorge that needed to be captured on the road to València. They were followed by six hundred British, Dutch and Spanish musketeers. The prince was in fact leading them to the fort which he intended to attack at dawn. Unfortunately, by the time they arrived it was broad daylight; they had lost the advantage of surprise. They went for it all the same. Arriving at the walls despite heavy fire, they leant the ladders against them … and found they were too short! They had little choice but to retreat to cover. The prince moved to seize another small fort which was giving cover to reinforcements coming up the hill from Barcelona, but getting there meant hazarding the murderous fire from Montjuïc. In what was a devastating blow to the allies and the Austrian cause, Prince George of Hesse Darmstadt was hit in the thigh and died from huge loss of blood soon after. The next day an allied shell hit its target and blew up the magazine in the fort at Montjuïc. With Caracioli amongst the dead, the garrison surrendered.

Guns from the fleet then began their bombardment of Barcelona and two and a half thousand seamen landed between the hill and the city walls. On 24 September a battery of guns began to pound the city walls. By 3 October the fifty-eight artillery pieces had created a breach large enough to persuade the governor to surrender. Even before the fall of Barcelona, towns all over Catalonia, from Tarragona to Tortosa, Lleida to Girona, declared for Charles. On 23 October Sir Cloudesley Shovel and most of the fleet sailed home. The expedition had achieved its objectives: Barcelona was theirs. Far off in the splendour of the Palace of Versailles an angry King Louis was about to react to the news by diverting his forces from Extremadura.

The overcrowded, uncomfortable living conditions in the barracks and convents of Barcelona were not conducive to the army's good health. Soon many fell ill. The problem was solved by dispersing the troops to various fortresses within the province. Meanwhile the Catalans carried the revolt through the province of València: town after town declared for Charles until they arrived at the gates of the city itself. They and Major General Basset-y-Ramos passed through without opposition.

A two-thousand-five-hundred-strong Bourbon contingent under

Lieutenant-General de las Torres, determined to reverse the Hapsburg tide, entered the north of the province of València from Aragon. After taking Montroy and Morella, it approached the town of Sant Mateu where Lieutenant-Colonel John Jones commanded a garrison of thirty Royal Dragoons, three hundred Catalan fighters and seven hundred Valencian militia. Neither side had artillery. After a thirteen-day siege, during which the defenders even used the pipes of the church organ for ammunition, de las Torres had news of a relief force on its way from Tortosa, and withdrew. He headed south, taking out his frustration on Vila-real and Quart with extreme brutality.

Meanwhile Peterborough's entire army arrived at València. This was excellent news for the earl, who had avoided a fight with a Bourbon army en route. València offered him a pleasant residence. He had escaped the company of the man he had grown to hate, the man he had come to Spain to support, King Charles.

Barcelona was now very vulnerable. The French forces totalling twelve thousand men were already in the peninsula, approaching the city from the west, and a further nine thousand French troops were ready to pour over the border from Rousillon in the north. And there was the sea, which would soon be busy with the French fleet from Toulon. All this against a garrison of just fourteen hundred, Peterborough having drained Catalonia of over five thousand men.

The peninsula-based French troops did not march on Barcelona with impunity. On 25 January, at San Esteban de Litera in Aragon, Colonel Wills and his four hundred and thirty men drove back the French vanguard. The following day four and a half thousand French attacked twelve hundred English and Dutch soldiers on a defensive hillside position; after seven hours of fighting, during which five hundred and fifty men were killed or wounded on the two sides, the French withdrew. The battle served only to delay the Bourbon advance, however: after it was over they continued to press on towards Barcelona. On 17 March, accompanied by King Philip, they crossed into Catalonia where they were constantly harassed by eight thousand armed Catalans.

April started badly for the defenders of Barcelona. On the 1st the French fleet sailed in; on the 2nd nine thousand from Rousillon came and on the 3rd Tesse's twelve thousand. In France King Louis XIV, called the Sun King after the bright star that illuminated the Bourbon banner, looked forward to the hasty restoration of Barcelona to his realm. Would Tesse be able to capture Barcelona before the allied fleet arrived?

The garrison of fourteen hundred included three hundred British guards. The chief engineer, the English colonel Lewis Petit, had overseen considerable improvements to the fortifications. Land reinforcements were on their way from different parts of Catalonia. Hastening up the coast was an allied fleet of thirty-nine British and thirteen Dutch ships with five thousand troops eager to respond to King Charles's appeal for aid. Admiral Sir John Leake ignored a bombardment of orders from Peterborough to ignore Barcelona and land the troops elsewhere.

Tesse wasted no time. An immediate attempt was made on Montjuïc. This first attack was repulsed by Colonel Hamilton's men, who had just marched in from Tortosa. On 5 April the arrival of reinforcements boosted the number of regulars at the fortress to three thousand six hundred, eleven hundred of whom were British.

As the besieging army erected its batteries, King Charles boosted the defenders' morale by riding round the city ramparts and out to Montjuïc. On 13 April guns began battering the walls of the fort, the defence of which was now under the command of the Earl of Donegal. Six days later the French navy began bombarding Barcelona. On 21 April breaches in the walls of Montjuïc were seen by Tesse to be adequate to justify a major assault. He had judged right. His troops stormed in. British losses totalled three hundred, including Donegal. That same day Peterborough arrived back in the area. The anxious King Charles urged him to attack Tesse but the earl had a better idea: that the king abandon the Catalans and escape!

Breaches in the walls of Barcelona grew wider under the pounding from an increasing number of guns. On 7 May news came that the allied fleet was approaching. The following day it began landing troops. The French ships did not linger. With no fleet, Tesse had no base; with no base it was best he left as well. After seven weeks of siege, his dispirited army trudged north to the French border, harried on land by well-organised armed Catalans, the *miquelets*. In the sky they were disturbed by an awesome event which the Sun King's soldiers could only see as a bad omen: in the middle of the day, the sun went out.

*

IT WAS EARLY IN 1706. With most of Tesse's French troops in Catalonia, the time was right for Galway and the nineteen-thousand-strong allied army (including two thousand two hundred British) to pour over the Portuguese border and strike at Madrid. Awaiting them at various fortresses were the Duke of Berwick's fifteen thousand three hundred Spaniards. The allies entered Spain and headed for Brozas where the duke, a marshal of France by now, waited with four thousand cavalry. As they closed in on 8 April Berwick withdrew. The castle fell after a fight.

The allies then headed north-west to Alcántara. Many place-names in Spain begin with the letters 'al', *al* being Arabic for *the*: Albacete (The Plain), Alcantara (The Bridge). Alcántara could not have been better named. It is a small, remote town with a grand six-arched Roman bridge spanning a gorge carved by the River Tagus on its way to Lisbon. The four thousand Spanish defenders fought bravely but, as allied artillery opened up a breach in the fortress walls sufficient for an assault, they chose to surrender. It was 14 April. This was an important victory, not least because the fortress contained five thousand muskets, seventy guns and an abundance of food and wine. After Alcántara the allies kept going, towns kept falling – Moraleja, Coria, Plasencia, Ciudad Rodrigo, Salamanca – and inexplicably Berwick kept retreating, all the way back to Madrid which he reached in June. There he was joined by King Philip, back from Catalonia. The army did not even make a stand in Madrid. It retired on the other side, the rest of Philip's court having fled to Burgos.

On 27 June 1706 Galway and the allied army entered Madrid; days later Charles III was declared King of Spain. Considering that Galway should have been leading a quiet life, it was a magnificent achievement for him. He urged Charles and Peterborough to come to Madrid as quickly as possible. Most Spanish towns and cities were sending in submissions to the new order but Galway knew that only the king's presence could consolidate Austrian rule. Clearly people in the capital were not over-enthusiastic about an absentee Austrian king set up by their traditional enemies, Portugal and England.

As Berwick retired still further towards the north-east, away from Madrid, Galway and his army left the capital to pursue him, passing through Alcalá de Henares on 11 July and establishing a camp at Guadalajara, an excellent defensive position. Learning that King Charles was at last on his way via Zaragoza, they pushed on to give him safe passage. Fifty miles north-east of Madrid, at Jadraque, their progress was halted by a force under French Major-General Fiennes. From an impregnable position, Fiennes prevented Galway from crossing the bridge over the Henares and the tide turned. Berwick received reinforcements of two thousand three hundred cavalry and nine thousand foot. The outnumbered allies began to retreat. Charles never arrived in Madrid. The people of New Castille switched their allegiance back to the Bourbons and the window of opportunity for Charles, opened so briefly by Galway, slammed firmly shut. Berwick did not attack the allies but simply cut off their route back to Madrid. On 4 August Bourbon troops were welcomed into Madrid. Philip V was again proclaimed king. The next day, too late, King Charles reached the allied camp at Guadalajara.

*

AFTER BARCELONA, Sir John Leake headed south, seeking the submission of another great Mediterranean port, Alicante. Distracted on the way at hearing the ancient port of Cartagena on the Murcia coast was well disposed to submission, he decided to head there instead. The city where Hannibal had once governed submitted on 24 June. Alicante, where Irish Major General Daniel Mahoni commanded a garrison of two thousand, was not going to fall so easily. Outside the town walls a much larger force of five thousand four hundred, including British foot soldiers, cavalry, marines and seamen as well as Catalans, waited for the ten British and Dutch ships to breach the defences for them. On 2 August the bombardment began. Within a week the town had been stormed, Mahoni and his men retreating to the castle that stands high on a huge rock. Mortars played on the defenders, causing many casualties. In the end it was not firepower that forced them to surrender on 11 September but the poisoning of their water supply.

A British force then headed down the road to Murcia. They took Orihuela and were within eight miles of their objective when they had to turn back for fear of being cut off from Alicante.

Leake proceeded with twenty-six ships to Ibiza where the governor submitted to the Austrian crown when they arrived on the 20 September. At Palma in Mallorca it took just a few shells to persuade the people to negotiate a surrender. On 1 October the small French garrison marched out and was replaced by a hundred marines.

*

GALWAY AND THE ARMY left Guadalajara on 11 August and marched to Chinchón, twenty miles south of Madrid. He was forced to conclude that his fourteen thousand against Berwick's twenty-six thousand men could not succeed in retaking Madrid. They were cut off in the west so would have to head for València and the fleet. Leaving on 9 September, they were joined a week later by Lientenant-General

Wyndham's troops which had been occupied in the reduction of
Requena and Cuenca.

Berwick's army should have been wearing bright orange jackets,
such was their stewarding role for Galway's retreating army. True, he
did harass the rearguard and try to overtake at one point but, having
failed in this, he turned towards Murcia. The allies crossed into the
province of València on 28 September. They were safe, but in the
remaining months of the year, all over Spain, from Cartagena and
Orihuela to Cuenca and Alcántara, the hard-earned gains of 1706
slipped back into Bourbon hands.

*

AN EXPEDITIONARY FORCE with eight thousand two hundred troops
on board sailed from Portsmouth on 10 August 1706. They were to
land in the province of Guyenne on the west coast of France and raise
a Protestant revolt. Driven back to Torbay by bad weather, by the time
they set off again their objective had changed. The odds of success in
Guyenne were considered too low. They were now directed to strike at
Cadiz in Spain. While the fleet was at Lisbon the objective changed
yet again. They were now to reinforce Galway in València.

They landed at Alicante on 8 February 1707. The British hoped to
combine with Spanish and Dutch forces and strike out at Madrid for
a second time. The others, including Charles, preferred a defensive
strategy. Galway was left standing as allied troops dispersed across
València and Catalonia to take up defensive positions. He was deprived
of more than ten thousand men for a final, decisive battle with
Berwick. His new plan was to follow the Rio Turia from its mouth at
Grao near the city of València back to the watershed in the mountains;
from there they would follow the Tagus that sprung from the other
side and flowed towards Madrid. First he needed to guarantee València's security by destroying the French magazines in Murcia. The job
was nearly done, facilitated by Berwick's customary withdrawals,
when news came that the Duke of Orleans was approaching with eight
thousand reinforcements for Berwick. Galway would have to attack
Berwick before Orleans arrived.

On 25 April 1707 Galway and his army of fifteen and a half thousand men came to a field outside the small walled town of Almansa
(then in Murcia, now in Castilla La Mancha). A third of his force
was British, a half Portuguese; the rest were Dutch Huguenots and
Germans. They approached Berwick's army. Half French and half
Spanish, they had a worrying numerical advantage of ten thousand.

Soon after 3 o'clock the allies attacked. It was not to be their day. Portugal would one day build a great army but their soldiers on the field that day were poorly disciplined. Many fled. The vicious fighting lasted two hours, after which four thousand allied troops, mostly British, Dutch and Huguenots, lay dead or wounded. Bourbon losses were higher but undoubtedly they were the victors. Worse was to come for the allies. Next day two thousand more of their number who had retreated to the hills were surrounded and taken prisoner. Galway, himself with sabre cuts to the face, led his troops back to Ontinyent in València.

The sick and wounded were embarked on ships of Admiral George Byng's fleet which had arrived at Alicante days before the battle. Galway then marched north to Tortosa in Catalonia where he intended to rebuild his army. He left behind a number of fortresses still in allied hands. The Duke of Orleans, disappointed at arriving a day too late to share the victory, secured the surrender of Requena before departing for Aragon. Berwick took possession of València and demolished its walls before heading north after Galway.

Berwick's cruel Lieutenant-General D'Asfeld arrived at Xàtiva where Galway had sent Lieutenant-Colonel Campbell with seven hundred troops. The citizens and *miquelets* fought valiantly, keeping the general out of the town for two weeks. When he finally entered, he vented his anger on the populace by murdering every one of them. Three and a half weeks later Campbell, whose men had been holding the castle, ran out of water and surrendered. Xàtiva was later razed to the ground; only the church was left standing. Colonel Stewart, who had been fighting off a siege at Alzira with eight hundred men, also surrendered. Both men must have thought they had secured an excellent deal when they were allowed to march out with their weapons and promised an escort back to their army in Catalonia. Little did they know that the escort would attempt to exhaust them by taking them a very long way round.

By late June the besieging Bourbon army facing Denia numbered nine thousand men. Within the walls a garrison of a hundred and eighty-five English and three hundred and sixty Spanish troops was supported by two and a half thousand Valencian soldiers and armed citizens. On the 30 June Bourbon guns began battering the town walls. A wide breach was opened up but two assaults were desperately fought off. D'Asfeld tried to intimidate the defenders by threatening to execute every one of them, women and children included, if they did not surrender. They were not going to give way now. Two further assaults were repulsed. After twenty-seven days of siege D'Asfeld, who had lost more than three thousand men to the defenders' three hundred, lifted the siege.

After a lull in the fighting over the hot summer, the action moved north to Lleida in Catalonia. Orleans, who had earlier retaken Zaragoza without a fight, lay siege to Lleida. The Bourbon army was now twenty-two thousand nine hundred strong. After his mauling at Almansa, Galway had rebuilt an army of fourteen thousand six hundred. He was close to Lleida but on the wrong side of the River Segre. On the Lleida side, Berwick posted fourteen thousand troops to prevent the allies from crossing.

Galway had to stand by whilst Lleida was bombarded. Its garrison of two thousand six hundred included three British regiments under Major-General Wills. On 14 November, after six weeks of siege, the remains of the garrison marched out with the honours of war and joined Galway. James, Duke of Berwick, after reducing Morella in València, went to Madrid and then to France. His war in Spain was over.

*

THE FRENCH HAD BEEN DEFEATED in Italy. A short journey away many German troops were now free to join the allies in Spain. The British government, the Emperor and King Charles now agreed that the Germans should form the core of the army. The Portuguese went home to defend their own frontier. Galway, nearly sixty years old, his right hand missing since Badajoz and blind in one eye after the sabre slash at Almansa, wanted to go home too. Too highly valued, he was allowed to leave Catalonia but only for Lisbon, where he assumed the role of ambassador. The new commander of the ten-thousand-two-hundred-strong allied army was the experienced and accomplished German field marshal, Count Guido von Staremberg. Major-General James Stanhope commanded the two thousand English.

The new allied army's first task would be to relieve the fortress of Tortosa which Orleans invested on 11 June 1708. There four thousand two hundred men defended the town against twenty-two thousand Bourbons, including the notorious D'Asfeld. The attack began on 21 June. The defenders fought well, making sallies and maintaining murderous fire on the attackers, who lost fifteen hundred men. After nearly three weeks and whittled down to half their original strength, the defenders' only hope was the arrival of Staremberg. There was no sign of him. The allied army was still awaiting the arrival of five thousand eight hundred troops from Italy. Fearing the kind of retribution of which D'Asfeld was capable on such occasions, the governor of Tortosa capitulated on 10 July.

Fifteen days later the allied reinforcements landed. Five hundred British and two thousand five hundred Germans sprung a surprise attack on the town in December but after a couple of days of fighting, which saw heavy losses of some four hundred on each side, they withdrew.

*

ADMIRAL OF THE FLEET Sir John Leake commanded operations in the Mediterranean in 1708. That summer he collected King Charles's betrothed from Italy and carried her to Barcelona. The marriage of King Charles and Princess Elizabeth of Wolfenbuttel took place on 1 August.

Thereafter the fleet sailed for Sardinia, an extensive fertile island under Bourbon control. Close to Italy, it had the advantage of a large fortified port. On board were six hundred British marines and a thousand Spanish troops under Major-General Wills. The fleet arrived off Cagliari, the island's capital, on 11 August; it fell as easily as Mallorca. A few shells hitting the town and the landing of the troops and nine hundred seamen was enough for the locals. They forced their governor to capitulate. The Spanish troops were left behind and the fleet sailed for Menorca, an island with the largest deep-water port in the Mediterranean, Mahón. In friendly hands it would be an ideal winter station for a fleet which could then protect British trade in the Mediterranean, currently threatened by growing French naval forces at Toulon.

Not for the first time did the British capture for Charles III and the Austrian party a place of immense strategic importance and not for the last time would British ships, troops and governors still be there long after their support for Charles had passed into history. Menorca was under British control for most of the eighteenth century. Like Gibraltar, Menorca merits its own chapter.

*

D'ASFELD AND HIS TWELVE HUNDRED men renewed the siege of Denia on 2 November. The garrison of two hundred and twenty-seven British troops was under the command of Lieutenant-Colonel Perceval. The governor, Valeo, commanded an unknown number of Spanish troops. On 12 November the attackers poured through a breach in the town walls and occupied the lower ward. D'Asfeld dealt with the inhabitants in his usual rough way. Ten days later, with provisions running out and no sign of their appeals for relief being answered, Perceval and Valeo surrendered.

The victorious D'Asfeld headed for the last remaining allied stronghold in València – Alicante. High on the rock, the governor, Major-General John Richards, was ready. He had spent nearly three years fortifying the place, preparing for this day. D'Asfeld, who now commanded a siege army of fourteen thousand, pondered below. The fortress's lofty position, two hundred feet above him, would render an artillery bombardment ineffectual. Instead he would tunnel into the rock and plant an enormous mine. The resulting explosion would shatter the castle above and bring it tumbling down with its shocked garrison. After nearly three months of mining, two of Richards' officers from his eight-hundred-strong garrison of English and Huguenot troops were invited to inspect the mine and consider whether they really wanted to be overhead when the explosives went off. They must have been aghast at the sight of fifty-two tons of gunpowder, in twelve hundred barrels, packed into the hollowed out rock. But it was a big rock. Richards rejected three separate appeals to surrender.

Early on the morning of Monday 3 March 1709 the sight of people streaming out of the town below warned the garrison that the big blast was imminent, though they knew not what to expect. A modest rumble? A thundering bang and nothing more? A devastating earthquake? The governor and senior officers stood on the parade ground in an attempt to inspire confidence. At 6 o'clock the almighty explosion rocked the fortress. Fissures opened up across the parade ground as the rock split open and into these chasms fell Richards and fifty others. They stood no chance: the openings immediately slammed shut again. But the castle survived intact. The garrison stayed on, watching the sea for the fleet.

Seven weeks later, more than four and a half months into the siege, it finally arrived: twenty-three ships with fourteen hundred heavy guns with which to batter the besieging army and thirteen thousand soldiers and seamen ready to form an invasion force. After the garrison's remarkable stand, it looked as if the last allied stronghold in València would not fall. This was not the case. Admiral George Byng and Lieutenant-General Stanhope concluded that a landing was not practical. They treated with D'Asfeld, embarked the garrison and sailed away.

Over on the other side of Spain, the allies suffered another reverse.

The Spanish Bourbon general the Marquis de Bay and his fifteen thousand Spanish soldiers had crossed into Portugal and taken up a position east of the River Caya. De Bay hoped that the Allies would cross the river and attack. Galway, in charge of two thousand eight hundred British troops, knew that the side that chooses the battle location has the advantage. He did not care to fall for it. The Portuguese commander, the Marquis de Frontreira, disagreed, however, so over the river they went. Frontreira's guns opened the combat and his cavalry as good as finished it as they fled from the field. Both British brigades found themselves isolated. One managed to retreat in square despite being attacked on all sides, the other surrendered. There were five hundred casualties on each side that day; the difference was that the Bourbons took nearly a thousand prisoners. An infuriated Galway would never allow his troops to fight with the Portuguese again.

*

THE FOLLOWING JULY the advantage again swung towards the allies. Deprived of French troops and a French commander, the twenty-two-thousand-strong Bourbon army was now totally Spanish. Its commander was the Marquis de Villadarias, already known to the British for his unsuccessful siege of Gibraltar five years before. Benefiting from considerable reinforcements, Staremberg decided to go on the offensive. His army now totalled twenty-four and a half thousand men, four thousand two hundred British, fourteen thousand German and the rest Dutch, Spanish and Portuguese. His objective was the Pass of Alfaraz, north of Lleida. Learning this, the Bourbons set off in that direction but several miles to the south, at Almenara, their way was blocked by a detachment commanded by Stanhope. Standing off until early evening, Stanhope then ordered a cavalry charge. After a short battle the Bourbon army retreated towards Lleida. Nearly a thousand of their troops were killed or wounded, and four hundred on the allied side, 208 of them British. The allies took 322 prisoners.

With victuals in Lleida no longer sufficient to sustain them, the Bourbon army withdrew west to Zaragoza. The allies followed, taking Aragonese towns as they went. Close to the Aragonese capital the twenty thousand Bourbons, again under the command of the Marquis de Bay, turned to face the twenty-three and a half thousand allied troops. Among the allies was King Charles. King Philip remained in the city, ill with a fever. At daybreak on 20 September 1710 the artillery on both sides began a furious cannonade which lasted until midday.

Then, from the right, came the Spanish cavalry. One of their commanders was the former Governor of Alicante, the Irishman Lieutenant-General Daniel Mahoni. They beat their way through the lines to the supply train and slaughtered the mules. However, in the centre the Germans effected a rout of the Spanish infantry. This proved decisive. Within two hours the Bourbon army was in retreat. They had lost three thousand men killed and a larger number, four thousand, were taken prisoner. As Philip and his army withdrew north-west towards Tudela, Charles entered Zaragoza. The allies had lost two thousand men but for them it was a victory of great importance. Once again, Madrid was theirs for the taking.

After securing the remainder of Aragon, the allied army followed the River Henares to the capital which Philip's court had vacated for Valladolid. The advance guard under Stanhope entered Madrid on 21 September. Charles followed a week later and must have been disappointed by the coolness of his reception. But at least he had turned up this time. Stanhope soon left Madrid, intending to follow the Tagus west for a rendezvous with the Portuguese army. It was not to be. The Duc de Vendome, sent by King Loius to replace the Marquis de Bay, blew up the bridge over the Tagus at Almaraz in Extremadura.

After securing two of the three Spanish provinces that bordered France, why had the Allies not made it three by conquering Navarre? Why did they not cut Bourbon lines of communication and prevent King Louis from sending reinforcements? As the Bourbon army at Talavera grew stronger, benefiting from Castillian sympathy to their flag and open supply lines to France, the allies faced local hostility and, worn down by dwindling supplies, desertion and illness, decided to get out. The tide had turned once more. On 11 November Staremberg pulled out of Madrid, moving his troops to Ciempozuelos and Chinchón not far to the south. At the beginning of December his army headed towards Aragon. By the 3 December Philip was back in Madrid and by the 15th Charles was again in Barcelona.

It was during this withdrawal to Aragon that the main part of the British contingent met with disaster. Marching separately from their comrades they were oblivious to the fact that a Bourbon detachment was hard on their heals. The 2,536 officers and men settled in for a couple of nights in the walled town of Brihuega unaware that they were about to be surrounded. On realising his predicament, Stanhope sent a request for assistance to Staremberg and rapidly prepared a defence. On 9 December, after Stanhope had refused to surrender,

Vendome's artillery opened fire. During the afternoon the breaches were stormed and bitter house-to-house street fighting ensued. By 6 o'clock three hundred English soldiers were dead and a further three hundred lay wounded. There was still no sign of Staremberg. Ammunition was running low. Stanhope was forced to make a tough decision: 1,936 men surrendered. Stanhope's Spanish holiday was to last nearly two years.

What had kept Staremberg? He had been at Cifuentes, just fourteen miles away, but so careful had the messenger been not to encounter the enemy that he had taken the best part of a day to get there. Staremberg, no doubt assuming that Stanhope could hold out for a time, had waited until the following morning before setting off. Even then he had not covered the ground quickly. When the allies found their route blocked by Bourbon soldiers at 6.30pm, just four miles from Brihuega, little did they know they were already too late. The thirteen-thousand-seven-hundred-strong Allied force, eight hundred and eighty of them British, had taken up positions on the heights of Villa Viciosa. Next day Vendome, leading twenty thousand eight hundred men, ordered his twenty-eight guns to open fire. The allies responded with their own artillery. For ninety minutes the air was filled with cannon shot. The combat that followed bore similarities to the Battle of Zaragoza. Here too, the Spanish Bourbon cavalry successfully charged through the lines to the supply train, attacking the mules, and here too the battle ended with the Bourbon army leaving the field.

Villa Viciosa was the hollowest of victories. The allies lost three thousand men. The British contingent, isolated by the Spanish cavalry, had virtually been wiped out. Although the Bourbon army lost four thousand, Staremberg knew it had been only temporarily delayed. It would soon be back in pursuit. Having learned of Stanhope's surrender, the allies went on their way, abandoning guns and supplies for lack of mules to carry them. On 6 January 1711 they reached Barcelona.

In 1711 seven new English regiments arrived in the peninsula. Their new commander and ambassador to the court of King Charles was the Duke of Argyle. In December that year, five hundred and fifty British infantryman led by Colonel Edward Stanhope, brother of James, were part of a four-thousand-strong allied force that went to relieve the castle at Cardona, fifty miles north-west of Barcelona. A Bourbon army of three thousand men was besieging the castle, perched spectacularly high up on a steep hill above the town and river. After two days of fighting, on 22 December the Bourbons withdrew. Amongst the allied dead was Edward Stanhope. For the rest of the British it was a case of 'happy Christmas, the war is over' as the Duke of Argyle, unconvinced of Westminster's continued support for the war, took his troops off to Menorca. On the Portuguese side, Galway had already returned home.

Little of consequence happened in the following months as the war in Spain petered out. In August 1712 Britain, Spain, Holland and France suspended hostilities. The Tory government had succeeded the Whigs with promises of concluding the war which latterly had given the public little to cheer about. More significantly, on 17 April 1711 Emperor Joseph had died and the Hapsburg Empire had passed to his younger brother Charles, who had promptly left Spain for good. The result was that the Grand Alliance could no longer support him. An Austro-Spanish empire would have been just as undesirable as the Franco-Spanish one that they had been opposing for a decade.

The peace became official when Great Britain, Spain, Holland, France and Portugal signed the Treaty of Utrecht in 1713. One of the conditions of the treaty was that France and Spain should never share the same king, so the allies had achieved what they had set out to do. They had prevented the emergence of a mighty Franco-Spanish empire that would have controlled world trade and grown ever more powerful with new conquests. Great Britain had also won a couple of bonus prizes – Gibraltar and Menorca.

CHAPTER 9

The Pillar of Hercules

Gibraltar lies like a huge monster, stretching far into the brine…
A terrible couchant lion whose stupendous head menaces Spain.

George Borrow, *The Bible in Spain*, 1843

IN AN ANCIENT TIME man, with his aptitude for the imaginative and romantic naming of places and things, bestowed upon the two mountains at the western end of the Mediterranean the title of Pillars of Hercules. The African pillar is the highest and bulkiest, but lacks shape. In striking contrast, its European brother rises almost vertically from the sea to its 1,398-foot summit. The African pillar is named Djebel Musa (Mount Musa) after the Arab conqueror of the Maghreb, the area that is today northern Morocco, Algeria and Tunisia. The Arabs named the northern pillar after Musa's Berber freedman, Tarik, who landed there on 27 April 711. But Djebel Tarik was always going to be a difficult name for non-Arabic speakers and so it was that Africa's gateway to Europe, Spain's gateway to Africa and Britain's gateway to the Mediterranean came to be known as *Gibraltar*.

Back in 711 Islam was a new religion. Just eighty years had passed since Mohammed's acclamation in Mecca and it was only thirty years since the Maghreb had fallen to the forces of Islam. After landing in the area of Gibraltar, Tarik had gone on to conquer a large part of Spain, so much in fact that he upset Musa, who felt his own achievements were being overshadowed. Musa crossed to Spain, caught up with Tarik in Toledo, whipped him and put him in chains. For his trouble Musa was then summoned to Damascus by an enraged Caliph who subjected him to sun torture and then made him spend the rest of his days as a beggar. The dispute did not stop the conquest which reached all of Spain save a small part of what is now Asturias on the Bay of Biscay.

The Arabs or 'Moors' were in Spain for such a long time that their society was to evolve differently from that south of the strait. In 1068 the Arabs of Seville and Algeciras felt sufficiently threatened by the new militant and fundamentalist Almoravid dynasty in Africa as to

113

build Gibraltar's first fortress. About this time the Christian reconquest was starting to gain momentum. In 1085 Alfonso VI, King of
Castille and León, shocked the entire Islamic world by taking Toledo.
Reluctantly the Spanish Arabs called in the Almoravids from south of
the water. They came and in October 1086 slaughtered twenty-four
thousand Christians at the Battle of Sagrajas, near Badajoz.

Less than a century later it was the Almoravids who were nervously
looking south at the latest warlike fundamentalists, the Almohades.
History repeated itself. This time it was Alfonso VII's taking of
Córdoba – the jewel in the turban of Moorish Spain – that encouraged
the Spanish Moors to call in help from Africa. In 1146 the African
Arabs came, and regained Córdoba. Their leader Emir al-Muminin
ordered the building of a city of victory on the slopes of the rock of
Gibraltar. It was probably never built. The emir's successor was preoccupied with developing Seville: the Giralda Tower and the Patio de
Naranjos that he built for his great mosque are now greatly admired
by tourists as parts of the cathedral.

In 1309 a small fortified town stood on Gibraltar. We know this
because in that year King Ferdinand of Castile and León sent the Archbishop of Seville to lay siege to the place, which at that time was part
of the Moorish kingdom of Granada. The ferocious attack forced the
thousand or so Moors inside to surrender. After nearly four hundred
years of Arab rule Gibraltar was once more part of Christian Spain –
but for how long?

In February 1333 Abd'l Malik, the one-eyed son of the new ruler of
Fez, arrived to lay siege to Gibraltar. The town was vulnerable. Its military governor Vasco Perez de Meira had been pocketing the money
meant for the garrison, its fortifications and food stocks – and he had
made yet more money selling food to the Moors. Four months passed
and no relief came from Alfonso XI and his treacherous nobles. The
Spanish Admiral Joffre tried catapulting bags of flour to the now
starving garrison but it was no good: on 17 June the well-fed Vasco
Perez surrendered and left for Africa. Gibraltar was Arabic once more.
Alfonso's subsequent siege failed. The job done, before taking the boat
for Africa Malik ordered improvements to the fortifications including
the construction of a huge keep that stands to this day.

By 1342 Alfonso was ready for attempts on Algeciras and Gibraltar
once more. He started with the former – that was the larger. Alfonso's
army terrified the besieged Arabs as it deployed a weapon that had
scarcely been used by an attacking army before – the cannon. His
efforts were boosted by assistance from some English fighters. In May

1343 Henry Lancaster, Earl of Derby, and William Montague, Earl of Salisbury, visited with a band of knights to investigate the chances of a dynastic alliance with Spain against France. While there, what better way to please their hosts than fight beside them? They fought hard and impressed the Spanish, though no dynastic alliance resulted. Algeciras finally fell in March 1344. One of the terms of the truce with the Hassan of Fez was that Alfonso agreed not to attack Gibraltar for ten years. The Spanish king did not have to wait that long to launch an attack on the Rock: Hassan was deposed in 1348. Now it was the turn of the walls of Gibraltar to experience cannon fire for the first time. Their deployment was not decisive, however; the Black Death was coming to defeat the besieging army. It swept through the troops and finally, in March 1350, claimed the life of the king.

In the fifteenth century Berber pirates were based at Gibraltar. They were a particular menace to Enrique, Count of Niebla, who had land and business interests in the area. He decided to do something about it and gathered five thousand troops for the job. One day at the end of August 1436 his men began landing below the town. As the tide rose and caught them against the sea wall they withdrew to their boats and disaster struck as Enrique's overburdened craft overturned. The Moors dragged his drowned body from the surf and sliced its head off before stuffing it in a wicker basket which was hung high from the fortifications. It was a brutal provocation to any knight, but their infighting and treachery, which meant that the reconquest was taking the best part of a millennium, now ensured that Enrique's body would swing a while before it received a Christian burial.

Twenty-six years later the Moors finally lost Gibraltar for good. Alonso de Arcos, the military governor of Algeciras, was tipped off that Gibraltar was defenceless as many of her residents had gone to Granada to pay homage to its new king. Alonso gathered two hundred and sixty soldiers and set off. He also requested help from other towns and from other local nobles, the Duke of Medina Sidonia and the Count of Arcos. Help came, but instead of the more the merrier it became the more the messier as squabbling broke out over who should accept the surrender of the willing garrison commander Muhammad Khaba. After withstanding the first assault, the garrison had offered to surrender if they could leave peacefully with their families and movable goods, and receive compensation. Farcically the besiegers replied that they would have to await the arrival of their superiors before anything could be agreed. The first senior figure to get there was Rodrigo, son of the Count of Arcos. The Moors tried to surrender to him but he preferred to wait for his father and the duke. Looking around for someone else, anyone else, to accept their surrender, the Moors found the Knights of Jerez willing to take the glory. As the knights entered the town, a red-faced Rodrigo rushed in behind them with his three hundred lancers. He was then double-crossed for a second time as the Duke of Medina Sidonia turned up and, behind his back, accepted the surrender of the castle. The angry Rodrigo was relieved to see his father arrive at last and the tale he told incensed the count, who challenged the duke to a duel. The duke refused to fight and sat tight until the count departed. The duke took down the wicker basket that contained his father's body and buried it in the Tower of Homage. So Gibraltar, the symbol of Spain's shame, the disembarkation point of the Arab conquest, was again Christian – and Christian it would stay.

Far away, at the opposite end of the Mediterranean, another country had grown powerful and built a strong navy. Its great distance away did not nullify its threat to Spain's security for the Turks had bases at Algiers and Tunis under the command of the infamous Barbarossa. In July 1540 a hundred Turkish slaves who had been working in the docks at Gibraltar escaped to Algiers, where they told their countrymen of the extreme vulnerability of the town's defences. A raiding party assembled, rowed across the sea, landed and walked in. In the panic that followed twenty-six residents were suffocated in the desperate crush at the castle gate, which had been closed to them by the governor. The town was plundered and sixty-three women and children were carried back to the ships. Instead of heading straight back to Algiers, the raiders waited for hostage money. This was a fatal mistake: it gave the Spanish time to despatch a naval force. The Spaniards caught up with the raiders, overpowered them and not only rescued the captives but also released seven hundred and fifty Christian galley slaves and took four hundred hostages. The extra defences that were added to ensure that such a raid could not succeed again were, however, insufficient; Gibraltar continued to suffer small incursions. It was ironic that the country that now controlled most of Central and South America and was growing fabulously rich should be unable to defend its own coasts. Much of that South American wealth was being minted into silver coins called 'pieces of eight'. These evolved to have the Spanish coat of arms on one side and two vertical lines representing the Pillars of Hercules on the other. The pillars of Gibraltar and Djebel Musa have proved an enduring design, one that today makes the dollar sign so distinctive.

The Spanish navy defeated the Turks at the Battle of Lepanto in 1571 but they still had the Barbary pirates to contend with. There was then a dramatic shift in who Spain regarded as her main enemy. Another foreign country, this one angered by the commercial damage being done by Spain's presence in the Netherlands, was determined not to let her pocket all the riches of the New World with impunity. That country had a large navy manned by sailors whose animosity towards the Spanish was fuelled by tales of the brutal Inquisition. Spain had despatched the Armada but when that failed the English were emboldened to enter the Mediterranean for a fight. Here the first Englishman to make a name for himself was John Ward. After deserting from the navy in 1604, he and a rabble of other deserters headed south from Plymouth. On the way they overpowered a number of other vessels and so arrived at Tunis with a small squadron. Ward struck a deal with the Bey of Tunis, Kara Osman, agreeing to share half his profits with him if the English pirates could base themselves there. Over the next five years Ward's growing fleet of sailing ships ravaged Mediterranean galleys until their destruction in Tunis by a Spanish squadron under Don Luis Fijado, newly freed from other duties after a Spanish truce with the Netherlands. The English pirates regrouped, however, and within a couple of years they had forty ships. Their crews were boosted by refugees from the ethnic cleansing now going on in Spain, where everyone of Islamic origin had been ordered to leave.

In 1620 eighteen ships under the command of Sir Richard Mansell sailed into the Mediterranean on the pretence of being an expedition against the Barbary pirates. At the time Britain and Spain were close to reopening hostilities so Spain had more to fear from the presence of Mansell's guns than any pirate. Interestingly, the English crews were permitted to land at Gibraltar and were able to observe the town's much improved fortifications. In the end, the expedition did not go beyond reconnaissance.

Five years later Britain, having worked out that control of trade routes meant wealth and power, decided that it wanted Gibraltar. Any harm done to Spain would be an attractive bonus because, for the second time in recent years, a British king's attempt to secure a Spanish bride had ended in humiliating failure. The whole country and not just King James I, or now King Charles I, felt insulted. Sir Edward Cecil, Viscount Wimbledon, commanding ninety ships and ten thousand men, sailed south with orders to capture the treasure fleet, seize a port and attack Spanish ships. The new defences on the

Rock served to deter Wimbledon who decided instead to raid Cadiz. Early in November his men landed, drank a lot of wine, caused a lot of damage, and left. As Wimbledon headed home to severe criticism he sarcastically suggested a Spanish defence policy: 'If the King of Spain will defend his country, let him lodge wine upon his coasts, and he may overthrow any army with it.'

On 30 January 1649 Charles I was executed in Whitehall. As the leading general in the new republic, Oliver Cromwell was obliged to maintain the momentum of military success. Besides uniting the British Isles, he looked west towards the Caribbean and America and resolved to establish an empire from Spanish possessions. Admiral Sir William Penn sailed to the Caribbean while Admiral Robert Blake cruised off southern Spain pretending to look for pirates but really making sure that the Spanish fleet did not leave. Blake was very convincing, earning welcome after welcome at Spanish ports such as Alicante and Cartagena before blotting his copybook at Malaga where his sailors incited local anger by ridiculing a religious procession. It was 1655. With Penn on his way, Blake was now ordered to intercept the treasure fleet. The poor state of his ships, however, meant that he could not remain at sea much longer; he sailed for England before any laden prize fleet appeared on the horizon. In May Penn was in the Carribean: repelled from Santo Domingo, he successfully took Jamaica for the British republic.

Spain declared war on Britain in February 1656. Blake sailed south again, this time with a new commander, General John Montague. A letter came from Cromwell in May ordering them to consider Gibraltar but lack of confidence of success and the poor prospects of plunder deterred them from making the move. Eventually Blake sailed to Santa Cruz de Tenerife where he captured a vast fortune aboard sixteen galleons but succumbed to scurvy before he could enjoy it.

In 1693 four hundred English merchant ships heading for the Mediterranean rounded Cape St Vincent on the south-west tip of Portugal to be met by ninety-two ships of the French navy. The convoy's nineteen-strong military escort was powerless to prevent the onslaught so the merchant ships scattered. Fifty were sunk and twenty-seven were captured but some made it to the shelter of land. A number reached Gibraltar where four warships sought to protect them. For nine days twenty French ships bombarded the harbour and the town. There were a further nineteen merchant losses before the French exhausted their ammunition and departed.

France's threat to British trade in the last decade of the seventeenth century looked set to increase in 1700 when a grandson of the French king ascended the Spanish throne. The threat that a Franco-Spanish empire would be to trade everywhere stirred Britain to form a Grand Alliance with Holland, Portugal, Austria and Denmark. Its demand was for the people of Spain to reject Bourbon King Philip V and recognise the Hapsburg Charles, Archduke of Austria, as King Charles III of Spain. On 15 May 1702 Queen Anne and her allies formally declared war on the Bourbon Empire. Admiral Sir George Rooke led a force to capture Cadiz but seventy-seven years after Viscount Wimbledon's wry observations the wine got in the way again. The invaders stopped at El Puerto de Santa María, drank rather a lot, smashed up the place and re-embarked after three weeks as local resistance grew.

On 1 August 1704 Admiral Sir George Rooke's fleet sailed into the bay at Gibraltar. At 3 o'clock in the afternoon eighteen hundred English and Dutch Marines went ashore on the isthmus, thereby cutting residents of the Rock off from mainland Spain. Further troops were landed. Thirty Spanish horsemen emerged from the fortress but quickly ducked back inside when allied troops opened fire. The commander of the attack, Prince George of Hesse Darmstadt, called on Governor Don Diego de Salinas to surrender the fortress and forwarded him a letter from the would-be Charles III, asking that the people proclaim him king. The reply came the next morning: Gibraltar and its five hundred and fifty armed defenders were loyal to King Philip. The English and Dutch ships took up their positions; next day many of their 1,490 heavy guns opened fire, causing priests, women and children to flee to the south end of the Rock. When the six-hour bombardment ceased, two hundred seamen stormed ashore to seize an abandoned fort. As they poured over its walls there was a terrific explosion as the magazine blew up, killing forty and injuring another sixty. More men arrived to secure different vantage points and set up a camp. The prince again demanded that the governor surrender. This he did on 4 August, but only seventy inhabitants opted to swear allegiance to Charles III and stay. The rest, some four thousand, went into exile, disgusted at the behaviour of many of the 'liberators', particularly their disrespect for places of worship. Gibraltar became Hapsburg Charles III's first foothold in Spain. The fact that 98 per cent of the Spanish residents left is of fundamental importance: it created a vacuum that over the years was to be filled by immigrants.

The French Mediterranean fleet under the Lord High Admiral of France, the Comte de Toulouse, was despatched to recapture the Rock.

His fleet encountered the allied fleet off Malaga on Sunday 24 August and a bloody battle was fought, as described in the previous chapter. Despite the high casualties, neither side gained any immediate advantage but in the longer term the French were deterred from tackling the British fleet again.

Charles III's two square miles of Spain provided a gateway to his country. Gibraltar was a point of access for the allies whose ships would now be able to support and supply a military push into Spain. Its strategic importance was immense, enabling its masters to control entry into the Mediterranean. It was perhaps the most strategically important place of all time but if Prince George and his garrison of two and a half thousand men were to keep control they would need a lot of good fortune. The Anglo-Dutch fleet needed cleaning and refitting; the Portuguese troops required training, and reinforcements could take months to arrive. The Bourbons realised there was no time like the present to recapture the place.

On 24 August the eleven-hundred-strong vanguard of a Spanish force under the Captain General of Andalucia, the Marques de Villadarias, arrived to begin the siege. That same day the Anglo-Dutch fleet which had crossed the straits to take on water from the North African coast was attacked by a French fleet which had managed to position itself between the allies and Gibraltar. It was not an epic battle; no ships were sunk or captured though there was a heavy loss of men. The allied ships returned to Gibraltar to offer what protection they could to the garrison in their weakened state. Meanwhile, on the Bourbon side, thousands were sailing and marching towards the area to swell the ranks of the besieging army to seven thousand.

On Sunday 26 October 1704 the bombardment began. Breaches were opened in the Round Tower and St Paul's Bastion and it did not go well for the defenders. The governor was mortally wounded, the commander of the marines was killed and many others lay suffering from wounds and other illnesses. Hesse did not have enough men to defend the place. He positioned some at fixed points but kept a large number centrally so that they could be deployed quickly wherever needed. As darkness closed in on the evening of 10 November a local goatherd led five hundred Spaniards up the precipitous east side of the rock to the summit. The next day, as they anxiously awaited the main force of fifteen hundred that was meant to follow them, Hesse's central reserve force struck with ferocity. Of the three hundred attackers that were killed, some perished as they tumbled down the treacherous escape route. That the fifteen hundred Spanish had not come was most likely due to the fact that, shortly after the departure of the initial five hundred, news reached the Bourbon camp of the imminent arrival of Admiral Leake's squadron. When he came, Leake sailed into the bay, opened fire and sank one of the French warships. Three others were beached and torched by their crews; another two managed to slip away.

The Bourbon army maintained its bombardment into December and the number of the garrison fit for duty in Gibraltar fell to a thousand. The siege army was also having problems: the rain filled and muddied their trenches and their manpower was diminished by sickness and desertion. Help was at hand for the Gibraltar garrison. Twenty transports carrying ammunition, provisions and two thousand five hundred reinforcements had set sail from Lisbon. Off Cape Spartell the convoy, which had the protection of just four warships, assumed that Leake had come to meet them when across the waves they saw a fleet flying British and Dutch flags. Leake, however, had been prevented by high winds from leaving the bay. This was a French fleet – as revealed by a change of flags. The convoy made a dash for it. Most of the transports escaped but one was sunk and three were captured. The lucky sixteen reached Gibraltar the week before Christmas.

Late in December 1704 and on New Year's day two sorties successfully sabotaged the Bourbon trenches. At the end of January 1705 the four thousand seven hundred outside Gibraltar were joined by four and a half thousand reinforcements, many of whom were soon in action. In February Villadarias ordered one more attempt. He was about to be replaced by the French Commander in Spain, Marshal de Tesse. His men attacked and stormed the Round Tower. They held it for just an hour, then the garrison counter-attacked.

As Hesse received further reinforcements his adversary, Marshal Comte de Tesse, grew very dispirited. His gloom was temporarily lifted when eighteen French warships arrived at the end of February but descended again when Rear Admiral Pointis, feeling that the weather was against any enterprise, ordered all but five of the ships to sail away again. A few days later Leake arrived to find these five also leaving. He pursued them and engaged them off Marbella, capturing three and sinking two.

Tesse realised he would be no more successful than Villadarias. He could not see the Bourbon army recapturing the rock unless the Spanish committed a lot more resources, and he had no confidence that this would happen. On 12 April King Louis XIV of France ordered that the twelfth siege of Gibraltar be lifted. Throughout April sixty thousand Bourbon troops pulled out. It was a great victory for the House of Austria. King Charles's foothold, his gateway to the rest of Spain, had been secured. Had the Bourbon land forces been better supported from the sea, they would almost certainly have succeeded. Far away, the valiant defence of the Rock passed into the national consciousness of the British people, most of whom did not even know who King Charles was.

Later that year, on 2 August 1705, King Charles III visited Gibraltar but already the British Ambassador in Lisbon had written suggesting that, should Charles be unsuccessful in taking the Spanish throne, Britain should hold on to the Rock. The War of the Spanish Succession continued over the next few years until, on 17 April 1711, Emperor Joseph died and the Hapsburg Empire passed to his younger brother – who was Charles. The Grand Alliance could now no longer support him, the prospect of an Austro-Spanish empire being just as undesirable as the Franco-Spanish one which had been opposed for a decade. In 1713 the war-weary parties concluded a peace with the Treaty of Utrecht. Philip V was recognised as King of Spain (France agreeing never to unite with Spain under one king), Spain gave up the large part of Italy that it held and Britain gained Menorca, a thirty-year monopoly of the slave trade in Spanish colonies, and Gibraltar.

Articles X and XI of the Treaty both start in the same way:

The Catholic King does hereby for Himself, His heirs and successors, yield to the crown of Great Britain …

but they continue very differently:

Article X: … the full and entire propriety of the Town and Castle of Gibraltar … but … the Catholic King wills, and takes it to be understood, that the above named propriety be yielded to Great Britain without any territorial jurisdiction …

Article XI: … the whole island of Menorca, and doth transfer thereunto for ever all right, and the most absolute dominion over the island …

The phrase 'absolute dominion' was not used for Gibraltar because Britain was being granted only the use of the town, port, castle and other fortifications, and this 'use' was subject to certain conditions, one being that no Jews or Moors should live there.

Philip and Spain opposed granting Gibraltar to Britain and in all truth the British government was not keen to accept it: Menorca provided a perfectly good base in the western Mediterranean. But in between them stood some very cunning French politicians. They convinced Philip that not surrendering the Rock put his throne at risk and they convinced Britain that Spain was offering the territory. France's objective was simple – to create a permanent source of friction between the two countries, in which Spain would be encouraged to side with France. The plan worked for nearly a hundred years, until Napoleon's brutal occupation replaced subtle political manoeuvring.

Ever since 1713 Spain has claimed, with justification, that the treaty is invalid, having been signed under duress; even if they had willingly signed it, there is nothing in it alluding to British sovereignty. Any rights that the treaty did grant to Britain were, moreover, nullified almost from the start by Britain's failure to meet certain conditions, such as the expulsion of Jews. The British government tried several times to offload Gibraltar but as time went by public opinion in Britain hardened against ever letting it go. The army loathed it: there was little to do there except drink. As the years passed Gibraltar's original small Spanish population was supplemented by immigrants from places like Genoa and Malta. They mixed and intermarried, producing a new breed, the Gibraltarians, who were not Spanish and did not wish to see their standard of living drop by re-absorption into Andalucia, a desperately poor province from which many were migrating to seek a better life in South and Central America. The Gibraltarians felt all the less inclined to be Spanish because of the degree of harassment by Spain.

The year after the Treaty of Utrecht was signed, Philip V married an Italian princess, Isabella, who was determined that Spain should recover the Italian possessions it lost at Utrecht. Britain was trying to achieve a peace in Europe and so offered Spain Gibraltar in return for renunciation of the Italian claims. Secretary of State General James Stanhope must have appreciated that it was hardly a balanced offer – a fortress in exchange for a wealthy and diverse country – and in truth the forces that Spain was assembling for the Italian campaign could easily have taken Gibraltar by force. The offer was in any case ignored, Spain's focus being on Italy, all the more for Isabella having managed to place an Italian cardinal, Giulio Alberoni, in the post of Spanish chief minister. Spain went on the warpath, taking Sardinia and invading Sicily. On 31 July 1718 Admiral Byng aboard the flagship *Barfleur*, his fleet having entered the Mediterranean to prevent Spain from occupying Sicily, encountered the Spanish fleet off Cape Passaro on the south-east tip of the island. Although Britain and Spain were not at war the guns on the *San Isidro* opened fire and the two fleets were immediately locked in a bitter and bloody confrontation in which twenty-two Spanish warships were lost. The human casualties in what has been called either the Battle of Passaro or the Battle of Messina Straits included Admiral Castaneta who died of wounds aboard the *Real Felipe*. The destruction of the Spanish fleet would make military attempts on the Rock all the more difficult. Spain reacted by recognising the pretender James III as king of England and seizing the ships, goods and property of all Britons in Spain. Britain declared war, as did France who sent an army into the Basque country of northern Spain. At its head was James, Duke of Berwick. With the Royal Navy giving offshore support, Berwick's forces took Hondarribia, Pasaia, San Sebastián and Pamplona. Alberoni did not win the war he had started. Worse, in the long term, was that he passed up a golden opportunity of regaining Gibraltar before the British had become too attached to it.

In June 1721 King George I wrote to Philip promising the restitution of Gibraltar once the consent of Parliament had been obtained; he did not expect this to take long. In return Philip restored Britain's trading privileges in the Indies. For a time Philip really believed he had won Gibraltar back; but he grew nervous, then frustrated, then angry at Parliament's continued failure to consent. He delivered a blow to Britain's trade in the West Indies by granting most favoured nation status to the Ostend East India Company, so making it a powerful rival. He then made two marriage pacts with Charles of Austria which promised an uncomfortable shift in the balance of power that could last for years. Britain reacted by withdrawing King George's commitment. That prompted Philip to declare Article X null and void due to Britain's breaking of so many conditions, admitting Moors and Jews and conducting external trade.

Full of bravado, the Count de la Torres ignored the lesson of the twelfth siege – that Gibraltar could not be taken without support from the sea – and mounted a thirteenth siege with an army of seventeen thousand. On 22 February 1727 the British defenders, who numbered around five thousand, opened fire on the trenches being dug on the isthmus. A month later the attackers started an intensive bombardment that lasted ten days. The garrison was fully stretched as it struggled to maintain its own fire, remount displaced guns, and stay sober. At least they had nothing to fear from an intrepid Spanish goatherd this time: all paths had been removed. What tipped the scales on the garrison's side was the fleet under Admiral Sir Charles Wager which kept them supplied and rained heavy fire down on the attackers.

Another massive bombardment in May did not provide the count with the breakthrough he needed. In June a British shot penetrated his powder magazine and caused an almighty explosion. Eleven days later, on 24 June, he agreed to a truce. The siege that had cost the lives of one hundred British and seven hundred Spanish was over. The Treaty of Utrecht had given Britain the right to participate in the highly lucrative slave trade with the Spanish colonies. Britain's participation brought accusations of abuse by the Spaniards who were also angered by the activities of English loggers on the Honduran coast and a boundary dispute between British Georgia and Spanish Florida. In 1738 Captain Robert Jenkins appeared before the House of Commons to tell of his mistreatment by the Spanish coastguard whilst innocently pursuing his business in the Caribbean. He regaled the right honourable gentlemen with his tale of how, seven years earlier, the Spanish *Guarda Costas* had boarded his Glasgow brig, the *Rebecca*, mistreated his crew and, worst of all, cut off one of his ears. Captain Jenkins then produced the ear. It was a highly effective propaganda stunt. The act roused the House and public to such anger that Britain, despite the better judgement of Walpole's government, once again found itself at war with Spain. This time the conflict, which became known as the War of Jenkins' Ear (1739-42), was not played out in and around Gibraltar but in the Americas. Governor James Oglethorp of Georgia led an invasion of Florida. Protected from the French on his western flank by the friendly Creek, Cherokee and Chickasaw Indians, his forces captured the forts of San Francisco de Pupo and Picolata and besieged St Augustine before eventually backing off when his rear guard was threatened. The Spanish then attacked Fort Frederica on St Simon's Island off the Georgian coast but were repulsed at the Battle of Bloody Marsh. The only other notable events in this stalemate of a war were some naval engagements in the West Indies involving a fleet under Admiral Edward Vernon that seized Portobello in Panama.

While Queen Isabella had inadvertently helped keep Gibraltar British by turning Spain's attentions to Italy, her son Charles intended to get it back. He ascended the throne in 1761, just a year after King George III began a reign that was to last for sixty very eventful years. That year Spain signed a treaty with France that obliged Spain to fight a war with Britain; before she could do so, Britain declared war on her and promptly relieved her of Havana and Manila.

In 1766 the weather nearly put Gibraltar back into Spanish hands. Unusually heavy rains and two hailstorms flooded the town, smashed windows and dislodged earth and rock higher up the mountain, which then crashed down onto buildings and fortifications causing severe damage. Across the isthmus in Spain the Spaniards were suffering too but the governor of the Campo, the Spanish zone bordering Gibraltar, knew that this would be a good time to reclaim the Rock. King Charles, preoccupied with internal affairs, rejected his suggestion.

However, when Britain's North American colonies declared independence that same year, Spain saw it as the ideal time to take back Gibraltar, but the task was now greater than ever before, the garrison's resident military engineer Colonel William Green having spent the previous two decades making the place impregnable. On 21 June the Campo's governor informed General Elliot, Governor of Gibraltar, that he had received orders to cut off the Rock by land and sea. Three weeks later a new governor arrived in the Campo and fired a shot; the defenders fired a hundred in return. By September 1779 fourteen thousand troops had arrived to lay siege to Gibraltar, which was protected by about one third of that number. On 12 September the defenders opened fired again on the busy Spanish lines. The Spanish had tried to take care of the sea approach this time; out on the waves Admiral Barcelo completed the blockade with nine warships and numerous other craft. Within the town the streets were ploughed up so that shot stopped where it fell; towers and steeples were demolished so as not to be used by attacking gunners to find their range. Food was scarce in the town but from the outset privateers slipped through Barcelo's leaky blockade. In January 1780 Admiral Sir George Rodney arrived with four Spanish ships captured in a battle off Finisterre. The fleet disembarked a thousand Highlanders and badly needed food supplies and embarked many women and children before sailing away. Gibraltar was left in uncertainty to contend with malnutrition, caused by the lack of fresh produce, and a deadly smallpox outbreak. The British continued to bombard Spanish lines throughout 1780. In June Barcelo sent in six fire-ships which were towed away by the Royal Navy before they could inflict any damage. The fact that the Spanish did not attempt a land attack was probably due to negotiations going on behind the scenes. Encouraged by the French, each country mistakenly believed the other was putting out 'peace feelers': Spain therefore wanted to talk about Gibraltar and Britain about anything except the Rock. Diplomatic initiatives only worsened relations between the two sides.

The screws tightened on the Rock when in January 1781 Spain and Morocco signed an agreement that cut Britain's supply line from North Africa. Food stocks were now so low that even the young children of soldiers were going short. As rations dwindled, prices spiralled. On April 12 Admiral Derby arrived at the head of a massive supply fleet of over a hundred vessels and prompted a Spanish bombardment that damaged buildings and revealed to the inhabitants the huge stockpiles of supplies the Gibraltar merchants still had in store. The incensed soldiers not surprisingly helped themselves, drank too much and ran out of control for a couple of days. The heavy bombardment continued until the end of the month.

The second anniversary of the siege passed. Far away in Virginia Lord Cornwallis surrendered to a Franco-American army at Yorktown in what proved to be the most decisive battle of the American War of Independence. Britain would now no longer be preoccupied with America; and she would be all the more determined to hang on to her European possession. The French were also now in a position to give Spain a helping hand.

The ever-encroaching siege works were by this time giving serious cause for concern. On the night of 26/27 November 1781 over two thousand men from the garrison poured out of Gibraltar and attacked the Spanish front line. They spiked guns and laid powder trails, then re-entered Gibraltar by the light of the huge blaze they left behind them. In 1782 a Frenchman, the Duc de Crillon, took over the command of the siege and increased the size of the army there to thirty-one thousand. At the same time the French supervised the construction of ten floating batteries, huge unsinkable, gun-filled hulks with sloping roofs to deflect shot and internal water systems to prevent fire. They would be sailed up to pummel the western defences before three hundred landing craft would carry troops ashore. But the Duc de Crillon and his chief engineer, Jean Claude d'Arcon, had not counted on the defenders' secret weapon – the roast potato. Roast potatoes were shot heated in a kiln until glowing red, loaded into guns and fired off. On 8 September 1782 the 'spud guns' caused great damage, igniting roaring fires behind the Spanish lines. Next day the long-planned Franco-Spanish assault began with a bombardment from the hundred and ninety land guns. On 13 September the hulks moved into position and opened fire: Gibraltar faced a furious cannonade from both land and sea. But that night two of the hulks blew up as fires ignited by roast potatoes reached their magazines. The attackers lost confidence. They fired the remainder of the hulks to prevent them from falling into the defenders' hands. The garrison turned from trying to kill the attackers to trying to save them, plucking them from the sea before they drowned. The following month Admiral Howe arrived with ammunition and sixteen hundred reinforcements but the bombardment from the lines continued; 1782 drew to a close and the siege entered its fifth year. In January a peace treaty was signed at Versailles and on 2 February the longest and last siege of Gibraltar was lifted. Over a quarter of a million shots had been fired at the garrison since 1779 but they were the last: it would never be attacked again. In March the Duc de Crillon and the Governor of Gibraltar General George Elliot discussed the siege as they toured each other's defences and dined together. In those three and a half years, three hundred and thirty-three of the defenders were killed but three times as many died of sickness. We do not know how many in total died on the Franco-Spanish side but nearly two thousand perished whilst manning the floating batteries.

In 1796 Spain successfully cooperated with France to clear the Royal Navy out of the Mediterranean. Early the following year Britain hit back when Admiral Sir John Jervis aboard the flagship *HMS Victory* encountered the Spanish fleet under Admiral Juan de Cordova off Cape St Vincent on the south-west tip of Portugal. The British were outnumbered twenty-seven to fifteen but managed to capture four ships and inflict massive damage and casualties on the rest.

At a time when a young Corsican artillery expert was rising fast through the ranks of the French army, the major threat to peace in Gibraltar was from within, from drunkenness and indiscipline among the seven-thousand-strong garrison. Old Cock of the Rock, General Charles O'Hara, Governor of Gibraltar, took an average of £100 a year from each of the ninety taverns so hardly favoured a fall in consumption. How would he then pay for his two expensive mistresses? In 1802 O'Hara was succeeded by Edward, Duke of Kent, who instilled some discipline and limited the troops' choice of tavern to just three. It provoked a Christmas mutiny that might have been more successful had the participants not been so drunk.

In 1798 Nelson sailed from Gibraltar to Egypt. It was the midsummer and Napoleon was celebrating the fall of Alexandria, victory at the Battle of the Pyramids and his entry into Cairo when Nelson arrived and annihilated his fleet at the Battle of the Nile.

In July 1801 Admiral Saumarez sailed from Gibraltar with six ships to confront three Frenchmen anchored off Algeciras. The British came off worst but decided to pursue the victors who were being escorted to Cadiz by five newly arrived Spanish ships. Two of the Spanish vessels, the *Real Carlos* and the *San Hermenegildo*, were enormous, with 112 guns each. On the night of 12 July Saumarez aboard the *Superb* slipped between these two giants, fired a broadside at each, and sped away.

The two Spanish ships each took the other as the enemy, opened fire, caught fire, collided and blew up with the loss of seventeen hundred lives.

In 1804 Gibraltar's public enemy number one was no longer drink; neither was it the guns of France or Spain. The scourge of the community was now yellow fever, which claimed 40 per cent of the fifteen thousand inhabitants. At the end of that year Spain was again at war with Britain. On 21 October 1805 Spain lost her fleet off Cape Trafalgar, on the Spanish Atlantic coast between Gibraltar and Cadiz. A week later the severely battered *HMS Victory* carrying the body of Lord Nelson was towed into Rosia Bay in Gibraltar. A few days later the great flagship left for England. In the Trafalgar cemetery you can see the grave of a Royal Marine captain, Thomas Norman, who died from wounds received whilst serving on *HMS Mars*.

Without a fleet to invade Britain, Napoleon tried a new tactic to bring her to her knees. In 1806 he issued the Berlin decrees, forbidding any country in Europe to trade with her. Portugal's defiance and the subsequent Peninsular War are covered elsewhere in this book. Another important breach in Napoleon's continental system was obviously Gibraltar. The merchants there made the most of it. British ships would disembark cargoes that would then be re-embarked on ships from neutral countries for delivery to enemy ports; and goods from enemy ports arrived at Gibraltar. If questions were asked about their origin a privateer might claim the goods to have been 'captured'. Guerrillas in Spain established a network for the clandestine movement of arms that would continue to be used for smuggled goods from Gibraltar after the war. The garrison feared attack from French troops but Napoleon did not want a place that in his view defended nothing, intercepted nothing, cost a fortune and spoilt Anglo-Spanish relations.

The Treaty of Utrecht clearly stated that goods could be brought into Gibraltar only if they were 'for the use of the garrison, the inhabitants and the ships which lie in the harbour' so, from a Spanish point of view, all other trade was illegal. It was never going to be easy to claim that everything was for internal consumption: by the middle of the century tobacco imports equated to one ton for every male adult! Smuggling was facilitated by easily-bought officials at the frontier. Many slim people crossed the frontier into Gibraltar in the morning only to return later suffering from a sudden onset of obesity.

In the nineteenth century the civilian cultural life of Gibraltar developed apace. Denied access to the garrison library, the populace set up its own and its committee became a representative voice of the people. A yacht club, a jockey club and a theatre were also established. In 1830 Britain started to treat Gibraltar as a civilian community first and a garrison second, changing its status to that of Crown Colony and giving it a civilian police force. All the time Spain still yearned for the return of Gibraltar but was preoccupied with revolutionaries, rebel colonies, military risings and the Carlist Wars.

The history of the colony is full of the tales of great ships that sank within the harbour or close by. In 1891 the *Utopia* was heading south with passengers excitedly anticipating a new life in Australia. They were probably apprehensive as well: not only was there a lot of ocean to cover but Australia was in the middle of a deep commercial depression in which companies were failing, banks crashing and families starving. The 551 passengers never reached their Utopia. The vessel collided with *HMS Anson* in Gibraltar harbour and sank.

The passing years brought great improvements in the range, accuracy, velocity and impact of artillery. Gibraltarians knew this as the fortress had its share of super-guns. These advances served to undermine Gibraltar's use as a naval base as any ship stopping there could easily be reached by armour-piercing shells fired from guns mounted along the Spanish coast and in the hinterland. It was a good time to be friendly with Spain. Britain duly abandoned the Sultan of Morocco as its ally against Spain and helped the Spanish, still wounded by the loss of Cuba and the Philippines, to obtain part of Morocco. In 1906 Anglo-Spanish relations were further improved by the marriage of Queen Victoria's granddaughter Ena to King Alfonso XIII of Spain.

When World War I broke out in 1914, Spain played no part. Thanks to this, Gibraltar was able to have a role, albeit a limited one. It could do little about German U-boats and battleships that slipped through the straits into the Mediterranean to destroy five million tons of allied shipping (eight million was lost in the rest of the world) but it could supply facilities for the repair and victualling of ships, and be a starting and finishing point for convoys. The war saw the loss of several more ships near Gibraltar including the *Britannia*, which went down with the loss of a thousand lives following a U-boat attack. As in the Napoleonic Wars, the civilian population prospered during the hostilities. There was plenty of work in the dockyard and plenty of trade as they supplied the large number of ships that called in. Of the eighteen thousand civilians only seventy-six joined the British Army or Royal Navy but others made a useful contribution to the allied war effort by raising enough money to buy an aeroplane, a gesture that they were to repeat three decades later when they bought a Spitfire.

Spain's demands for the return of Gibraltar have long been under-mined by the fact that she herself owns two enclaves on the North African coast. One of them, Ceuta, consists of five square miles, mak-ing it twice as big as Gibraltar; it has a superior natural harbour and, being directly opposite the Rock, it has the same strategic importance. Spain and Britain have seriously considered the possibility of an exchange; during the First World War General Primo de Rivera openly suggested such a deal. It did not happen because Britain knew that Morocco would never accept what was seen as part of her land being traded by two foreign countries, because there were fifty thousand Spanish residents in Ceuta and because the British public were emo-tionally attached to the Rock.

After the First World War Gibraltar's civilian population took con-trol of local administration. A City Council was established with seven elected members.

When the Spanish Civil War broke out in 1936 Gibraltarians had an uncomfortably close view of the return of Spain's Army of Africa and the bombing of Tetuan, Algeciras and La Línea. On 21 July the *Miguel Cervantes*, the *Libertad*, the *Jaime I* and the *Churruca* arrived in the har-bour; next day some of their crews went ashore. The first two ships were heavy cruisers, the third a battleship and the fourth a destroyer, so policemen on the quayside were surprised to see no senior naval officers coming towards them. In fact the highest ranked Spaniard was a mere petty officer and traditional military formality was miss-ing amongst the others. The policemen suspected the truth: that the crews had responded to the orders of the Republican navy minister to overpower their officers and take over the ships. Not surprisingly the officers of the Royal Navy, deterred by mental images of their Spanish fellow officers being manhandled overboard, refused to meet the committee's request for coal. If they wanted coal they would have to buy it from a merchant. The merchants agreed to supply the coal if the Spanish released all the officers. The ships left without fuel. Clearly the mutineers had taken no prisoners. General Franco's nephew, who had been Captain of the *Libertad*, was no more.

Southern Andalucia fell to Franco early in the war. After his troops occupied Malaga, in February 1937, life on Gibraltar returned to normal. The war had come very close, but it had now gone. The Governor of Gibraltar knew that at any time Franco could close the frontier and deprive the town of the thousands of workers that crossed every day. Franco might decide that those fit men should be fighting in his army instead of contributing to the economy of an old enemy.

However the governor also realised that, for that poor area of Spain, Gibraltar was a money spring; the authorities would be reluctant to lose the £3,000 in workers' wages that entered Spain every week. On 1 April, three days after his Nationalist troops entered Madrid, General Franco announced the surrender of the Republican army.

Five months later Britain declared war on Germany. Gibraltar was vitally important to the allies because so much of the fighting was focused on the Mediterranean area. The civilian population enjoyed brisk business and plentiful work as once more Gibraltar became the starting and ending point for convoys. Then in May 1940, as Italy's entry into the war seemed imminent, the decision was taken to evacuate civilians: fourteen thousand were taken to Casablanca, another two thousand to other parts of the world. Britain's first hostile action against Italy was the seizure of five ships in Gibraltar harbour. With the fall of France, the Royal Navy was concerned about the fate of French fleet: it would be totally unacceptable for it to be absorbed into the German fleet – a real possibility with the collaborationist Vichy government – so if it did not join the allies it would have to be blown out of the water. The deadline passed on 3 July and the Royal Navy opened fire on the French fleet at Mers-el-Kebir in Algeria. Thirteen hundred French sailors were killed and Gibraltarians in French Morrocco were left looking for another home. Twelve thousand were evacuated to London, a city people were normally evacuated from; the remainder went to Jamaica, Madiera and the Azores.

Hungry Spain, bled weak by the savage Civil War, was in no position to threaten Gibraltar alone but it would be a different story if she entered the war alongside Germany and Italy. The Germans already had a plan for the taking of Gibraltar: they called it Operation Felix. The British went on a diplomatic offensive in Madrid. Fortunately Franco did not trust or like Hitler; he was probably afraid of him. If German troops entered Spain, like Napoleon's troops they could not be trusted to leave again. Hitler chose not to walk in without permission: to do so would provoke a vicious guerrilla war which could prove his own 'Spanish Ulcer'. The British crossed their fingers, hoping Franco would continue to sit on the fence. They knew, however, that there was a real possibility that they might lose Gibraltar, so they drew up a plan to take a Spanish possession that would offer continued control of the western entrance of the Mediterranean and which Franco could not defend in the face of their vastly superior sea power. Operation Puma was designed to take Gran Canaria. Britain needed to occupy Atlantic islands; if she did not, the Germans would. There was also Operation Thruster, aimed at occupying the Azores; if Germany controlled them, Britain's trade routes with the Americas would be threatened. When in July 1941 Franco delivered a very anti-British and pro-German speech, Puma was upgraded to Pilgrim: this plan included thirty-five ships, two fighter squadrons and twenty-four thousand men.

The war, and Spain's preoccupation with getting back on its feet, meant that the authorities in Gibraltar were able to press on with a project which would have attracted huge opposition in peacetime. Thousands of tons of rock were tipped into the sea to create an all-weather runway out in the bay. When finished it was just over a mile long. Meanwhile a huge network of tunnels was excavated throughout the rock to accommodate everything from living quarters to hospitals and storage areas.

From early 1941, when General Erwin Rommel initiated his offensive against the British in North Africa, Malta assumed vital importance in the disruption of supply lines from Italy; in turn Gibraltar became essential for maintaining supplies to Malta. After 1941 the convoys that battled through to Valetta did so more for Malta's sake. A fleet named Force H that included the *Ark Royal* operated out of Gibraltar to protect the life-line. It was a bitter blow when, in November 1941, the *Ark Royal* was holed by a torpedo from a U-boat and joined the list of great ships that have sunk near Gibraltar. The siege of Malta tightened. Bombs rained from the sky as fewer and fewer of the supplies got through. Then in November 1942 Montgomery's Eighth Army defeated Rommel's Afrika Korp at El Alamein and the tide turned. The people of Malta were later collectively awarded the George Cross for standing strong in such adversity. For enabling them to do so, much credit must go to Gibraltar.

Churchill strongly believed in the importance of the Middle East to Britain. If Hitler were to seize control of the Iberian peninsula, communications with that zone would be seriously threatened. Operation Pilgrim was not the answer. If Hitler was to control the Mediterranean by seizing all the countries on its northern shores, the answer was to control the ports and overland routes on the southern shores. And so Operation Torch was developed. Gibraltar was hugely important to the build-up of forces prior to this operation. Somehow over four hundred aircraft were crowded onto the airfield and a similar number of ships gathered in the bay. It could not be helped that many of those planes occupied space on the so-called 'neutral ground' of the isthmus. Britain knew that there would be a lot of German pressure on Franco:

tolerating the military build-up meant that Spain's neutrality was benefiting the allies more than Germany. But Britain need not have worried. By then Franco believed that the allies would win the war. Operation Torch began early in November 1942. Within six months the Axis had left Africa and Gibraltar's part in the war was all but over.

Gibraltarians returning home from Britain were smarting from the contemptuous way they had been treated by their hosts, and Spain's role in the war had made them feel equally alienated from that country. They concluded that they were a people and nation with their own characteristics setting them apart from all others. They appreciated that there were not enough of them for full independence but that would not stop them from grabbing all the civil and democratic rights a British citizen was entitled to. After the war the people of Gibraltar pushed for self-government. In 1945 the City Council for the first time had a majority of elected members over nominated officials. But local ambitions went far beyond keeping the streets clean: the desire was for real power and real government, the power to make laws and control the economy. These powers were achieved five years later when the Duke of Edinburgh opened the Legislative Council. At first the majority of its members were nominated but by the end of the 1950s the majority were elected. In 1954 Her Majesty Queen Elizabeth II paid a visit: her loyal subjects were elated to see her. Gibraltarians today can be forgiven for believing that another visit is long overdue. In 1964 a system of government and opposition was introduced and Sir Joshua Hassan was elected as the first Chief Minister. Five years later Gibraltar had a new constitution and a House of Assembly. The elected government controlled everything except defence, internal security and foreign affairs. The preface to the constitution states that Gibraltar will not be passed to the sovereignty of another state against the free and democratically expressed wishes of its people. In a referendum in 1968 12,168 voters chose to retain the links with Britain; just 44 opted to become Spanish. In 1969 Britain ceased regarding Gibraltar as a colony: it was now the City of Gibraltar, one of Her Majesty's dominions. This was an interesting way to deal with United Nations demands to terminate the colonial situation there. Franco reacted by closing the border. This was a disaster for the families of the five thousand Spanish employees who could no longer get to work in Gibraltar. Many of their jobs went to Moroccans. In 1973 Gibraltar joined the European Economic Community as a dependent territory of the United Kingdom, which joined as a member state. The border was reopened for pedestrians in 1982, but not fully until February 1985 as part of the price Spain paid for joining the EEC the following year. They were not happy about this and chose to make crossing as painful as possible; they also refused to treat Gibraltar as a fellow member of the European Union. Spain still forbids air and maritime links with Gibraltar and operates the border in such a way that it can take hours to cross. There are no red and green channels. In 2002 98.97 per cent of voters in a referendum rejected the idea of Britain sharing its sovereignty over Gibraltar with Spain.

So what of the future? Is Gibraltar destined to be reabsorbed into Spain or will it continue to be British? Geographically, Gibraltar is obviously part of Spain, and so many terms of the treaty that made it British have been broken as to render it obsolete. However, since the treaty was signed two factors have combined to take the argument from the black and white to the highly complex and debatable. Firstly, a community of Gibraltarians with roots as diverse as Genoese, Savoyard, Portuguese and English, going back hundreds of years, has grown up on the Rock; secondly, international norms of democracy and self-determination have emerged. But when the people of Gibraltar claim the inalienable right to choose their status then Spain returns to Article X of the Treaty of Utrecht whereby Britain agreed that, if she ever surrendered control of Gibraltar, she would return it to Spain. Handing over control to the residents was never an option.

Although the people of Spain are generally united in the belief that Gibraltar should be Spanish, they do not attach much importance to the issue. No politician will admit as much, and anyway Gibraltar will always be a useful distraction. Spain consists of fourteen distinct and autonomous communities – such as Galicia and Aragon. In the past mountains, rivers and sheer distance contrived to keep these people apart, hence the rich diversity in culture, cuisine and even language that exists to this day. It follows that Catalans care very little about an Andalucian territorial dispute. Why should Asturians, at home in their lush green valleys beside the Atlantic, concern themselves with whether a very large, distant, arid and largely untilled region of Spain regains two square miles of land?

The prolonged British confrontation with Spain cannot be good for the two countries. The British government would love to settle the Gibraltar question and usher in a new era of Anglo-Spanish relations, but that wrongly suggests that Gibraltar is the only point of friction in the relationship. Spain's attitude to Britain will always be tempered by the fact that she needs the custom of the ten million British holidaymakers who go there every year.

Spain's biggest mistake has been to maintain a hostile attitude towards the community on the Rock. Spanish officials consistently flout the spirit of the EU by making the crossing of the border with Gibraltar as painful and long-winded as possible, and Spanish politicians frequently snipe at the colony. Even the sinking of a heavily laden Greek-owned oil tanker off Galicia in 2002 was blamed on Gibraltar. This attitude frustrates Gibraltarians and makes them more determined than ever to maintain their separation. If Spain is really serious about winning back this one-thousandth of a per cent of its potential land area then its border officials, government and media need to embark on a permanent charm offensive towards the people of Gibraltar. They should stop accusing Gibraltar of being a haven for money launderers and drug smugglers; they should stop spoiling the view and polluting the water (Gibraltarians have had to put up with a huge oil refinery being built across the bay); they should invest heavily in the Campo so that Gibraltarians would desire to work and play there. Integration would then begin. One day the citizens of Gibraltar might conclude that they did not mind being part of Spain after all. Until Spain changes tack then 99 per cent of the citizens will continue to vote 'No' to a change of sovereignty.

Every now and then some poorly read British politician will seek to gain political points from Spain by selling the small, loyal Gibraltar population short. Then the protests of the residents begin and the politician will pick up a history book and read about how the Rock stood firm through all those sieges, and conclude that perhaps their career would not best benefit from removing a symbol for strength, solidity and loyalty from the national consciousness.

CHAPTER 10

Menorca Britannica

The Catholic King does hereby for Himself, his Heirs and successors, yield to the crown of Great Britain, the whole island of Menorca, and doth transfer thereunto for ever all right, and the most absolute dominion over the island, and in particular over the town, castle, harbour and fortifications of the bay of Menorca, commonly called Port Mahón, together with the other ports, places, and towns situated in the aforesaid island.

Extract from Article 11 of Treaty of Utrecht, 1713

It is Our Resolution not only to preserve to you your Religious and Civil Rights, but to render you a rich and flourishing people by encouragement of your Trade and Navigations.

Queen Anne, 1712

ABOUT ONE HUNDRED AND THIRTY miles south-east of Barcelona in the Mediterranean Sea lies the second largest of the Balearic Islands, Menorca. Towards the end of the seventeenth century Britain was becoming wary of the build-up of French naval strength, coupled with the growth of a powerful base at Toulon, which threatened her substantial Mediterranean trade. A local base for the shelter and maintenance of the British fleet was required. Mahón, a deepwater port at the eastern end of Menorca, less than two hundred miles from the French coast, was the ideal candidate. Britain did not invade in her own right but in the name of the Hapsburg King Charles III, who encouraged the action. Today, nearly two hundred years after the end of the third British occupation, few people in Britain know that Menorca was once an important part of the Empire.

The First Takeover

IN SEPTEMBER 1708 the British fleet approached Menorca which was defended by no more than three hundred Spanish soldiers under the hated General Davila. The repression being suffered by the Menorcans meant that they did not object when twelve hundred marines commanded by Lieutenant-General James Stanhope landed at Cala Alcaufar, south of Mahón, on the fourteenth of the month. Meanwhile the ships of Sir John Leake, Admiral and Commander-in-Chief of the British Mediterranean fleet, bombarded Fort San Antonio on the north coast of the island. With little loss of life this fort soon surrendered; the news served to demoralise the occupants of Fort San Felipe near Mahón, before which Stanhope's men placed their cannon, and it capitulated on 29 September, the day after the artillery opened fire. With the capital Ciutadella surrendering peacefully, the island had fallen with only forty dead and wounded on the British side. The defeated prisoners were taken by allied ships to France and Spain. The disgraced General Davila did not wait for his court martial to announce his punishment: he threw himself from his cell window in Cartagena. Curiously, the guards buried him where he fell.

Four years after occupying Menorca in the name of Charles III, the British Government found a good reason for not handing it over to his control. They had originally backed him in the face of a threateningly large Bourbon empire but Charles's ascension as Holy Roman Emperor meant that the Hapsburg empire now represented the greater threat and Britain was obliged to switch its support to the Bourbon Philip V. In 1712 a British governor arrived, Union flags replaced Spanish ones and officials were made to swear allegiance to Queen Anne. The cession of the island to Britain was confirmed by Article 11 of the Treaty of Utrecht.

Having taken Menorca, Stanhope and company now looked at how they should go about defending the island. Two hundred and fifty miles of coastline meant that this would never be a simple task even with a large garrison and good infrastructure for the rapid deployment of troops. They must have concluded that, although it would be almost impossible to protect Menorca from a large invasion force striking from, say, Toulon at short notice, they could at least ensure that there was a stronghold where the garrison could shelter until the Royal Navy arrived with reinforcements, unrivalled firepower and the ability to cut off enemy supplies. Immediately work began on Fort San Felipe on the south side of the entrance to Port Mahón. Stanhope thought that it would require an expenditure of £60,000 to make it impregnable. Twelve hundred men were brought from Barcelona. San Felipe, with its massive proportions and eight hundred pieces of artillery, was the Malta of the eighteenth century; it certainly looked impregnable. But the truth was that the erratic and uncoordinated nature of its construction meant it was less formidable than it looked. There had been no master plan. It was so big that it required an enormous garrison to protect its walls. Despite the massive expenditure the quality of the

construction was poor in places; some of the engineers had cut cor-
ners in order to pocket a dishonest profit. The fort's security was further compromised by the existence of a suburb called the Arabal which
had grown up right next to it. An attacking force would be able to
approach under cover all the way to the walls. Although it was obvious that the settlement needed to be moved, this was not done for
fear of the disquiet it would cause amongst the population. In 1710
the Marlborough Fort was constructed in Cala San Esteban just south
of Mahón.

Much of the opposition to British rule came from members of
the Church and the nobility, who in the main were residents of the
capital, Ciutadella. Their incredulity at seeing their power snatched
away must have been greatly increased when they learnt that they no
longer resided in the capital. The only part of the island that really
interested the British was the vast deep water port of Mahón over
thirty miles away, and it was to Mahón that they moved the seat of
government. A shipyard was built on the north side of the port and a
hospital on Isla del Rey, or Bloody Island as the British called it at the
time.

By establishing civil order, reforming the administration, building
an infrastructure and improving agriculture, Britain aimed to raise
Menorca from being simply a place of strategic military importance to
one enjoying profit and prosperity. There is no doubt that the Menorcan economy did profit from the reforms, but Britain's economy did
not. The island's most direct gain was from the visits of the fleet
and the huge amount of money spent on improving the defences and
servicing the garrison. In 1800 there were thirteen thousand British
soldiers on Menorca. In just eighteen months the British spent over
£1¼m on the island. Towards the end of British rule Admiral Lord
Nelson's fleet frequently visited Mahón as it fought to contain the
activities of Napoleon. The port was able to cope with thirty-two ships
of the line at once.

Of all the lieutenant governors of Menorca, it was the first, Richard
Kane, who contributed most to progress on the island. Having moved
the seat of government, he instigated the construction of an east-west
road between the former and current capitals. At the eastern end of
this *Cami d'en Kane* there stands today a memorial to this man who
gained the respect of the locals. In Mahón, under his auspices, the
naval dockyard was built. As well as instigating public works he strove
to make farming more efficient by bringing in agricultural advisors
who introduced new livestock and plants. The most obvious visual

evidence of this today is the familiar sight of the black-and-white British Friesian cow. Other improvements included schools for all, a printing press and the introduction of standard weights and measures.

While the lieutenant governor was responsible for the effective running of the island, the governor's position was purely nominal. Between 1736 and 1756 that post was occupied by three men whose approach to the job can be inferred from the fact that not one of them ever set foot on Menorca. The main charges against lieutenant governors were that they were lazy, corrupt or dictatorial. Anstruther and Johnstone were accused of raising taxes for their own enrichment; Winyard infuriated the population by permitting the navy to recruit two hundred sailors by means of a press-gang.

The British never found it easy working with the system of government that existed when they arrived, but on balance it was in their interests to work with the elected *jurats* who legislated in assemblies called *universities*. After all, Article 11 of the Treaty of Utrecht stated: 'Her royal Majesty of Great Britain moreover engages, that she will take care, that all the inhabitants of the said island, both ecclesiastical and secular, shall safely and peaceably enjoy all their estates and honours...' The truth was that the British did not consider these *jurats* up to the job. Many were illiterate. As Menorca's prosperity grew, the island needed well-informed civil servants, not ignorant peasants responsible only for the management of a pittance in their own households. The *universities* invested a lot of money and effort in sending agents to Britain to air their grievances. Don Juan Bayarte went to London in 1718 to protest against robbery, rape and murder committed by British troops, inadequate compensation for seized cattle, forced labour on the roads, the expulsion of Menorcans from their homes to accommodate troops, indecent searches and the unlawful imprisonment of *jurats*. Replying to the secretary of state, Kane admitted that the list of grievances was largely accurate; it was true that there had been many problems when the garrison arrived, but discipline had now been restored. Two soldiers were hanged and others less severely punished.

Besides its loss of power, the Church in Menorca found it hard to stomach submission to a Protestant sovereign, something which went against its belief in papal supremacy. Kane, a Presbyterian who earlier in his life had survived the siege of Londonderry, typified a British administration which could not trust a clergy that still supported the continuation of the Spanish Inquisition. The head of the Church in Menorca was a vicar-general appointed by the Bishop of Mallorca in whose see it lay, therefore allegiance was divided. The Church was distressed by British complicity in the arrival of non-Catholic immigrants such as Greeks and Jews. Objections were raised when a Greek Orthodox church was built in 1754, and there was resentment because much of the profit those foreigners made left the island. The single event during British rule that most upset the Church was part of a problem which troubled the administration and sharpened Menorcan resentment – the poor behaviour of the garrison. In 1749 three nuns of good family background were helped to escape from Santa Clara convent by three British soldiers. The girls took instruction in the Anglican faith, were converted, and then married the soldiers. A great furore followed. Two Catholic priests were allowed access to the girls to try to persuade them back into the fold but whatever pressure was brought to bear was not enough; the girls went off to make their lives in England. All Lieutenant Governor Blakeney could do was decree that in future soldiers should shun escaping nuns. A relation of one of the women later failed in an attempt to abduct her and bring her back to face the justice of the Spanish Inquisition in Mallorca.

The prospect of continuing to be burdened with the increasingly undisciplined troops worried the Menorcans considerably when they learned in 1712 that the island was to be signed over to British rule. Although members of a well organized and effective fighting force, most early recruits to the British Army were pretty low-life; their only motive for joining up was that the army offered an alternative to a life of crime and punishment. Rarely rotated with fresh troops from back home, the soldiers on Menorca were consumed with boredom and found relief in drunkenness. Uneducated and insensitive to local feelings, they inevitably drew charges of disrespect for the local religion. Their drunken antics frequently attracted vengeful shots from peasants' slings, and these were lethal weapons in the hands of men who had over-developed arms from their constant use.

THE SEVEN YEARS' WAR was sparked off in 1756 when the Austrian Hapsburgs attempted to win back the rich province of Silesia, wrested from them by Frederick II (Frederick the Great of Prussia) in the War of the Austrian Succession (1740–8). The great European powers all took sides and, unsurprisingly in view of their colonial struggles in North America and India, Britain and France stood in opposing coalitions. Great activity around the French Channel ports deliberately gave the impression that an invasion of England was imminent. The Royal Navy's attention was being drawn away from France's real objective, Menorca, which by then had been in British hands for forty-eight years. The thinking behind France's resolution to capture the island was, firstly, that it would benefit her alliance with Spain; secondly, it would prejudice Britain's Mediterranean interests and, thirdly, strike a blow to her national pride. Appeals to London from Menorca went unheeded despite growing evidence of France's real intentions. In the end, the response was too little too late. Admiral Byng set sail with undermanned warships and, as he entered the Mediterranean, General Fowke, Governor of Gibraltar, defied orders to provide the squadron with a battalion of infantry.

The French expeditionary force was formidable, consisting of twelve thousand soldiers, an armada of two hundred merchant ships, twelve warships and five frigates carrying 894 guns. Two days after the invaders landed near Ciutadella on 18 April, the British garrison of three thousand retreated into Fort San Felipe. The former capital Ciutadella, home to many who had lost their power under British rule, welcomed the invaders. French progress east to Mahón was slowed down by the destruction of bridges and the placing of obstructions on the road. At least the invaders had a road to follow, but they were handicapped by the same problem that had slowed down the British advance from their landing place to Fort San Felipe many years before – the crippling lack of oxen and carts.

Eighty-four-year-old Govenor William Blakeney anxiously awaited the arrival of the fleet of Admiral Byng, Commander-in-Chief of Mediterranean forces; only he could prevent the fall of Menorca. There had been a small British force of three warships and two frigates in Port Mahón but this had left to avoid being trapped.

On 19 May, a week after the French batteries had opened fire on San Felipe, Byng's force of thirteen ships of the line, four frigates, a corvette complete with 874 cannon, and four thousand soldiers to reinforce the garrison, arrived off Cape Favarix. Next day it faced La Galissoniere's twelve warships and frigates which had been patrolling to prevent British naval intervention. The ships on both sides opened fire. It was a half-hearted confrontation; the adversaries were too far apart to cause much serious damage. With losses of just 45 dead and 162 wounded, Admiral Byng decided not to risk another confrontation with the French squadron and retired to the defence of Gibraltar. He believed that landing reinforcements on Menorca could enable it to hold out for only a little longer and add to the number that must fall into enemy hands. That he did not even remain to harass French lines of communication would later cost him dearly.

The action at sea cheered the French; they continued the bombardment of Fort San Felipe, keen to finish the job before the arrival of Admiral Hawke. On the evening of Sunday 27 June they assembled in the main street of the Arabal for the assault. At ten o'clock the attack commenced and for three hours the fighting raged. The French ascended the walls and occupied three redoubts as well as many subterranean passages. Their losses were just 248 killed and 412 injured. With many of the fort's guns dismounted, Blakeney's position was untenable. The defenders, who had begun with insufficient numbers, had suffered 398 casualties during the siege; they faced an enemy outside with twelve thousand men to call upon. Worse still, they faced enemies within in the form of low morale and disease. On 29 June, more than two months after the French had landed, the surrendering garrison marched out with flags unfurled and drums beating. The Duc de Richelieu refused to accept the defeated governor's sword and instead warmly embraced the eighty-four-year-old man. The British left Menorca on ships bound for Gibraltar on 10 July 1756, passing Admiral Hawke on the way. Later Hawke arrived off Menorca but sailed away without carrying out his orders of effecting a blockade against a well-stocked garrison of six thousand men.

With the battle in the Mediterranean lost, accusations and recriminations were flying about back in Britain. Newcastle's government was the first casualty. Blakeney was blamed for surrendering too soon though few could genuinely have believed that he could have held out against such overwhelming odds for two long months until the arrival of Admiral Hawke. In the end he was cleared of blame and received a baronetcy. Admiral Byng was not so lucky. After he was tried and convicted his life was finished by a firing squad aboard the warship *St George* in Portsmouth harbour. Ironically it was to be a Frenchman who would create the most lasting and most sympathetic memorial to Byng's unfortunate demise. In his great satirical work *Candide*, Voltaire refers to the admiral's execution '… to encourage the others'.

The Second Takeover

SEVEN YEARS LATER the British were back. On 10 February 1763, at the end of the Seven Years' War, defeated France returned Menorca to Britain in a peace treaty signed in Paris. On 3 July Admiral Brest's English squadron arrived in Mahón; the following day the French force departed. The Menorcans accepted the change placidly, remembering that British rule had been less oppressive than that of their most recent landlords.

Having lost Menorca only seven years previously, the British administration and military leaders must have come up with some good ideas to stop such a thing happening again. It is therefore surprising that they were so slow to address the chief weakness of Fort San Felipe: the location of the suburb of the Arabal just below its walls. Perhaps it was simply that the main concern of the new lieutenant-governor, James Johnstone, was how best to fill his own pockets. Later Governor General John Mostyn organized the demolition of the Arabal, finally achieved in 1779. New housing for the displaced community was build near Mahón. First called Georgetown, its name was later changed to Villa Real de San Carlos in honour of Charles III and later still shortened to the present name of Villcarlos. Objections to the move were subdued by the payment of compensation and the fact that most of the three thousand people who left the 904 houses behind depended on the garrison for their livelihoods.

Eighteen years later, in 1781, when most of Britain's military resources were committed in America, Spain's Charles III decided it was a good time to snatch back Menorca and Gibraltar. Gibraltar, as we have seen, proved too tough a nut to crack, but Spain was heartened by successes against the British in Honduras and the Gulf of Mexico. As Spain was enjoying some prosperity and progress at this time, Menorcans were known to favour a return to its dominion. The Spanish fleet was now the second most powerful in the world. Spain did not set out to recapture Menorca alone: it would be done jointly with the French, who would provide the general-in-chief of the expedition, the Duc de Crillon.

London responded to appeals for help from Governor James Murray and despatched five warships and seven transports to Mahón in April. Murray did his best to organize the defence of the two-hundred-and-fifty-mile coastline but he had just eighteen hundred men for the job. The port of Mahón was blocked by sinking thirteen boats, and chains were stretched between the shores.

The Franco-Spanish expedition sailed from Cadiz on 23 July 1781. The force of 7,802 soldiers and 264 cannon aboard two warships, two frigates and twenty-two smaller vessels travelled via Cartagena where it picked up nineteen more warships and four frigates. The Duc de Crillon's force landed unchallenged at Cala Mesquida, just north of Mahón, on 19 August. The invaders were welcomed into the capital and the British retreated to Fort San Felipe. Despite the speedy fall of most of the island, the Duc de Crillon would have to wait more than five months for total victory. Having assumed that the element of surprise could win the day, no siege machine had been brought along. Keen to conclude the matter quickly, de Crillon offered Murray a bribe of £1m. It was turned down.

The bombardment of San Felipe was at first met by a spirited defence including a number of successful sorties. Soon the lack of fresh food and the unhealthy subterranean accommodation saw the onset of illness within the fort. The besiegers sympathised to the extent of sending in medicines and vegetables for the inhabitants whose numbers included a hundred and fifty women and twenty-one children. Not until 6 January did they launch a major offensive. After four weeks of uninterrupted fire, those inside decided they had had enough. One hundred and seventy-one days into the siege the garrison had been reduced to seven hundred and fifty able-bodied men. On the morning of 4 February a white flag appeared above the ruins. The British counted 59 dead and 149 wounded as a direct result of the bombardment, but scurvy had claimed far more – a hundred dead and eight times that number sick. The nine hundred and twenty emaciated figures that marched out in full military dress were a shocking sight for the fifteen thousand Spanish, French and German soldiers who had come to take their place. Spain welcomed back Menorca, then ordered one of the greatest acts of unilateral disarmament ever. Charles III's government concluded that Menorca would cease to be a target for foreign takeovers if it had no defences. Ignoring the fact that the island's strategic position was the main reason it so tempted foreign powers, orders were given for the destruction of Fort San Felipe. Six months later one of the world's greatest and most expensive fortresses was no more.

The Third Takeover

SIXTEEN YEARS LATER, Britain's third takeover of the island was precipitated by the march of Napoleon. In 1796 France and Spain, drawn together in enmity towards Britain, signed a defensive and offensive treaty. In 1798 Malta's fall to the French was answered by Nelson's destruction of the French fleet at Abukir. Britain's fleet now controlled the Mediterranean and needed a naval base to secure its position. Spanish attention also needed to be diverted from Lisbon, which had a port that was of immense value to the Royal Navy

The Spanish were now about to pay the price for their puzzling act of unilateral disarmament. Governor Brigadier Juan Nepomuceno Quesada's defence was further weakened by his dependence on mercenaries of dubious loyalty and the disinterest of the Menorcans who had not found rule from Madrid to be any better than rule from London. The Spanish declaration of war against Britain in 1796 was not accompanied by the strengthening of Menorca's defences. The island was felt to be exposed, yet numerous appeals to Madrid for reinforcements were ignored. Quesada had to make do with the limited forces he had available, 1,371 Spanish soldiers, 2,300 Swiss mercenaries and a hundred cannon. There was no local contribution towards defence.

The British squadron was sighted from the highest point on the island, Monte Toro, on 7 November 1798; it stepped ashore at Cala Mola and Addaya on the north-east coast. Brigadier Quesada despatched Field Marshal Christobal de Rutiman to defend the landing point but by the time he arrived four hundred and forty of his 1,320 Swiss mercenaries had fled. Those that stayed managed to contain the invaders but then, to Quesada's great disappointment, the force which had been well supplied retired on the grounds that they had nothing to eat and no ammunition. Quesada could not mete out exemplary punishments for fear of losing the rest of the mercenaries. As the British force marched south to seize Mercadal, and thus cut off east-west communication, Mahón was left undefended as Quesada's Spaniards retreated into the walled city of Ciutadella which he hoped to defend until reinforcements arrived.

On 9 November two English frigates and five large transports arrived off Mahón. Colonel Paget landed and was offered the keys by the town councillors. Back in Ciutadella the citizens, indifferent to who ruled them, were keen to avoid any risk to their lives and many abandoned their homes. Quesada was pressed to avoid exposing the populace to any fighting. The approaching British lacked the great numerical superiority which the Spanish thought they had but positioned themselves to give the impression of a formidable four-mile front complete with artillery. The trick worked. After a symbolic exchange of cannon fire on the 15th, Quesada's council took the only option apparently open to them and surrendered. The island had fallen without the loss of a single man. Six hundred Swiss mercenaries who decided to remain on the island enlisted in the British Army.

*

NINETY-FOUR YEARS after Charles III's requests for a landing in Menorca were answered the British were tricked by the French into handing it back to his son Charles IV. By the time the British realised Napoleon's duplicity, Menorca was already back under the authority of Madrid.

At the end of 1801 peace seemed like a good idea to both Britain and France, but for totally different reasons. Britain welcomed an end to a greatly draining business whilst Napoleon saw it as an opportunity to prepare for further conquests. By the Treaty of Amiens, signed on 23 March 1802, Britain was to leave Menorca, Malta and Elba in return for Napoleon's leaving Egypt. With the arrival of six hundred troops under the Captain General of Mallorca on 14 June the last British troops sailed away. Hastily revised orders that troops should not after all abandon Menorca, following the revelation that Napoleon had not evacuated Egypt, came too late.

Whitehall certainly did not miss the expense of maintaining the garrison in Menorca. The need for a port in the Mediterranean was satisfied by Malta, the place where Horatio Nelson could be near the wife of the British ambassador in Naples, Sir William Hamilton.

*

SOME ASPECTS OF THE BRITISH LEGACY in Menorca fundamentally affected everyday life, others were just interesting details. One sees in many societies that when people do not have a strong outside threat to unite them they tend to fight amongst themselves. So it was with the Menorcans. Prior to Stanhope and Leake's arrival they had commonly carried weapons which they did not hesitate to use, especially if there was a family vendetta. The British banned such weapons and instilled a respect for law.

The most visable British legacy must be Mahón. After its elevation to capital it developed considerably, in contrast to Ciutadella which retained much of its old-world charm. Today when cruise ships arrive in Port Mahón they pass the abandoned British naval hospital on Isla del Rey. As their vessel moors, passengers will notice that just across the road from the quay there is a working gin factory, a testament to the favourite tipple of the English in the eighteenth century, which became the preferred spirit of Menorcans as well. If passengers look to the top of the cliff they will see buildings with sash windows, one of several British architectural features that persist locally. Inside those houses much of the furniture is in the English style. The clearest legacy in the countryside is the British Friesian cow. While the British absorbed the word 'mayonnaise', from *mahones* (of Mahón), the local language contains a number of hispanicised English words such as *grevi* (gravy), *xel* (shell) and *joques* (jokes). On the Spanish mainland, Fool's Day falls in December but in Menorca it falls on 1 April.

CHAPTER 11

London's Plaza Mayor

Es de advertir que la marina subsistente a Inglaterra, no es otra que la antigua española.
One is to observe that the navy that England sustains is none other than the old Spanish one.

Joaquin Aguirre, early nineteenth century

IT WAS AT THE 'HEART OF EMPIRE'. It has been the place to celebrate everything from international football victories and the New Year to the ending of world wars. It is the scene of mass meetings and demonstrations. Yet this most British of places has an Andalusian name, that of a cape that juts out into the Atlantic Ocean some thirty miles south-east of Cadiz. Completed in 1843, Trafalgar Square, with its fountains and four huge bronze lions, is dominated by a 185-foot-high column on the top of which stands the 18-foot statue of Admiral Lord Nelson. We tend to think of the Battle of Trafalgar as a great British naval victory over just the French, but the fleet that was so decisively defeated on that autumn day in 1805 was in fact Franco-Spanish.

*

THE GREAT SPANISH SHIPBUILDER Jorge Juan y Santacilla took advantage of a rare period of peace to visit England in 1749 to research naval design and defences. He persuaded some English shipbuilders to return to Spain with him at the end of his visit. Among them was Matthew Mullan who later designed the largest warship to be built anywhere in the world in the eighteenth century. Launched from the Spanish colonial dockyard in Havana, Cuba on 3 March 1769, the enormous four-thousand-ton *Santisima Trinidad*, held together by iron bolts six feet long, was built to carry eleven hundred men and 136 guns.

Twenty-eight years later she faced the British at the Battle of Cape St Vincent. After the battle, during which she was almost totally dismasted, Vice Admiral Mazarredo recommended beaching her at Cadiz as a stationary gun platform. He was ignored and she was overhauled.

149

Eight years later, captained by Commodore Francisco Javíer de Uriarte y Borja and with Admiral Báltasar Hidalgo de Cisneros on board, she sailed north with the combined Franco-Spanish fleet to Cape Trafalgar.

HMS Victory approached with the intention of attacking the French flagship, *Bucentaure*. It was midday as the ships ahead and astern of *Bucentaure*, the Spanish *Santisima Trinidad* and the French *Redoutable*, peppered the sea before *Victory*. The churning sea became a wall of fire as *Victory* neared the *Santisima Trinidad* and the French ships that now included *Héros*. *Victory* wanted to pass astern of the *Santisima Trinidad* and forward of the *Bucentaure* so that she could pierce the enemy line and fire point-blank broadsides into the stern of the Spanish giant and the bows of the French flagship. But they were so closely packed together that *Victory* was forced to pierce the line astern of the *Redoutable* which followed the *Bucentaure*. *HMS Victory* became engaged in a furious fire-fight with the *Bucentaure* and *Redoubtable*; Admiral Lord Nelson was felled by a French sharpshooter's musket ball as *Victory* was still managing to score hits against the *Santisima Trinidad* with her port guns. The British ships in *Victory*'s wake, in particular the 98-gun *HMS Neptune*, also bombarded the Spanish ship. *HMS Leviathan* came up to give her some more but before she could the great main and mizzen masts of the *Santisima Trinidad* came crashing down. *HMS Conqueror* gave her a broadside and the splintered foremast also crashed down. *HMS Africa*, a ship with less than half the guns of the Spanish giant, arrived and seeing no flag flying, all her masts being down, despatched a party to take possession. The party soon returned having been informed they had assumed wrong: the *Santisima Trinidad* had not struck her colours! It was some hours later that the drifting giant finally surrendered to *HMS Prince*.

An enormous explosion in the magazines of the French ship *Achille* signalled the end of the battle at 5.45pm. Nelson had achieved annihilation: eighteen prizes to zero. The British, Spanish and French respectively suffered 448, 1,038 and 3,370 men killed and 1,241, 1,385 and 1,160 wounded.

After the battle a huge storm blew up. Of the Royal Navy's eighteen prizes, twelve were snatched away by the raging elements and plunged to the bottom of the sea or smashed against rocks. Two escaped. Unable to hold on to the others the difficult decision was taken to scuttle them. So it was that the mighty *Santisima Trinidad*, so beautifully crafted from Cuban hardwoods and until so recently the pride of the Spanish navy, was sent to her final resting place on the sea floor. The *Santisima Trinidad* was just one of fifteen Spanish ships that made up nearly half of the Franco-Spanish fleet at Trafalgar. How was it that Spain was so involved with French naval activities? Why were ships of the Spanish navy at the Battle of Trafalgar?

During the eighteenth century the Spanish navy saw a great revival. An impressive 227 warships were built as Spain sought to protect her empire and trade which stretched from Louisiana to Lima, from Melilla to Manila. She built fine ships, the envy of the British, and despatched navigators and explorers all over the world. The Spanish king who gave most to this naval renaissance was Carlos III who reigned from 1759 to 1788. Unfortunately his judgement was clouded by Anglophobia, which led to some costly wars with England and even costlier alliances with France. His paranoia stemmed from an incident at Naples in 1744 when Commodore Martin led some ships of the Royal Navy into the bay and landed to demand that Carlos, then King of Naples, withdraw his army from the conflict with Britain's ally Austria. The king tried to negotiate but the impatient naval officer had no time for games. Consulting his timepiece, he instructed the seething, humiliated monarch to get on with it – within the hour. Carlos obeyed but vowed to build a navy capable of avenging the insult. Early in his reign, fuel was added to his fire when the English temporarily occupied Havana. Subsequently he backed the revolt of the American colonists against Britain between 1779 and 1783 and squandered huge resources on trying to recapture Gibraltar.

The year after Carlos III was succeeded by his son Carlos IV, Spain's royal family was appalled to hear of the brutal treatment meted out to their fellow Bourbons by the French revolutionaries. The Spanish ruling classes all abhorred the way so many of their French contemporaries had lost their heads before the baying crowds and in 1793 Spain was driven to join an alliance of most of the monarchies of Europe, Britain included, known as the First Coalition. Two years later Spain's concerns about revolutionary France were outweighed by her nervousness over British intentions in the Caribbean. By August 1796 Spain and France were again allies and by the Treaty of Ildefonso she agreed to contribute fifteen ships to a Franco-Spanish fleet. Six months after the treaty was signed the Royal Navy did much to peg back the threat of the combined fleet by soundly defeating a large Spanish force off Cape St Vincent. On that day, 14 February 1797, Admiral Sir John Jervis commanded fifteen warships that included *HMS Victory* against twenty-seven under Admiral Juan de Cordova, including the *Santisima Trinidad*.

Later that year a soldier called Napoleon Bonaparte clambered his way to power in France. An artillery officer by profession, he was bent on military aggrandisement and led his armies into other European states at will. If they opposed him, as the Austrians did, his massed batteries of guns and endless columns of infantry swept their troops from the battlefield. The world war created by him reached places as far apart as Scandinavia and South Africa, the West Indies and Egypt. Great proud nations like Russia were forced into 'friendly' treaties by the little Corsican who even had Pope Pius VII rush across the Alps to crown him Emperor. From 1803 Napoleon began working on his plan to invade Britain. This was necessary for three reasons: firstly, Britain's control of the seas was getting in his way; secondly, her huge subsidies were sponsoring resistance in Europe; thirdly, in his words, 'We have six centuries of insults to avenge.' The invasion plan was for a combined Franco-Spanish fleet to wrest control of the Channel from the Royal Navy long enough for an invasion force of a hundred and eighty-eight thousand to sail across from Boulogne. The prospect of invasion terrified the British populace, especially in southern England. To ensure that the Gallic cock might never roost in the British oak, the Royal Navy had the difficult task of blockading ships of the combined fleet not only in French ports but also in Cadiz, El Ferrol and La Coruña. It was an extremely long blockade, stretching all the way from Cadiz to Boulogne, and it was only temporarily effective. What Nelson wanted was for the combined fleet to come out and fight: its annihilation would sink the threat of invasion. There could be no peace without a big battle first.

In 1803 Spain was not actually at war with Britain, she was officially neutral. In October France coerced Spain into supplying and repairing French warships in Spanish ports, for which she would be paid six million francs a month. As the agreement was under duress Spain could still claim to be neutral. Sir William Cornwallis, who commanded the forty-three battleships and frigates enforcing the blockade, watched the situation carefully. At first the only ships prevented from leaving Spanish ports were French warships, but he ordered the boarding of all neutral ships leaving French ports in order to obtain information. Increasingly suspicious of Spanish intentions, he then gave orders to prevent 'neutral' Spanish warships from leaving El Ferrol. Additionally, fearing that returning Spanish treasure ships might fall into French hands, he ordered that they be intercepted. On 5 October 1804 three British frigates attempted to detain four such treasure ships approaching Cadiz. A battle ensued during which one

Spanish ship, *La Mercedes*, was sunk and the others were captured. *Medusa*, *La Fama* and *La Clara* were taken to Gibraltar where their rich cargos, including over one million gold dollars and three million silver dollars were unloaded. Spain was provoked into throwing off the mantle of neutrality and declaring war on Britain on 12 December 1804. They must have laughed in Paris. It was so easy. Spain was no longer a reluctant ally but a committed supporter, determined to help France do as much damage to Britain as possible. On 4 January 1805 Admiral Frederico Gravina signed a Franco-Spanish pact that virtually handed control of the Spanish navy to Napoleon.

The hysteria and panic that gripped the British public might have been less had they realised what problems faced the French in assembling their invasion force. The logistical nightmare was from the start beset by concerns over finance, design, materials, manpower and security. Ports from Dieppe to Flushing lacked the capacity for so many ships and had to be expanded. Had the new works only to provide shelter from rough sea they would have had to be extensive, but they had also to offer protection from British bombardment. The French set about building more than two thousand vessels to carry troops to Kent but the 'Emperor's New Boats' were to be almost totally unseaworthy due to their flat-bottom design. No one dared tell the emperor until it was too late. The weather was not kind to the flotilla and Napoleon courted disaster when, on 20 July 1804, he ordered a review at Boulogne even though it was known that a storm was approaching. He must have felt inexcusably foolish as he observed upwards of twenty boats and hundreds of men perish needlessly in the surf before him. The anxieties of the British public might have been eased yet further had they understood the state of mind of the man commanding the Franco-Spanish fleet, Vice-Admiral Pierre-Charles Silvestre de Villeneuve: he considered the chances of Napoleon's invasion plan succeeding to be 'utterly impossible'.

On 30 March 1805 Villeneuve sailed from Toulon. The squadron joined Admiral Gravina's ships at Cadiz on April 9 and the next day the two fleets left port. The blockade had been breached; now there was a force out there big enough to confront other sections of the cordon. The Royal Navy did not know what Villeneuve and Gravina intended. The obvious move would be to sweep up the coast, roll up the blockade, collect compatriot ships at El Ferrol, Rochefort and Brest, then proceed to the Channel. Instead, they headed for the West Indies where Napoleon ordered them to attack British islands while waiting for more ships to break out of the blockade. Nelson followed in hot pursuit, desperate to engage the enemy but aware that he might be falling for a French trick to draw British ships away from the main theatre of battle. Nelson arrived in Barbados to find that no-one had seen the French fleet. He continued to search the seas, later discovering that he had come very close to meeting it. Learning Nelson's whereabouts, Villeneuve had decided to ignore orders and return to Europe. Nelson followed, to the south, before heading for Gibraltar.

Sailing off El Ferrol, the men on board the *Prince of Wales* were the first to catch sight of the homecoming combined fleet. On the foggy afternoon of 22 July 1805 the opposing fleets lined up for battle. The Spanish fired first and launched themselves wholeheartedly into the fight; all but three of the French ships stood off. The action lasted from just after five o'clock until dark. The British captured two Spanish ships, the *Firma* and *San Rafeal*, and took twelve hundred prisoners, themselves suffering nearly two hundred killed and wounded – enemy casualties were more than double that, most of them amongst the brave Spanish who had fought so hard with so little support. The Battle of El Ferrol might have continued the next day but neither side made a move. The fleets drifted apart and the chances of further action receded.

Napoleon now ordered the increasingly despondent Villeneuve to the Channel without delay. The British no longer wanted to block the combined fleet in port: the Royal Navy yearned for what Nelson had wished all along, for the enemy to come out and face attack. Villeneuve left El Ferrol on 10 August but, incredibly, instead of sailing for Boulogne, where Napoleon waited, he turned left and headed down the Iberian coast towards Cadiz. The emperor was beside himself with fury; his chances of invading England were being sabotaged by his most senior admiral! He considered his options. If he could not trust Villeneuve even to turn up, how could he rely on him to gain control of the Channel? The strength of the invasion force had peaked. Most of its members had long thought theirs an impossible mission. Napoleon came to a decision: from now on he would not rely on procrastinating, depressed ex-aristocrats bobbing along on the ocean – he would get on with what he himself was best at, commanding conquering armies across the landmass of Europe. He left Boulogne. How wasteful the whole venture had been – but he would cover the cost with the wealth of the next nation to be subjugated. However, he was not to forget the invasion fiasco. Villeneuve would be summoned to explain his actions. There would certainly be fireworks at the palace that night.

Down at Cadiz Villeneuve had no intention of disembarking and travelling to Paris, or of setting sail again. From port he could see the British frigates that Nelson was using as bait to entice his fleet out. Nelson himself was waiting beyond the horizon with twenty-seven warships. Villeneuve learnt that a carriage was hastening south from Madrid with a certain Vice-Admiral Francois-Etienne Rosily-Mesros who had orders to take over his command. He did not wait for the humiliation; he ordered his fleet to set sail immediately. Rosily's carriage pulled up at an almost empty quay. Of Villeneuve's thirty-three warships, fifteen were Spanish. The Spanish officers were only too aware of the risk they were taking following an incompetent foreign commander to do battle with the most formidable navy in the world.

The British frigate *Euryalus* sprinted from Cadiz to give Nelson the good news that the enemy was out. At dawn on Monday 21 October 1805 Nelson's fleet eyed the Franco-Spanish fleet several miles off Cape Trafalgar. Later that morning, as the fleets converged, a famous signal was run up the rigging of *HMS Victory*: 'England expects that every man will do his duty.' The British flagship led the way into battle.

Of the eighteen ships that the Royal Navy captured at Trafalgar, nine were Spanish. The great storm intervened, sending some to the bottom of the sea and allowing one to escape. In the end, of fifteen Spanish ships at Trafalgar, seven (*Argonauta, Monarca, Montones, Neptuno, Rayo, San Francisco de Asis* and *Santisima Trinidad*) were lost in the great storm, four (*Bahama, San Agustin, San Ildefonso* and *San Juan Nepomuceno*) remained captured, and four (*Principe de Asturias, San Justo, San Leandro* and *Santa Ana*) returned to Cadiz.

The huge Spanish flagship, *Principe de Asturias* (another product of the Havana shipyard), got away but Admiral Gravina was fatally wounded during a bombardment by *HMS Dreadnought*. One of the admiral's aides-de-camp was Miguel de Alava who, ten years later, was to find himself on Wellington's staff at Waterloo. Just before retiring on the night of that battle, Wellington and Alava would share a toast to the memory of the Peninsular War.

In addition to the *Santisima Trinidad* and *Principe de Asturias*, the other very large Spanish warship in the Trafalgar contingent was the *Santa Ana*. She had more crew aboard that day than any other ship, an incredible 1,118, so it was not surprising that, when she entered the battle early against Admiral Collingwood's *Royal Sovereign* and received a broadside, she suffered many casualties. Her crew fought bravely for two hours before the wounded captain was persuaded by his ship's total dismasting and the carnage of 340 casualties that surrender was the only option.

The fate of the *Santa Ana* goes a long way to explaining why the Spaniards lost so badly. Collingwood described the ship as 'a Spanish perfection' at a time when Spain's feats of navigation and exploration were second to none, but Spain's warships were let down by her crews. British crews trained and trained and trained until they could load, fire and sponge over three times faster than their adversaries. They spent much longer at sea, much of it on blockade duty, so could turn their ships on a sixpence. The Spanish found it hard to find skilled manpower for their magnificent ships amongst the yellow-fever-ravaged southern coastal populations. The *Santa Ana* may have been crowded that day but skilled men were lacking and there was a disastrous division between soldiers and seamen, which had also been the undoing of the Spanish at the time of the Armada. Finally, it must be remembered that there was a never a huge amount of enthusiasm for fighting beside the French.

With just ten ships left, the combined Franco-Spanish Fleet effectively ceased to exist. Spain was no longer capable of participating in a major operation against British war or merchant ships. The blow to Spanish sea power, however, did not result in the loss of the South American colonies as has often been suggested: the rush to independence was triggered by the mother country's loss of sovereignty when Napoleon's troops invaded in 1808, and it was encouraged by the revolutionary philosophy of the time. Interestingly, unlike the French, the Spanish did not view Trafalgar as a disaster. Her captains returned home not to shame and dishonour but to promotion. Several are honoured to this day, having ships in the modern Spanish navy named after them. Villeneuve's return home was less auspicious. He never faced Napoleon but his brutal murder in a Rennes hotel room was almost certainly the work of the emperor's men.

Joaquin Aguirre's assertion, quoted at the start of this chapter, that England's navy was none other than the old Spanish one, is obviously an exaggeration; the truth was, however, that between the battles of Passaro in 1718 and Trafalgar in 1805 twenty-five captured Spanish ships joined the Royal Navy. The *San Agustin* was burnt but the other three Trafalgar prizes went on to fly the royal ensign. Such was the superstition around renaming a ship that *Bahama* and *San Ildefonso* kept their names and *San Juan Nepomuceno* was merely shortened to *San Juan*.

CHAPTER 12

Sharpe's War

Even as they fought in file they lay,
Like a mower's grass at the close of day
When his work is over on the levelled plain,
Such was the fall of the fallen slain.

Lord Byron

THANKS TO THE NOVELS of Bernard Cornwell and the subsequent television series, the war that the British and their allies fought against Napoleon's troops in the Iberian Peninsula between 1808 and 1813 has been the focus of renewed interest. The tales of Riflemen Captain Richard Sharpe and his friend Sergeant Patrick Harpur are set against a meticulously researched background of great historical accuracy. Whether read as fact or fiction, the history of the Peninsula War with its epic battles and fascinating events is a magnificent story.

Napoleon would have liked to invade Britain and subjugate a stubborn obstacle to his plan for European domination. Seeing that this might be beyond France's means, however, he settled for trying to stifle his enemy by cutting off her oxygen of free trade. He prohibited every country in Europe from trading with her but, far away in the south-west corner of Europe, little Portugal refused to bow to the Frenchman's dictat. Half her trade was with Britain; obeying the command would have been economic suicide. Napoleon answered Portugal's disobedience by sending an army under General Junot through Spain to occupy the country. The imperial troops reached Lisbon on 30 November 1807.

Spain had permitted the French forces to pass through her territory; nevertheless in the spring of 1808 France decided to appropriate the whole of the peninsula. Spain's King Ferdinand was imprisoned and Napoleon's brother Joseph enthroned in Madrid. Both Iberian nations appealed to Britain for help. In view of Portugal's stand, Britain was morally obliged to answer her call. Spain and Portugal rose up. A British expeditionary force sailed for Portugal and the Peninsular War began.

The expeditionary force under the thirty-nine-year-old Lieutenant General Arthur Wellesley landed at Figuera da Foz in Portugal on 1 August 1808. Sixteen days later, from the castellated walls of the medieval town of Obidos, Wellesley spied the French four miles off at Rolica. Knowing he had the numerical advantage of three to one but that French reinforcements were not far away, he ordered an attack. However, as the French withdrew to a steep gullied ridge, a battalion in the British centre, the Worcesters under the command of Colonel Lake, attacked prematurely, forcing a full offensive in their support. Superior British numbers were almost neutralised by the steep gradient and the spirited French defence. Finally the British reached the crest and the French withdrew. The first victory had been achieved at the expense of 479 casualties compared with 600 for the French.

Four days later, on 21 August, Wellesley's army defeated the French for the second time. Many features of the Battle of Vimiero were typical of encounters which were to follow on the seven-year road to Waterloo. This time it was the French who attacked; it was Wellesley who chose a ridge. He ordered his troops to lie down on the reverse slope thereby reducing the danger from the French artillery; this also prevented the enemy from making an accurate assessment of British numbers and positions. The French advanced in columns, only to be checked by the British line which was able to fire more shots at one time. Then the British soldiers broke line, fixed bayonets and charged. Wellesley turned defence into attack by sending in the cavalry which charged – and sadly went too far, losing all control. Nevertheless it added up to a fine victory, assisted by the introduction of Major Shrapnel's new shells which exploded mid-air, raining lethal fragments on the columns below. The Convention of Cintra brought an end to hostilities, the French agreeing to leave Portugal. Wellesley also went home.

Lieutenant-General Sir John Moore took over command of the British army and soon learned that Rolica, Vimiero and the Convention of Cintra had touched a raw nerve in Napoleon. How dare a mere expeditionary force humble the greatest army in the world! The emperor sought retribution: he would personally lead the two hundred thousand men of the Grand Imperial Army over the Pyrenees into Spain and, with the fifty thousand troops already there, clear the peninsula of all opposition, especially the British whom he called 'the hideous leopard'. On Christmas Day 1808 Sir John Moore at Sahagún decided that his far smaller army of thirty thousand had no option but to run, to quit Spain before the overwhelming French force caught up with them. He ordered a retreat north-west to La Coruña where ships of the Royal Navy would meet his troops to take them home.

The 312-mile retreat to La Coruña was despised by the troops, who wanted nothing more than to stand and fight an enemy already defeated at Rolica and Vimiero. Moore could have made a stand at Astorga but he was reluctant to risk the only army England had. Three and a half thousand of his troops took a more southerly route towards Vigo as, unbeknown to them, Napoleon himself left the pursuit and returned to Paris.

The ordeal of those who pressed on towards the Atlantic was terrible. The elements threw everything they had at them: torrential rain, snow and biting winds. When the paths across the mountains were not covered in treacherous ice they were deep in slush or thick mud. The situation was made worse by the lack of food, fuel and shelter, and by boots that fell apart leaving men to hobble along barefoot. Many suffering from fatigue and exposure collapsed at the roadside. However, valiant rearguard actions prevented the pursuers, who were also suffering, from capturing any guns or colours. It was difficult to maintain discipline in a sullen, hungry, weary army and many broke ranks to loot and pillage. Some took out frustrations on the local population, angry that they had been risking their lives for Spain while the local men stayed at home. Many broke into wine vats, only to be amongst the stragglers captured by the French in the following hours.

On 11 January the army finally entered La Coruña but the ships of the Royal Navy were nowhere to be seen. They found themselves in a strange situation, not knowing who would come first, friendly ships from across the sea or enemy pursuers over the hills. Both parties arrived, the navy on the 14th, the French the following day. Having enjoyed the pick of local stores and keen to avenge their tormentors, Moore's army was prepared to fight but they dared to hope it might not come to that as embarkation continued apace without a French attack. Then early in the afternoon of the 16th the French guns opened fire on British positions around Monte Mero. Troops on their way to the ships turned back to fight. In the battle that followed the French were contained and then pushed back. General Sir John Moore saw his troops gain the upper hand shortly before he was fatally wounded. In his stirring poem, Charles Wolfe movingly described...

The Burial of Sir John Moore after Corunna

Not a drum was heard, not a funeral note,
As his corpse to the rampart we hurried;
Not a soldier discharged his farewell shot
O'er the grave where our hero we buried.

We buried him darkly at dead of night,
The sods with our bayonets turning,
By the struggling moonbeam's misty light
And the lantern dimly burning.

No useless coffin enclosed his breast,
Not in sheet or in shroud we wound him;
But he lay like a warrior taking his rest
With his martial cloak around him.

Few and short were the prayers we said,
And we spoke not a word of sorrow;
But we steadfastly gazed on the face that was dead,
And we bitterly thought of the morrow.

We thought, as we hollowed his narrow bed
And smoothed down his lonely pillow,
That the foe and the stranger would tread o'er his head,
And we far away on the billow!

Lightly they'll talk of the spirit that's gone,
And o'er his cold ashes upbraid him –
But little he'll reck, if they let him sleep on
In the grave where a Briton has laid him.

Sir John Moore was one of eight hundred dead left behind as, two days after the battle, nineteen thousand troops headed home on board the one hundred and ten ships. Although the French had succeeded in throwing the 'hideous leopard' out of Spain, they had not had it all their own way. There was still plenty of resistance separating their positions and the Pillars of Hercules – and they had lost Portugal.

Three months later Wellesley returned to the peninsula, landing at Lisbon on 22 April 1809. His first task was to secure Portugal again. The French under Marshal Soult had retaken the northern half of the country. Using the navy to outflank the enemy, he pushed them northwards, back to Oporto on the north side of the deep, wide gorge through which flows the River Douro. The French destroyed the bridge, made sure that there were no boats on the south bank which could be used to cross the great river and prepared themselves for an attack from the west, assuming that the British would use the navy to ferry troops from the south to the north bank. Wellesley arrived on the south bank where the likes of Sandeman, Taylor, Dow and Cockburn made their port. Every year special boats brought the grape harvest downstream from the vineyards to these lodges. As Wellesley pondered what to do a Portuguese barber rowed over from the city side of the river with news of where four such vessels were moored, unguarded by the French, on the north bank. Quickly they were collected and the crossing began. By the time Soult's shocked west-facing army realised that the British were establishing themselves behind them on the same side of the river, it was too late. In the fighting that preceded their retreat, the French suffered losses of three hundred plus fifteen hundred taken prisoner. The British lost just 123. Wellesley must have considered it a fine day's work as he dined on the meal which had been prepared for Soult in the Palacio das Carrancas.

Back in Spain the British planned to cooperate with the Spanish against the French, not an easy task in a country with no central government and an unreliable army led by General Cuesta, a man of questionable usefulness. The chosen place was Talavera on the road west of Madrid. Wellesley knew that if he moved fast the allied army would have an advantage of more than two to one over the French: fifty-five thousand British and Spanish against Marshal Victor's twenty thousand. But the advantage melted away as Cuesta's army, having failed to arrive for a joint attack on the morning of 23 July, curiously pursued the withdrawing French only to face a counter-attack. As the Spaniards went off on their own, the French force swelled to forty-six thousand with the arrival of King Joseph's men. Now Victor had a two-to-one advantage.

To the west, Major General Robert Crauford's light brigade, desperate to reach Talavera in time for battle, had started its epic and arduous march which would cover over fifty miles in twenty-five hours. Normally armies did not march in the fierce heat of the day but Crauford had received a despatch from Wellesley urging him to hurry east. Moving along poor roads, the men were encumbered by their heavy uniforms, shakos, packs and weapons. They suffered terribly from exhaustion and dehydration. Many collapsed by the roadside and two committed suicide. Most were carried along by a combination of the discipline imposed by Crauford and their eagerness to join the fighting.

The allied positions stretched out in a rough line to the north of the city of Talavera. The dominating feature was a hill called the Medellin against which the French concentrated their attacks. These began on the night of 27 July when two thousand Spanish troops panicked, fired at an enemy too distant to harm and looted supplies as they fled to the rear. General Cuesta was as outraged as Wellesley and ordered two hundred to be shot, a number which was reduced to forty after representations from the British commander. Next morning the first French artillery bombardment of the day preceded the first of many marches of their columns of infantry against the thin red line which, as at Vimiero, appeared as if it would be easy to pierce but held due to its capacity to bring more arms to bear. The French attacks lasted all day but never managed to break through. They ceased as Joseph left for Madrid, which he understood to be under threat from a Spanish army under Venegas.

As the light brigade closed in on Talavera they were shocked to meet a column of refugees, English and Spanish, crowding the route and speaking of the defeat of the British army. Finally, unhappily too late, they arrived at 6am on the 29th to learn that victory belonged to the allied army but at the expense of a quarter of their comrades, 5,365 men. The French had lost 7,628, a higher figure but a lower percentage of their strength on the day. The horror of that battlefield, where so many wounded lay dying amongst the dead, was increased by the grass catching fire, hastening many to a death far more agonising than the one they had expected.

The battlefield is today crossed by a motorway, the construction of which meant digging up many British graves. Protests at the time led the Spanish government to agree to the erection of a monument to the battle. Dedicated in 1990, it is a large pyramid formed by three concrete motorway supports with a bronze wreath at the summit. To see the most impressive monument to the war, you have to go to Oporto where, in the Boavista area, there stands an enormous column topped by a lion crushing an eagle. Below, the joint civilian and military struggle is brilliantly depicted by bronze figures whose expressions of determination and distress are so convincing that they cannot fail to leave an impression of the horror and heroism of those days. The Battle of Talavera was important as it was the first reverse for the French in Spain. The allied leader Arthur Wellesley was created Viscount Wellington of Talavera in recognition of the achievement. The

Spanish went on to defeat the French again at Tamames in October before suffering overwhelming defeats at Ocaña and Alba de Tormes in November. The British stayed in Spain until 9 December, then returned to Portugal for the winter.

Determined once again to drive the British from the peninsula, Napoleon despatched a hundred thousand troops, raising his total there to three hundred and twenty-five thousand. He also sent the able but reluctant Marshal Massena. Against such huge numbers Wellington's priority was survival and the defence of Portugal. He would be patient and bide his time before returning to Spain. To ensure that the only army Britain had was not driven into the sea he planned and built the 'lines of Torres Vedras', a series of defensive fortifications across the Lisbon peninsula. In late September, as Massena's army moved towards Lisbon, Wellesley's British and Portuguese army took up positions on Busaco Ridge. They thoroughly battered and repelled their assailants, then withdrew behind the impassable lines of Torres Vedras. Massena pursued, not expecting to find such a barrier. In mid-November his frustrated army withdrew having lost twenty-five thousand to starvation and disease.

Far to the south, a long way from the main theatre of war, a garrison of twenty-six thousand British and Spanish troops had held out in Cadiz against a besieging French army of twenty-five thousand since January of the previous year. Then in January 1811 the besieging force was reduced to fifteen thousand when a large proportion left to support Marshal Soult's attempt on Badajoz. Those in Cadiz saw their chance. Cadiz stands on a peninsula and this had enabled the Royal Navy to keep supplies flowing in over the past year. Now it was planned that thirteen thousand men would slip out of Cadiz by sea, travel east and disembark behind the investing French, provoking an attack. At the same time four thousand of General Zayas' Spaniards would pour out of Cadiz.

The British force under sixty-two-year-old Major-General Sir Thomas Graham sailed from Cadiz on 21 February, disembarked at Algeciras and joined General La Peña's Spanish force of eight thousand on the road back to Cadiz, at Tarifa. Progress was too slow: General Zayas made his sortie from Cadiz before Graham and La Peña were in position. Not surprisingly General Zayas was defeated. The French now knew what the plan had been; they decided that they would do the attacking. As La Peña changed his plans, cooperation broke down and Graham's force of five thousand was left to take on nine thousand French under Marshal Victor. On 5 March, Dilkes' brigade and

Browne's battalion attacked the French on Barrosa Ridge; once again the superior firepower of the line overcame that of the column. A mile to the north, two thousand six hundred men of the light battalion, also in line, held four thousand French. Then Wheatley's brigade joined in and fierce fighting ensued. To the delight of the 87th, they captured the first example of a prize that would be dearly sought after by every regiment all the way to Waterloo – a French eagle. Unable to make their superior numbers count, the French withdrew. Although not a major battle, it was a fine victory in view of the odds, and the allies had managed to keep their losses down to 1,740 against 2,400 of the enemy.

The main theatre of war in 1811 was on the Spanish-Portuguese border. On a similar latitude to Madrid, and not far from Portugal, stands the Spanish fortress city of Ciudad Rodrigo. Going south, about half-way to the sea, and on a similar latitude to Lisbon, is another great fortified city, Badajoz. Ciudad Rodrigo and Badajoz straddle the two most important roads between Portugal and Spain. The French needed these roads and their fortresses in order to invade Portugal for the fourth time. Conversely Wellington needed to secure them before he could take his campaign east across Spain. On 3 May Marshal Massena headed west from Ciudad Rodrigo with an army of forty-eight thousand. Fifteen miles west Wellington, with ten thousand fewer chose the last village in Spain, Fuentes de Oñoro, to make a stand. The French launched their attack against the village in the afternoon. The bitter street fighting soon reduced the single-storey houses to rubble and filled the narrow streets and alleys with bodies. The allies were driven out before two Highland regiments recaptured the village. The following day there was a truce, the only warfare being psychological: the French held parades and the British played football.

On 5 May the British were forced to realign as a massive force of seventeen thousand French infantry and four thousand cavalry swept in from the south instead of the east as their army had done two days before. South of Fuentes de Oñoro, where today a line of white stones with E on one side and P on the other mark the border, the beleaguered and isolated 7th division found itself surrounded by hundreds of French cavalry. The light division went to meet them and covered their withdrawal with a highly disciplined, simple but masterly manoeuvre. The only way infantry could survive a cavalry attack was by grouping into tightly packed squares with all bayonets facing out. They formed into seven such blocks and, although surrounded by

French cavalry, infantry and artillery, refused to panic as they slowly withdrew in formation back to their lines. The withdrawal covered three miles and must have required nerves of steel as three thousand cavalry milled around waiting for a chance to pounce. Never was endless drill on a parade ground so justified. It was not to be the only magnificent withdrawal that day: protecting the withdrawing squares, Captain Norman Ramsey of the Royal Horse Artillery stayed behind too long and was surrounded by the enemy. His gunners limbered up the two guns, mounted, drew their sabres and drove their charging horses madly through the enemy cavalry, emerging from the tumult to make it back to safety.

Back in the village the bitter fighting continued. The French captured it again, then fell back themselves in the face of the determined Connaught Rangers. A seventh French attack failed; it was to be the last. The allies counted 1,545 losses against 2,192 of the enemy. Three days later Massena withdrew. The battle virtually destroyed Fuentes de Oñoro. In one of his despatches Wellington asked the British government for money to rebuild it. Today, although it is a charming old village filled with humble stone houses, it is obvious that the money never arrived.

One hundred and eighty miles to the south General Beresford had been investing Badajoz. On 12 May, having heard that Marshal Soult's army of twenty-five thousand was marching northwards in his direction, he left Badajoz and transferred a few miles south down the Seville road to La Albuera. His army of twenty thousand British and Portuguese was joined by fourteen thousand Spaniards, something that Soult had not reckoned on. At nine o'clock on the morning of 16 May, in fields to the south-west of the village, the five-hour battle commenced as four thousand eight hundred of Zayas' Spanish division found themselves facing a huge onslaught by twelve thousand of the enemy. With great valour and despite large losses, the Spanish held their ground. The pattern had been set for a day in which the two sides fought at close quarters, inflicting and suffering great losses but not giving way. That day the allies were commanded by General Beresford whose style was less hands-on than Wellington's. He arrived with his army and let them get on with it. As a result mistakes were made but in the end it was probably his approach that won the day for the allies. The French were convinced that they had won but, unable to persuade Beresford that he had lost, they finally left the field in frustration. Marshal Soult summed it up, 'They could not be persuaded they were beaten. They were completely beaten, the day was mine and they did not know it, and would not run.' The British could argue that they had won: they were prepared to go on fighting when the French departed. The French disagreed and the name La Albuera was to be included on the Arc de Triomphe in Paris. Beresford's despatch carried news of a victory not in any great belief that it had been one but because Wellington did not like to upset people back home.

Losses on both sides were immense. The 57th was one of the regiments caught up in close-range fire between the three thousand seven hundred of Houghton's and Abercrombie's brigades and seven thousand eight hundred French. Colonel Inglis of the 57th knew that many of his men would be killed but he did not want them to die cheaply or easily. 'Die hard,' he urged them as 428 out of 616 fell. Later, when a rainstorm soaked the gunpowder and silenced the muskets, the sixteen hundred of Colborne's brigade did not have time to form squares before the arrival of the Polish Lancers, who promptly cut down thirteen hundred of them. The casualty list at La Albuera was, in this war, exceeded only by that of Talavera. The allies lost close on six thousand. Of these, 888 British soldiers were killed and 3,574 wounded. Estimates of French losses vary between six and a half and eight thousand.

Less than two years before the battle Lord Byron had rejoiced in the tranquillity of the place as he passed through on his way to Gibraltar to take ship to Greece. On learning of the battle he was driven to write about the contrast between the way he remembered it and how he now heard it reported.

> Oh Albuera, glorious field of grief!
> As o'er the plain the pilgrim pricked his steed
> Who could foresee thee in a space so brief
> A scene where mingling foes should boast and bleed!

Today every motorist and pedestrian arriving at La Albuera is reminded of the village's pride in its Peninsular War heritage by ceramic monuments with Byron's words below the heads of Spanish, British, Portuguese and French troops.

Despite the fierce fighting over the two most important routes between Portugal and Spain, little had been resolved. The following year control over them would have to be fought out all over again.

Napoleon made a mistake in 1812 that Hitler was to repeat a hundred and thirty years later – he invaded Russia, thereby opening up a second and very difficult front. Twenty-seven thousand troops were withdrawn from Spain. This still left a French army of 232,500 in the Peninsula but a considerable number of these was shackled by guerrilla activity. One such guerrilla, Julian Sanchez, whose band had seen action at Fuentes de Oñoro, had laid siege to the walled city of Ciudad Rodrigo. Wellington now intended to capture it, a task not expected to be difficult as the garrison numbered only two thousand.

Several hundred metres north of Ciudad Rodrigo, a ridge called the Lesser Teson runs parallel to the city walls; and a few hundred metres north of that is a higher ridge, the Greater Teson. The British planned to capture the Reynaud Redoubt on the Greater Teson and sap down to the Lesser Teson; here batteries would be set up to blow a couple of breaches in the city walls.

The French would not have been amused by the entertaining spectacle of allied soldiers competing in a field sports day had they known it was actually cover for a reconnaissance. With the necessary information gathered, a large storming party attacked the Reynaud Redoubt. The defenders put up little resistance. When one of their sergeants, about to throw out a fallen shell before it exploded, was shot dead an alarmed comrade kicked the shell away, but in the direction of the gate which was opened by its explosion. The British rushed in and took forty-eight prisoners.

The difficult and unpopular task of digging trenches in freezing cold weather continued. The breaching batteries opened fire at dawn on 15 January and by the 19th two breaches had been opened. This success, and the news that Marmont was concentrating nearby, led Wellington to order the storming of the city that night. The troops were delighted: they would escape from freezing trenches into a city full of plunder and other temptations. They hoped the French would not surrender and deny them the post-victory spoils.

At seven o'clock, following two successful diversionary attacks round the other side, a rocket signalled the commencement of the main assault. Tremendous fire from the defenders, including blood-curdling blasts of grapeshot, ripped through the ranks of the allies who found their way obstructed by ditches and metal obstacles; then in the greater breach a huge mine exploded. Designed to kill and maim attackers it did just that but also damaged the defence, enabling the 3rd division to enter the town. The light division succeeded in penetrating the lesser breach at the great cost of their most able commander, Major General Robert Crauford. Altogether 195 were killed and 916 wounded. Two thousand of the enemy were taken prisoner.

Having taken the town, the soldiers felt at liberty to do as they pleased. The inhabitants were in theory friends and allies yet the victors embarked on whatever depravity took their fancy. It must have been a strange sight indeed the next day as troops left the burning town wearing newly acquired coats, hats and boots and carrying hams, bread and even monkeys.

Today the pock-marked cathedral still bears the scars of that bombardment all those years ago. In a garden below its tower is a monument to the guerrilla Julian Sanchez whose investment preceded Wellington's arrival. Robert Crauford was buried below the lesser breach where he fell; a plaque marks the spot.

With the northern road between Spain and Portugal secured, Wellington now looked south to make the other his. Two months later his army besieged the fortress of Badajoz. Three weeks passed; trenches were dug, occasionally interrupted by very damaging French sorties. With the batteries established, 22,374 round shot were available for the sixteen nine-foot-long 24-pounders which began battering the walls. Supporting them were thirty-six more guns with 24,983 rounds of shot. The thundering guns pummelled the high walls until 6 April 1812, when news that Marshal Marmont and Marshal Soult were on the move persuaded Wellington to order the second storming in three months. The plan was to launch the main assault against the breaches on the south-east side. Two smaller forces would make diversionary attacks on the castle on the east side and the San Vincente bastion on the west. As at Ciudad Rodrigo, the spirits of the troops were high – less from the prospect of gaining military honours in the second great assault of the year than from the prospect of plunder and revenge. Sergeant William Lawrence of the 40th and his comrades George Bowden and Pig Harding had all been quartered at Badajoz after the Battle of Talavera so they knew where the shops were located. Having heard a report that three hours' plunder would be allowed if they succeeded in taking the place, they arranged to meet at the silversmith's shop.

The assault began at 10 o'clock that night. The frightful carnage that followed would cost Wellington three thousand men. As at Ciudad Rodrigo, the assailants charged blindly into a blaze of musketry and grapeshot and came up against unexpected obstacles. A strong beam full of sword blades blocked one breach and from behind it enemy muskets rattled away at all who approached. The 4th division never expected to find the ditch full of water, and one hundred drowned. The assailants kept pressing forwards despite the hail of musket balls, the murderous artillery fire and exploding grenades and mines. The noise was deafening as the sound of the guns, bugles and drums mixed with the shouts of men desperate for victory and its rewards. As they scaled the ladders, many fell backwards up to forty feet onto the bayonets of their own comrades. Below, the piles of bleeding, burnt, trodden, screaming and groaning men grew and the wounded struggled to free themselves from underneath. Upon the walls the French taunted their enemies and hurled down logs and rocks but the assailants were like men possessed: despite the gaps ripped in their ranks by the deadly fire, the men of the 3rd, 4th, 5th and light divisions refused to give up. Just as Wellington was considering calling his men off, the breakthrough came. On the walls of the San Vincente bastion the French had not been quick enough to push away Colonel Ridge's ladder and after dodging the vicious thrusts of pikes and bayonets he found himself on the ramparts with the accolade of first man into Badajoz. At the same time, in the other diversionary attack, the 3rd division succeeded in getting into the castle. It was two o'clock on the morning of 7 April. As thousands of assailants gained the walls, the time had come for the French to pay for their gallant defence. Even those trying to surrender were cut down on a night when the enraged victors showed little mercy as they embarked on a forty-hour binge of retribution and lawlessness.

Soon a large proportion of the brave victorious army was transformed into an intoxicated rabble of debauched plunderers. Defenceless inhabitants suffered shameful physical abuse and their property was smashed if it could not be taken away. Officers struggled and failed to maintain any semblance of order as indiscriminate firing filled the streets. Sergeant William Lawrence's planned meeting at the silversmiths came to nothing: Pig Harding had received seven shots to the body and George Bowden's legs had been blown off at the thigh; both men must have died instantaneously. Lawrence resolved never again to plan assignations in such fearful circumstances. Eventually a gallows erected in the main square on Wellington's orders had the desired sobering effect and the violence subsided. Readers of Peninsular War history will come across the theory that to this day a bad atmosphere pervades Badajoz due to the carnage wrought by the British after the battle. But any gloom today is more likely to stem from events that followed the fall of Badajoz to Franco's ruthless fascist forces in 1936: in just twelve hours, eighteen hundred suspected Republicans were rounded up and put to death by machine gun in the city bull ring.

Badajoz, the scene of such unspeakable suffering and misery for so many, was for one soldier, twenty-four-year-old Captain Harry Smith, the place where he found great happiness. The day after the storming two Spanish ladies fled from the city, making for the British encampment. One approached rifleman John Kincaid and begged that her young companion be given protection. Kincaid turned to Juana Maria de los Dolores de Leon and saw 'an angel – a being more transcendingly lovely I had never before seen – one more amiable I have never yet known.' Unluckily for Kincaid, Harry Smith was the more assertive knight: he stepped in to take her hand, marrying her soon afterwards. The popular officer and his beloved wife went through the remainder of the Peninsular War together. His career was a distinguished one, including the Battle of Waterloo. When General Sir Harry Smith was Govenor of the Cape Colony of South Africa, Juana was honoured in the naming of Ladysmith, which years later would ironically be the scene of another great siege involving the British Army.

Badajoz with its mighty walls had been in a fine state of repair with a strong garrison and plenty of supplies, so the French were shocked and bewildered by its fall. Wellington was equally appalled at losing nearly five thousand troops in the siege and assault. Studying the casualty list had the same effect on him as it did on one other occasion – he wept as he would do again after Waterloo. As the duke himself said, 'Nothing except a battle lost can be half so melancholy as a battle won.'

The capture of both Ciudad Rodrigo and Badajoz meant that Wellington's offensive against the French in Spain could truly begin. He would push into central Spain, towards Madrid, and divide Soult's army in the south from Marmont's in the north. General 'Daddy' Hill, so named because of his fatherly, compassionate attitude towards his troops, took eighteen thousand of their number to hold the south. The actions of Spanish troops and guerrillas were meanwhile preventing French forces from concentrating.

On 17 June 1812 Wellington's army liberated the university city of Salamanca. In the fields nearby a hundred thousand allied and French soldiers spent much of the following month marching up and down, trying to outmanoeuvre each other. On the night of 21 July there was a terrific thunderstorm and lightning killed several Inniskilling dragoons. Three years later, the night before Waterloo, there was to be another great storm, but as the Belgian rain drenched the soldiers' uniforms in 1815 it did not dampen the spirits of Peninsular veterans:

they would remember the events that followed the downpour on the plains of central Spain in 1812.

On 22 July the allies were moving west across the fields about five miles south of Salamanca; about a mile further south the French moved parallel to them: they wanted to get ahead of the British so that their front divisions could turn north and cut Wellington's men off from Portugal. In seeking to gain this advantage the most forward, westerly French division under Thomiere pressed on so hard that a dangerous gap opened up behind them. The following division under Macune lagged behind by about a mile and the whole French force now stretched out over four miles. Wellington saw his opportunity to hit Thomiere's isolated division and then attack the straggling force behind.

Thomiere's, Macune's and Brennier's divisions were all but destroyed. Then two of the French divisions which had been following thrust north to exploit a gap which had opened up between the British 4th and 5th divisions. Unluckily for them Wellington had anticipated this: Clinton's 6th division went forward to meet them. After some hard fighting the French, who had had five of their eight divisions mauled, broke and retreated east. It was an emphatic victory for Wellington's men. His losses were 5,214; Marmont's were over two and a half times that number and Marmont himself was badly wounded. As at Talavera, almost exactly three years before, the suffering of the wounded was horribly intensified by the flames which swept through the grass after the battle.

Wellington progressed towards Madrid, which his forces liberated on 12 August. The garrison of two and a half thousand in the forts of the Retiro surrendered in the face of artillery: inside were a hundred and eighty guns, twenty thousand muskets and two eagles. It is amazing that the eagles, so stoutly defended by their regiments in battle and so prized by every adversary of the French, should simply have been abandoned, not even hidden or smuggled away. After a month the allies marched north to drive General Clausel towards France. On the way was the castle of Burgos. Held by the French, it had to be taken before further progress could be made. Despite having only three guns, Wellington invested it on 19 September.

Far off in Eastern Europe Napoleon entered Moscow, not as a proud conqueror keen to inspect his new possession but as a dismayed spectator of a smouldering ruin. It really was quite unbelievable: he had marched his Grand Imperial Army all that way, only for the vindictive Muscovites to torch his prize. While Napoleon pondered his next move in Moscow, Wellington was also having a bad time, failing to add Burgos to his collection of three great victories savoured that year. Wellington had twenty-four thousand British and eleven thousand Spanish troops besieging Burgos; its castle had a French garrison of two thousand under the command of the very able General Dubreton. The main shortcoming of the castle was that it was overlooked by a hill. On the night of 19 September the fortification on San Miguel hill was attacked and taken at a cost of 421 losses compared with 198 on the French side. During the next four weeks four assaults against the castle failed whilst two sorties by the French achieved significant success. In total, the calamitous Siege of Burgos cost Wellington 2,064 casualties against 623 French. When news came of the combined threat from Soult, Joseph and Suchet against Hill there was no option but to lift the siege and head towards Portugal to try to join up with Hill.

While the Russians pursued the suffering French west during the terrible retreat from Moscow, in Spain the French pursued Wellington's troops as they struggled towards the Portuguese border. The French never charged, they just picked off stragglers. The hungry troops' flight was made miserable by cold and torrential rain. Despite the fact that there were no long marches – in fact there were considerable numbers of rests, and relatively little interference from the French – discipline began to break down. The situation was not helped by the fact that the road from Burgos to Salamanca passed through wine country. There had been a good harvest; the vats were full and many soldiers wasted no time in helping themselves. Many were captured, too drunk to continue the retreat and unable to defend themselves. On 6 November the French ceased their pursuit. Three days later Hill was in Salamanca with Wellington and by 18 November they were in winter quarters at Ciudad Rodrigo. During the retreat two thousand had died and one thousand had been captured. It was an inglorious end to a fine year but although Wellington regretted the blemish that Burgos represented on his exemplary record, his troubles had been small compared with those suffered by Napoleon in the Russian snow.

With Napoleon's power on the wane in central Europe, Wellington was determined that 1813 would be the year he finally bundled the French out of Spain. To achieve this he needed an army of greater numbers, whose ranks were more disciplined and less susceptible to ill health. These needs were addressed during the winter so that by the time the army was ready to march through Spain in pursuit of the

French forces commanded by King Joseph, their ranks had been boosted by five thousand new arrivals, they had countless hours of drill behind them and each infantryman's damp bivouac had been upgraded to a comfortable tent.

Against British hopes Napoleon did not elect to transfer troops from Spain to defend France from the attacks it faced from the east, so Wellington, who was now at last Commander-in-Chief of the Spanish armies, still had two hundred thousand French to contend with on Spanish soil. As before he had to ensure that they did not concentrate in one overwhelming mass. This was achieved in a number of ways including guerrilla activity, the coordination of which had become much easier as many of their leaders now held regular commissions in the Spanish army. Suchet's army remained in the east to oppose the sea-borne landings threatened by an Anglo-Sicilian force under Sir John Murray at Alicante.

The march north-east began on 22 May. This sweep, further north than the French had anticipated, sought not only to outflank the retreating French army but also to take advantage of the new supply route through Santander on the northern coast of Spain. There were several skirmishes on the way. The French army could easily have got away but they were determined not to leave Spain without the money, ornaments and art treasures that they had systematically robbed from dwellings, public buildings and places of worship all over the country. Not far from the French border, at Vitoria, they had to make a decision – abandon the treasure and escape or stand and fight. They decided to fight.

Assuming that Wellington would attack from the west, King Joseph placed his divisions in three defensive lines to the west of Vitoria. The battle began early on the morning of 21 June when the front line of the thirty-five thousand men of Gazan's division was attacked by the allies on its left, southern flank. Early in the afternoon Gazan's men faced another huge attack, this time on their right, northern flank. Already weakened by assaults from two unexpected directions, they now faced an onslaught from a third side – and this time it was the west. During the morning a forth allied column under Sir Rowland Hill had swept north and cut off the French escape route north of Vitoria. Gazan was driven back and attempted to form up next to the second line of defence, D'Erlon's division, but the allied pressure was too much; by five o'clock the French defence had broken and was retreating eastwards.

The allies pursued them until they came across thousands of

carriages full of riches and an abundance of food and wine. Even the new levels of discipline stood no chance in the face of such temptation and the troops just helped themselves. The wounded and dead French soldiers also offered rich pickings, having just been paid. A lot of troops made a lot of money that day, some as much as £1,000! It was a total and memorable victory. The allies lost just over five thousand men but the French lost eight thousand, 151 of their 153 guns and a treasure haul worth millions. The duke himself took care of over two hundred paintings stolen from the Spanish royal collection; they included the celebrated 'Waterseller of Seville', one of four paintings by Velazquez, as well as works by Goya and Rubens. Amazingly, when Ferdinand VII was re-instated as King of Spain, he allowed Wellington to keep them. Can he really have understood the enormous value of what he was giving away? Eighty-three of these paintings hang in Apsley House, the London home of the duke, which is open to the public.

After Vitoria Wellington's army was tantalisingly close to clearing the French out of Spain completely. There were only two main garrisons to go, San Sebastián and Pamplona, but if the allies thought that these would soon capitulate, leaving the march to the frontier free from the fear of being cut off from behind, Soult had his own ideas. On the other side of the Pyrenees he was busy reorganising the French army for a counter-offensive. The allies were now in the position of having to defend a long mountainous frontier behind which they had to stay back on the road, ready to concentrate wherever the attack eventually came. On 25 July, when Wellington was away investigating the failed assault on San Sebastián, sixty-one thousand French attacked at the passes of Maya (Puerto de Otxondo) and Roncesvalles. At both they were checked by the allies who, although heavily out-numbered, enjoyed favourable defensive positions. After the fighting the allies withdrew to the south.

Cole's force, which had been at Roncesvalles, withdrew down the road to Pamplona with Soult in pursuit. Six miles north of Pamplona, at Sorauren, eighteen thousand allies and thirty thousand French took up positions on facing ridges. Wellington returned and approached the allied lines. The master player took the stage and the crowds on one side of the theatre cheered, Portuguese and British alike acclaiming the one who was worth a thousand bayonets. Wellington did not enjoy such noisy public adulation but across the valley his adversary was finding it disturbing – so much so that he delayed the attack, allowing British reinforcements to arrive. The French attacked soon after noon the following day, 28 July. Several hours later they had lost around four thousand compared to the allies' 2,692 but the two armies still occupied their respective ridges. Two days later Wellington successfully attacked and sent the enemy retreating into France. Soult's counter-offensive was over.

There was still, however, the three-thousand-strong French garrison at San Sebastián to be dealt with. This town was located on an isthmus protruding seawards between the mouth of the River Uremea and a sandy beach. The town was on the landward side of the high headland on which stood a castle. After the siege guns had opened up what was deemed to be a sufficient breach the attack was set for 31 August. The fighting was bitter in a situation reminiscent of Badajoz. The day was carried only when the allied artillery, which was in some cases twelve hundred yards away, opened fire over the heads of the assaulting troops. This audacious act surprised the defenders without killing any of the attackers. The French ammunition was destroyed as the magazine exploded and the attackers surged into the town. After an hour of fighting in the streets the surviving defenders withdrew to the castle. The rampage began and one more Spanish town was to have its memories of liberation blighted by what its 'friends' did next – San Sebastián was all but destroyed by fire. Five days later mortar fire forced the troops occupying the castle to surrender. San Sebastián cost the allies 856 killed and 1,520 wounded. On the seaward side of the headland is a small British cemetery where lies Colonel Sir Richard Fletcher, the engineer behind the 'lines of Torres Vedras', who had died in the first, unsuccessful assault. Nearby is an impressive monument with soldiers and a cannon, and the tribute: 'To the glory of the victorious British Army which fought for the liberty of Spain and the glory of their own country.'

At the very western end of the Pyrenees, where Spain and France are separated by the River Bidasoa, there rises on the Spanish side the Ridge of San Marcial outside Irún. It was here that, on the same day as the fall of San Sebastián, General Freire's Spanish troops awaited the last major French offensive of the Peninsular War. Thick fog hid the French divisions that morning as they forded the river and started up the ridge. Though the Spaniards fought well, Freire was worried when the French temporarily established themselves on the western end of the ridge. Wellington turned down his request for assistance: British reinforcements were unnecessary; they would detract from what should be a totally Spanish victory. Further upstream at Vera a second French attack also failed. When rising

floodwaters prevented them from fording back the way they had
come, ten thousand were trapped on the wrong side of the river. The
only escape route was a bridge but here Captain Cadoux and eighty
rifles were determined not to let them retreat in peace. The French
crossed the bridge in the end but only after losing two hundred, including the divisional commander.

Spanish shrimpers enjoying a peaceful existence in Hondarribia at
the mouth of the Bidasoa could never have imagined that it would
be they who were to lead the victorious allies out of Spain and into
Napoleon's sacred land. But so it was. At low tide on the morning of
7 October 1813 they guided the troops across the estuary. Like Soult
five weeks before, Wellington chose Vera upstream as a crossing point.
There was some resistance at the coast and in the hills before the allies
successfully established themselves in enemy territory.

Two and a half weeks later Pamplona fell, freeing up troops for
the offensive into France. Wellington wished to push north to put
pressure on Napoleon but many of his Spanish troops had their
own agenda – revenge and plunder. As Goya's series of eighty-five
gruesome etchings under the title 'The Disasters of War' so vividly
illustrates, the civilian population of Spain had suffered dreadfully at
the hands of the French, and now the Spanish military had accounts
to settle. On 10 November the allies fought the French who had made
a stand south of the River Nivelle. During the battle some of the enemy
surrendered to Colonel John Colbourne, fearing that they were about
to be captured by the Spanish, a thought that horrified them. That
night the worst fears of many French civilians were realised when
a Spanish division wreaked terrible revenge in Ascain. Wellington,
who could not risk an uprising of the French civilian population,
reacted by sending many of the Spaniards home. Wellington was
also wary of a scheme whereby Napoleon's prisoner King Ferdinand
of Spain would be restored to his throne in Madrid in return for a
military alliance against Britain. This Treaty of Valencay was almost
certainly the result of Ferdinand's willingness to say anything to
win his freedom; it was unthinkable that Spain should genuinely
be uniting with a country which had just subjected it to six years of
savage repression.

Wellington's army, which still included several Spanish divisions,
continued to pursue Marshal Soult, fighting battles at the River Nive,
St Pierre and Orthez during the winter of 1813-14. On 10 April 1814
they attacked Toulouse at a cost of four and a half thousand men. The
losses could have been avoided had the participants known that six

days earlier Napoleon had abdicated. A week later Marshal Soult surrendered. The Peninsular War was over.

For Wellington and many of his troops, the start and middle of their road to Waterloo was in the Iberian peninsula. After his abdication, Napoleon was exiled to Elba but he escaped to raise another army. One hundred days later he was defeated at the Battle of Waterloo.

CHAPTER 13

The British Legion

I would not give a toss up for the choice between Don Carlos and Maroto,
the Queen and Espartero. They ought all to be hanged on the same tree,
to avoid the injury which might be done to a second.

Duke of Wellington

O NCE OR TWICE A WEEK, depending on the time of year, a large
car ferry travels from Portsmouth to Bilbao on the Basque coast
of northern Spain. It sails under the red, gold, blue and white
flag of the Peninsular and Oriental Steam Navigation Company
(P&O). Red and gold are the colours of the current Spanish royal
household, blue and white those of the old Portuguese monarchy. The
two royal households granted the company the right to fly their
colours in appreciation of its ferrying British soldiers who, in separate
Spanish and Portuguese civil wars, fought on behalf of liberal monarchs against despotic pretenders. It would have taken four journeys
by today's *Pride of Bilbao* to deliver the ten thousand members of the
British Legion who started disembarking further east along the coast
at San Sebastián in the summer of 1835. In a climate not dissimilar
to that of today, the British Parliament, press and public were bitterly
divided over participation in yet another foreign war. It must be noted
that this British Legion was nothing to do with the Royal British
Legion, the charity that today safeguards the welfare, interests and
memory of those who have served in the armed forces.

At the beginning of the eighteenth century, in both England and
Spain it was possible for either a man or woman to ascend the throne,
while neighbouring France permitted only male monarchs. Eager to
ensure that Spain and France were never united by a royal marriage,
England successfully encouraged Philip V to adopt France's Salic Law
of Succession in 1713. In 1830 Philip's great-grandson King Ferdinand, who had no sons, announced that his father had secretly
revoked the Salic Law, therefore his daughter Isabella would succeed
him. The king's brother Don Carlos felt cheated and, when Ferdinand
died in 1833, he and his 'Carlists' took up arms to fight for what they
believed to be his throne by divine right. Isabella was only three years

old at the time so her mother Maria Cristina assumed the regency. Her 'Cristinos' drew most of their support from liberals in large towns and cities who were keen to see more commercial progress, modernisation and democratisation such as was beginning to benefit some of their European neighbours. The Carlists represented traditional god-fearing feudal, agrarian communities and reactionaries who feared change and the chaos it might bring. They were strong in the north where centralisation threatened to sweep away regional privileges.

Even though Salic Law had suited them in 1713, the British Government and Prime Minister Lord Palmerston now backed Maria Cristina, mainly because she had introduced a limited amount of parliamentary democracy, anathema to the Carlists who strongly believed in the absolute power of the monarchy. Palmerston hastened to form a Quadruple Alliance with France, Spain and Portugal, principally to forestall unilateral French action that might give them undue influence in Madrid. Britain then wished to move Carlos away from the peninsula (he was in Portugal) to England, where he could be persuaded to renounce his claim. Accordingly in June 1834 Don Carlos, his wife, three sons, the Bishop of Leon and their retinue were collected by the Royal Navy ship *Donegal* and taken to Spithead, then on to Portsmouth. Don Carlos had acquiesced because, at the time, travelling via England was probably the easiest way of reaching his followers in northern Spain. The civil servant who visited him with the offer of a handsome pension wasted his time: Don Carlos did not believe he had the right to renounce a position bestowed by God and he certainly was not going to abandon loyal supporters who had risked and lost lives for his cause. In London he saw the sights and laughed off cautionary advice from the Duke of Wellington before slipping away to Brighton where, with new hair colour and no moustache, he embarked for Dieppe. After travelling across France on a Mexican passport he tramped over the border into Navarre and arrived at the village of Zugaramurdi. He had left his wife, the Portuguese Princess Francisca, at Alverstoke Rectory near Portsmouth, where she died after a short illness in September that year. The plaque on her tomb before the high altar of the small local chapel described her as Queen of Spain. She was a great loss to the Carlist cause: without her Don Carlos struggled to make decisions.

Don Carlos proceeded to the Carlist training camp at Elizondo. His arrival cheered the volunteers; equally, he must have been elated to see the fine guerrilla army taking shape under his brilliant commander Tomás Zumalacárregui. A veteran of the Peninsular War, he built up a

force of thirty-five thousand that brought most of the country between
Santander and Pamplona, with the exception of the big cities, under
Carlist control and enabled Don Carlos and his court to live in considerable comfort at their headquarters in Oñati. Further east the
Carlists were also making gains in Aragon, Catalonia and València,
where Ramón Cabrera was making a name for himself as much
through war crimes as military achievements. From his youth in
Tortosa, Cabrera had combined appalling behaviour with religious
fervour and now, with a force of four thousand men and several hundred cavalry, he terrorised Cristinos from his base in the Maestrazgo,
the mountainous area between València and Aragon.

Back in the Basque Country Don Carlos and his advisers decided it
was high time that a big city was added to their territory. Zumalacárregui agreed: with disorganisation and dissension in the Cristino
ranks an advance on Madrid was possible and, once Don Carlos was
installed in the palace there, the war would be won. Unfortunately for
Zumalacárregui Don Carlos was thinking not of Madrid but of Bilbao.
The Carlist court felt that if they controlled that city it would be
easier to import stores and arms and secure loans. Zumalacárregui
warned that taking it was not worth the lives that would be risked;
he felt so strongly that he offered his resignation which, not surprisingly, was refused. He was overruled. The siege began on 15 June 1835.
The following day he went up to the balcony of a building in Begoña
which, standing on a hill near the city walls, offered a superb view.
He took out the telescope the Duke of Wellington had used at the
Battle of Toulouse. It had been given to Zumalacárregui by Colonel
Gurwood who had visited Spain earlier in the year with Lord Eliot on
a mission to encourage both sides to end the atrocities, especially the
routine execution of prisoners. Zumalacárregui's presence on the balcony drew the musket fire of vigilant defenders and he was struck in
the right calf. It was a minor wound but incompetent medical attention meant that eleven days later he was dead. A conspiracy theory
surrounds his death. One of the surgeons had been an Englishman,
Frederick Burgess. His recommendation that the ball be extracted
immediately was overruled, and he was dismissed. The British Ambassador in Spain reported that 'Don Carlos openly expressed his joy …
upon being rid of a tyrannous subaltern.' The siege was lifted. The
Carlists were still in a position to win the war but the loss of 'Uncle
Tomás' was a huge blow. They needed to make haste now. The Cristinos were about to get the foreign intervention they so desired.

That same June the only man who was present at both Trafalgar and Waterloo, General Alava, now Spanish Ambassador to London, obtained Prime Minister Palmerston's permission to raise ten thousand British volunteers to fight the Carlists. The Peninsula veteran, and Member of Parliament for Westminster, Colonel de Lacy Evans, was chosen to command them. As a member of the Quadruple Alliance, Britain had pledged only naval assistance and this devious way of further intervening without commiting the British Army enraged Tory critics. The French did not formally intervene either, but the French Foreign Legion saw action in Aragon and Catalonia.

Recruitment was easy: there was high unemployment at the time and the agents were not fussy about character or physical fitness; neither were recruits deterred by Don Carlos's declaration that all foreign prisoners would be shot. The firm run by Wilcox and Anderson which later became P&O supplied a steamer, renamed the *Reyna Governadora* (Queen Regent), which carried the first five hundred men to an enthusiastic reception in San Sebastián on 10 July 1835. Their lodgings were in the Dominican friary of San Telmo which is today an art gallery. By the end of August the MP for Westminster had his mercenary army in place, ready to join a Cristino attack on Hernani, a Carlist stronghold just a few miles inland. The legionnaires were surprised and angry that the Carlists would not come out to fight like gentlemen; instead they held their ground, taking some prisoners and shooting the British among them. General Evans was impressed by his men's bravery but decided they needed another two months of training before engaging the enemy again. Many had come to Spain without ever having loaded a musket.

The Legion spent October in Bilbao before marching to Vitoria to join the Cristino army. Diverting through Old Castile to avoid the Carlists, they spent three weeks at Briviesca where the harsh Spanish winter closed in. Early in December they arrived in Vitoria. During the next four months a combination of atrocious accommodation, poor clothing, bad food, fetid wine and foul weather so weakened the men that a form of typhus claimed 819 of their number. Just eighteen hundred were sufficiently fit to take part in an inconclusive battle against the Carlists in January.

As British legionnaires needlessly perished in Vitoria, the inhumanity of the war in Catalonia darkened. In April 1835 Zumalacárregui and the Cristino General Valdés had signed up to the Elliot Convention, agreeing to the regular exchange of captives, the humane treatment of the sick and wounded and not to shoot prisoners. Unfortunately, outside the Basque Country and Navarre neither side felt that the convention applied to them. In January 1836 Carlists in a besieged castle threw a hundred and seventy Cristino prisoners over the wall and shot at them as they fell. In revenge, a mob in Barcelona ignored the weak protests of their authorities and stormed the forts to seize a hundred and seven Carlist prisoners to execute with sabre and shot. That same month Ramon Cabrera, the ruthless Carlist commandant-general in Lower Aragon, ordered the shooting of two mayors working with the Cristinos. General Nogueras, the Cristino commander in the same sector, then ordered his men to execute Cabrera's mother Maria Griño, a fifty-three-year old grandmother. Denied Holy Communion or last family visits, she was shot on 16 February. The outraged anti-war lobby in the House of Lords remonstrated that the Legion's presence in the peninsula meant that '... Britain was substantially participating in a cause and in a system of warfare which had been disgraced by atrocities and abominations unheard of in the history of any civilised country.' Any hope of humanity in the brutal war had disappeared. Cabrera replied by ordering the execution of four female Cristino hostages including the beautiful nineteen year-old Cinta Fos whom he had been expected to marry.

The Carlists knew that if they were to win the war they had to show themselves and their flag beyond their own established territories in the north. Early in 1836 a fighting priest called Batanero led two hundred and sixty cavalrymen south towards Madrid. It was too small a force to attack the capital but just getting close alarmed the Cristinos. The raid was so profitable that it looked more like an opportunistic, criminal foray by men determined to get rich under the cloak of a military cause than a serious element of an overall Carlist plan. During the summer another raiding column under generals Basilio García and Juan Balmaseda pressed south towards San Ildefonso de la Granja near Segovia, a beautiful royal palace in a mountainous setting with vast gardens, fountains and extensive woodland, where the royal family came to escape the heat of Madrid. Close to it, the generals discussed whether to attack. Again, personal gain was seen to be more important than the cause. Rather than entering to arrest the queen regent, they returned home with their profits. A column of some four thousand infantrymen under Miguel Gómez headed west through Asturias where it captured Oviedo before proceeding to Santiago de Compostela in Galicia. For six months it successfully evaded the attention of the Cristino general, Baldomero Espartero, before returning home a lot richer. It can be seen from these forays that, whilst the Carlists did not lack courageous and capable soldiers, they did lack an overall military plan and the central command crucial for ultimate victory. The blame for this lay squarely with Don Carlos. When asked for direction, he rarely provided it. In 1837, the same summer that an eighteen-year-old girl called Victoria awoke one morning in England to learn that she was queen, the Carlists finally formed a united front. They marched towards Madrid, Don Carlos among them.

After leaving Estella the Royal Expedition, so named because of the presence of Don Carlos, did not head directly for Madrid but turned first towards Aragon. It clashed with the Cristinos at Huesca and Barbastro, then entered Catalonia where it faced further opposition before arriving at the River Ebro a few miles north of Tortosa. There were no boats to be seen, the Cristinos having ordered that all in the area be taken away. With a huge natural obstacle barring their progress, no boats and the enemy closing in, the Royal Expedition was fortunate in the arrival of Ramon Cabrera, fresh from his latest victory near València where he was said to have dined afterwards whilst watching the execution of all the captured Cristino officers and sergeants. Cabrera had seized a large number of boats from a coastal village south of Tortosa, well outside the zone where the Cristinos thought they could be useful, and transported them across the mountains to the bank opposite the Carlist army. Cabrera now hoped for a march on Madrid but Don Carlos's staff preferred first to attempt Castelló de la Plana and València. They failed at some cost. Finally setting off for Madrid, they arrived at nearby Arganda on 12 September. Madrid seemed theirs for the taking. Soon Don Carlos would be celebrating its fall; their twenty thousand men would be unstoppable. But it was not to be. Don Carlos waited for a rising from within Madrid, and for a positive answer from the palace to his proposition that Isabella be betrothed to his son. Neither materialised. Meanwhile he was being told that the Cristino General Espartero would have to be defeated before Madrid was taken. The weak and indecisive Don Carlos, so close to his objective, turned to his expectant army and gave the order to retreat. Cabrera was livid. Perhaps some Carlists were pleased: an end to the war would have brought an end to their plundering.

After the premature and needless break-up of the Royal Expedition it could be said that Don Carlos and his descendants did not deserve to ascend the throne. On the other side, however, political infighting in the Cristino ranks and the many amorous liaisons of the queen regent meant that they hardly deserved to stay in charge either. The pleasure-loving queen regent, who had nine children by a guardsman she had secretly married, had little time for the various progressive and moderate chief ministers who formed a succession of unstable governments against a backdrop of risings and unrest.

We return to the fortunes of the British Legion after the Vitoria fever. Deaths and desertions meant that five thousand marched off to Santander in April 1836 to board transports taking them back to the besieged city of San Sebastián. That month Royal Marines garrisoned Portugalete at the mouth of the estuary that leads to Bilbao. Their presence was in response to Palmerston's instructions that the Royal Navy protect Cristino ports and assist in the recovery of those under Carlist occupation. On 5 May the British Legion went into action to raise the siege of San Sebastián. Assisted by fire from the *Phoenix* and *Salamander*, they stormed enemy lines on the heights overlooking the city. Three thousand Carlists abandoned rifles and supplies as they were driven from their positions. This first Cristino victory for some time was a fine one, greatly appreciated in Madrid. It was a rout in the Carlist heartland. Among the forty legionnaires killed was Lieutenant-Colonel William Tupper who is buried in the English cemetery on the headland of Monte Urgull which rises above the old quarter of San Sebastián.

On 6 June Royal Marines garrisoned at Pasaia, a port just a few miles east of San Sebastián, went to assist legionnaires facing a Carlist push to recover their lines on the heights. The Carlists retreated but took with them to Hernani seven legionnaires who were later shot. The following month a force of five thousand men including Royal Marines marched eastwards from Pasaia with the intention of taking Hondarribia (the last Spanish coastal town before France), the bridge over the River Bidasoa which linked Spain to France and the border town of Irún. The raid failed. Evans was incapacitated by illness, the wrong assumptions had been made about the enemy's preparedness and deployments were delayed. Despite temporarily securing the bridge, a full retreat back to Pasaia was called by the end of the day.

On October 1 the Legion successfully defended Pasaia against a Carlist attack at the cost of thirty-six casualties. Three weeks later the Carlists, desperate for money, began another siege of Bilbao. They had failed before, and now the task was even more difficult. There was a well-armed garrison within; Espartero, the new Cristino commander-in-chief, was on his way with an army and he would be assisted by the Royal Navy which was preparing to land men and guns from the *Saracen*, *Ringdove* and *Comet*. Interestingly, the British Legion was not involved. The Spanish and British forces entered Bilbao on Christmas day. The Carlists had failed again.

The Legion's two-year term was due to end in June 1837 so the Spanish command decided to use them in a grand push against Carlists positions before they sailed home. The plan was for three Cristino columns from Bilbao, San Sebastián and Pamplona to converge on the thirty-two thousand Carlists in Guipúzcoa. Evans commanded the San Sebastián column which included five thousand Spaniards, three thousand three hundred legionnaires, four hundred and fifty Royal Marines and eight gun batteries from the Royal Marine Artillery and Royal Artillery. On 10 March they attacked the Carlist positions in front of Hernani, then waited for the Pamplona column before attacking the town. After five days it had still not arrived: it had had to return to Pamplona on account of a terrible snowstorm. The San Sebastián column could wait no longer. It took the heights of Oriamendi above Hernani and the following day attempted to capture Hernani. Although they were outnumbered, the assault was going well until massive Carlist reinforcements poured through a gorge and recaptured Oriamendi. This new onslaught, combined with news that the Pamplona column would not be coming, prompted a retreat to San Sebastián. As for the Bilbao column, it had got only as far as Durango, some twenty miles south-east of Bilbao. The campaign failed for a number of reasons, not least because, unlike the Carlist forces, the Cristino columns had totally failed to converge.

The Carlist victory provided great impetus for the Royal Expedition which left Estella in Navarre on 15 May. Ironically, the departure of Carlist forces to join the Royal Expedition also gave the British Legion and their Cristino allies fresh impetus and a numerical advantage which enabled them to capture the heights of Oriamendi and Hernani with ease the day before the Royal Expedition moved off. After allowing the Legion the honour of being the first troops into Hernani, Espartero also allowed Evans to lead the assaults on Oyarzun, Irún and Hondarribia. Evans's ten thousand men, together with British regular seamen and marines, heavily outnumbered the Carlists defending Oyarzun and easily swept resistance aside. The reduction of Irún took a little longer. After eighteen hours of pounding the walls the Cristinos fought from house to house. Victory came on 16 May. Seeing white flags, some British dropped their guard and stepped into the open, only to be shot at. The Carlist commander was therefore somewhat surprised that, when defeat came on 16 May, Evans shot no prisoners. Hearing of his 'generosity', the Carlist garrison at Hondarribia surrendered on 18 May.

On 3 June 1838 General George de Lacy Evans began his journey home. Colonel William Wylde, who had been serving in Spain as the chief British commissioner to the Cristino armies, tried to persuade the legionnaires not to follow but to stay and enrol in a New Legion. The offer was accepted by 1,740 of them. After a heavy defeat near Hernani in September, worsened by their receiving no pay or supplies, they also returned home at the end of the year. The Royal Marines did not leave Pasaia until 1840 when Lord John Hay's squadron left the zone.

In the final analysis, the British Legion's limited contribution to the war was to help the disorganised Cristino army deny the Carlists total territorial control of the Basque provinces and towns. They encouraged a dispirited Cristino army at a time when many, including Sir George Villiers, the British Ambassador to Madrid, fully expected Don Carlos to triumph. The final cost to the Legion was 629 killed or fatally wounded in action while 1,850 more died from disease.

After the failure of the Royal Expedition, Don Carlos reshuffled his staff, nominating General Rafael Maroto as his commander-in-chief. Maroto believed the people to be tired of war and, having consolidated his position with some purges of extremists, went behind Don Carlos's back to open peace negotiations with Espartero. The mediator was Lord John Hay. On 25 August 1839 Don Carlos visited the army, ostensibly for a review but really to appeal to the troops to continue the war. They were not interested. A humiliated Don Carlos galloped off, a betrayed and fallen man. On 31 August Maroto agreed to a peace that confirmed his officers in their ranks and guaranteed back-pay if they joined the Cristino army. In front of the two armies Espartero embraced Maroto warmly and encouraged his men to do the same to their former adversaries. The treaty became known as the 'Embrace of Bergara'. Hundreds of miles to the east, Cabrera dismissed Maroto and his army as traitors and vowed to keep fighting. Nine months later, when Espartero had taken his stronghold at Morella and was closing in on his army at Berga, Cabrera also finally concluded that to fight on would merely waste lives. On 6 July he entered France. The war was over.

The end of the war did not bring lasting peace and stability. Their part in the First Carlist War propelled Spain's generals to the most powerful political positions in the land. In 1840 Maria Cristina, unable to bear being the puppet of Chief Minister General Espartero, herself went into exile. As Isabella grew up, the British strove to ensure that there was no prospect of her marrying a member of the French royal family. While King Louis-Philippe entertained Queen Victoria and

Prince Albert in Normandy, an agreement was reached by their ministers. After this meeting, improved Anglo-French relations were described as the *entente cordiale*. Espartero was forced out in 1843 and moved to London. To avoid further problems with regents, Isabella was declared queen, though still only thirteen. In 1846 the Carlists launched a guerrilla campaign that has alternatively been called the Matiners' War and the Second Carlist War. Cabrera returned for a while, as did Carlos Luis, Count of Montemolin, who had assumed the role of pretender in place of his father Don Carlos. In 1849 the count was engaged to an English commoner, Adeline de Horsey. Aware that this union was unacceptable to his supporters, he renounced his claim in favour of his brother. Unhappy that she was no longer a possible future queen of Spain, Adeline called off the engagement and the count was able to resume his position as pretender. In 1868 a revolution drove Isabella into exile. For a while the Carlists sought power mainly through parliament. Their party, which stood not just for a particular royal claimant but for traditional values, was supported by country people worried by the urbanization and industrialization of Spain. The political initiative failed, however, and full-scale war resumed between 1872 and 1876. When Spain was declared a republic in 1873 the Carlist fighters suddenly found themselves representing all monarchy and their numbers were boosted accordingly. In 1870 Isabella had renounced her rights in favour of her son Alfonso. In 1874 he was a cadet at the Royal Military College at Sandhurst, from where he issued the Sandhurst Manifesto, declaring that on his restoration he would establish a monarchy backed by a representative parliamentary government. The army in Madrid supported it and forced the unpopular republican government to resign. Alfonso left his Christmas lodgings at the Charing Cross Hotel and arrived in Madrid on 14 January 1875. That the Carlist cause was lost was reinforced by Cabrera's recognition of Alfonso XII as the legitimate King of Spain.

Cabrera's change of heart was partly due to the fact that he was now living the life of an English country gentleman. In exile he had met and married the very wealthy Marianne Catherine Richards. After honeymooning at Tunbridge Wells, they lived in Eaton Square in London for a few years, then moved to Wentworth, the estate near Virginia Water which became a golf club in 1924. Cabrera enjoyed foxhunting and years later General Franco would recount how Cabrera would always avoid the danger of unnecessary jumps because the only thing he feared in life was to die without glory. Cabrera met Alfonso, the Sandhurst cadet, at Wentworth. He purchased the land and underwrote the building costs of the Catholic Church of St Edward the Confessor in nearby Windsor. Every year on 24 May a mass is celebrated for Cabrera whose youngest son was buried there and is commemorated in a stained-glass window. There is a picture of Cabrera hanging in the office of the priest's house beside the church; it remains there because few appreciate that it is the face of a ruthless war criminal who shot eleven hundred prisoners of war. The Count of Morella, Marquis of Ter and Surrey country squire, died aged seventy-one in 1877 and was buried at Christ Church in Virginia Water.

Colonel Evans also prospered after the Carlist War, answering all of his critics by distinguishing himself at Alma and Inkerman during the Crimean War where he commanded a division.

CHAPTER 14

King Juan Carlos I's Grandmother

Always be a good girl and love your mother. If you do this, when you grow up and are big, you too will travel and you will come to this beautiful country. You will see for yourself how much you will like it and how happy you will be there.

Prince Henry of Battenberg in a letter to his daughter from Cadiz in 1896

KING JUAN CARLOS I of Spain is one-quarter British. His grandmother on his father's side was Queen Victoria Eugenia, the English wife of King Alfonso XIII. Obviously King Juan Carlos does not shout about it or it would not be such an obscure fact. He was almost certainly the favourite grandchild of Queen Victoria's Golden Jubilee granddaughter.

Victoria Eugenia Julie Ena was born at Balmoral on 24 October 1887 during an extended stay by the court on account of the extra rest required after the demanding schedule of the Golden Jubilee celebrations. Ena, as she was known in Britain, was brought up at court because her mother Beatrice, Queen Victoria's youngest child, was not permitted to leave the nest. While new arrivals in the British Royal Family were aplenty, Spain was not having the same good fortune. When King Alfonso XII died in 1885 the disappointment was double for he had not produced a male heir. Then, incredibly, the sad news of his death was followed by the joyful news that his wife was pregnant. On 17 May 1886 she gave birth to a son, Alfonso XIII. In 1905, when the king was nineteen, he came to England to find a bride. Up to that time four British monarchs, Richard I, Edward I, Henry VIII and Mary I, had taken Spanish spouses but it had only once happened the other way round, when Alfonso VIII had married Henry II's daughter Eleanor in 1170. That Alfonso had been King of Castile only; it would be another three hundred years before anything approaching a united Spain emerged from the reconquest. This was the first time a Spanish monarch had even visited England since 1557. Alfonso first set eyes on eighteen-year-old Ena at a Buckingham Palace banquet on his first day in London. It became clear to others that he was drawn to her during a performance of *Romeo and Juliet* at Covent Garden. She spoke no Spanish and he no English; he had deliberately avoided learning English since the loss of Cuba during the war with the United States. They got along fine in French.

Before Ena could marry Alfonso she had to join the Roman Catholic Church. This she did in a ceremony in March 1906 at the Miramar Palace in San Sebastián, the beautiful Basque seaside town that Queen Victoria had visited seventeen years before. On 31 May they were married in the Church of San Jeronimo in Madrid. The streets were packed with crowds of bouquet-throwing well-wishers desperate to catch sight of the fairy-tale couple on their way back to the palace. Unhappily one man pushing through the crowds came not to throw petals but a bomb. As the procession paused by the Church of Santa Maria in the narrow, congested Calle Mayor, Mateo Morral threw his deadly wedding present from a third-floor balcony at number 88. The blast caused carnage amongst outriders, onlookers and horses: twenty-four people were killed and a further hundred injured. The new queen got away with a huge fright and a blood-spattered wedding dress. Unfortunately the court and the people interpreted her stiff upper lip and determination to get through this cruel episode as coldness and insensitivity. This Protestant-born foreigner had already brought tragedy to their beloved king.

At that time the pressing priority in the early married life of a sovereign's wife was the production of royal heirs and, to general delight, on 5 May 1907 Ena gave birth to a son, Alfonso. A few days later, following his circumcision, his parents were horrified when he was diagnosed as a haemophiliac. His was a particularly virulent form of the disease. Alfonso, who had chosen to marry a strong, healthy woman from well outside the Spanish circle to strengthen his family line, was devastated to find that the ploy had failed because Ena was a carrier of the disease. Over the next eight years she produced four more sons and two daughters. Just one of the sons, Juan, born on 6 June 1913, was free from haemophilia.

Alfonso could not forgive Ena. He fell out of love; they began to live separate lives. She threw herself into charity work for the Red Cross and the Anti-Tuberculosis League; he threw himself into the arms of various women.

In 1921 the king decided that his position in a politically unstable Spain would be greatly enhanced if he could associate himself with a breakthrough in the stagnant thirteen-year-old Moroccan war. His enthusiastic public rhetoric was very likely combined with some behind-the-scenes encouragement to the army to take risks. They did just that and ten thousand paid the ultimate price in a ravine at Annual. As recriminations and enquiries edged closer to directly blaming the king for the disaster, General Primo de Rivera saw his chance. He knew that a *coup d'état* to replace parliamentary democracy with a military dictatorship would be accepted by Alfonso if it meant that any further enquiries into Annual would be quashed. So it was that Spain espoused an interesting combination of monarchy and dictatorship. However, by undermining the constitution in support of the one non-democratic element that could negate his personal embarrassment, Alfonso had demonstrated to Spain that the monarchy was redundant. The final signal that its time was up came in the municipal elections of 1931. The republicans and socialists swept the board.

At 8am on 15 April 1931 Ena and her children left the palace and drove to the station at El Escorial. Sir George Graham, the new British ambassador, was among those who waved off the departing exiles, who that evening checked into the Hotel Meurice in Paris. They were soon joined by the king who had taken a less direct and more secretive route out of Spain. Ena and Alfonso's marriage was over; they were destined to find homes in different places, he in Rome, she in Lausanne in Switzerland. In 1934 their daughter Beatrice had an accident whilst driving her nineteen-year-old brother. In normal circumstances it would not have been serious but minor bleeding killed the haemophiliac Gonzalo. Four years later his elder brother Alfonso died in similar circumstances.

King Alfonso XIII died in Rome in February 1941 and Ena became queen mother. The heir to the throne was Don Juan who, married to Doña Mercedes of Bourbon-Orléans, already had two healthy daughters and, crucially for the Bourbon lineage, a son called Juan Carlos. Ena saw much of Juan Carlos as he went to school in nearby Fribourg. She was concerned that the boy who was second in line to the throne was growing up speaking Spanish with a foreign accent and worked hard with him to improve his pronunciation.

In 1947 General Franco privately decided that the monarchy should be restored after his death, but not to Don Juan whom he had loathed since the start of the Civil War when the prince had attempted to join the republican forces. Instead Juan Carlos would be king.

Ena had always yearned to go back to Spain. The opportunity came in February 1968 when she returned to fulfil the role of godmother at the baptism of Prince Juan Carlos's son Felipe in Madrid. A huge cheering crowd greeted her and Don Juan at Madrid's Barajas airport. In the days following the baptism she met the dictator and gave a reception at the Liria Palace. When the time came to leave, she was waved off by an even bigger crowd, estimated at fifty thousand. Juan Carlos's grandmother Ena died on April 15 the following year, 1969. She was buried in the church she had attended in Lausanne, the Sacred Heart at Ouchy.

Juan Carlos has always been aware of the importance of the monarchy to an emerging democracy. He has always known that it was his grandfather's undermining of the system that had all but ended the Bourbon tenure forty years before he came to the throne. In his first message to the nation as king in 1975 he expressed his intention of restoring democracy and becoming king of all Spaniards, without exception. Later on his action in going on television saved the constitution, and democracy, on the night of 23 February 1981, when General Tejero held up parliament at gun-point in an attempted military *coup d'état*.

One wonders whether it has ever crossed the king's mind to one day bring his grandmother home to join the rest of the Spanish kings and queens in the vaults of the great monastery just down the road from the station where she caught a train so many years ago.

CHAPTER 15

The Sell-Out of the Century

I had come to Spain with some notion of writing newspaper articles but
I joined the militia almost immediately because at that time and in that
atmosphere it seemed the only conceivable thing to do.

George Orwell, *Homage to Catalonia*

I N THE SPAIN of the 1930s, sixty years after the last Carlist War,
there were still those who yearned for the throne to be occupied
by a descendent of Don Carlos. He would rule as an absolute
monarch in the fashion of Phillip II and bring back some of the old
glory. But by this time this was just one of many conflicting movements in Spanish society that clashed so much with one another that
the only way to settle things was by revolution or another civil war.
Despite the previous bloody conflicts it was this latest one that would
become known as *the* Spanish Civil War.

Among the other problems the scourges of *latifundia* and *minifun-
dia* blighted the primitive countryside. With the former, workers could
find only poorly paid employment on a daily basis on huge inefficient
estates. With the latter peasants rented smallholdings that were barely
big enough to provide basic subsistence. If the people suffering under
these systems had any complaints the brutal Civil Guard was there to
suppress protests. The education system promised little advancement
as it was mainly in the hands on the Church which, like the absentee
landlords, was determined to hold on to its wealth and power at the
expense of the populace. Many missed out on education altogether,
being forced to work from an early age in order to supplement
meagre family incomes. Illiteracy was rife.

One of the beauties of Spain for the visitor today is the rich diversity of the different regions and their inhabitants. These cultural and
linguistic variations are the result of isolated regional development
due to poor communications. The centralised power of Madrid was
unpopular; most regions felt that it was too remote to be able to
understand or deal with their particular needs. The Catalans resented
paying taxes to a city which had been Spain's capital for only three
hundred years; the Basques, Europe's only aboriginal race, disliked

being governed by politicians who did not speak their language; the Andalusians, many of whom lived in appalling conditions, could not see how Castilian rule benefited them at all.

The fact that the regions seemed to care little for the entity of Spain infuriated the army. Distrustful of a civil administration's ability to prevent Spain from tumbling into chaos, they intervened on no less than forty-three occasions between 1820 and 1923. The army's determination to ensure that things did not get out of control at home was exacerbated by its desire to atone for its recent humiliations abroad. In 1898 the colonies of Cuba, Puerto Rico and the Philippines had been lost during a war with the United States. These losses had marked the end of the Spanish empire. Nearer home, in 1921 Moroccan tribesmen destroyed a Spanish army of some twenty thousand.

Between 1931 and 1933 a government of socialists and liberals tried to implement a programme of social reform. It was extremely limited but reactionary landowners and the Church and army were alarmed at what was happening. In the absence of any electoral cooperation between the socialists, republicans and anarchists, the left lost out to a right-wing coalition at the next election in November 1933. The new right-wing government set about reversing the social reforms. In 1934, miners from the northern province of Asturias rose up to fight the establishment of what they saw as a fascist state. The rising was brutally put down: two thousand were killed or wounded. The army's reprisals were a taste of what was to come. Welsh miners petitioned the Spanish ambassador to release their Spanish counterparts, many of whom faced execution. Their newspaper demanded that the Asturian cause should not be undermined by imports from South Wales – their comrades' coal was not to be scabbed! All the factions and parties on the left now realised that they had to unite to defeat the right. Their Popular Front won the election of 16 February 1936 but the political temperature had been rising rapidly. Peasants seized land and churches were burnt. Supporters of the right-wing Falange fought street battles against socialists and communists. Worst of all were the tit-for-tat political assassinations. The murder of the militant monarchist Calvo Sotelo, who was in effect the leader of the opposition, forced the hand of a group of right-wing army officers who had been planning a rising. They saw the country descending into anarchy and chaos – the only way it could be saved was by the overthrow of the democratically elected government.

*

GENERAL FRANCISCO FRANCO, the chief of staff who had taken charge of the suppression of the Asturian miners' revolt, visited England in January 1936 for the funeral of King George V. He attended the service in Westminster Abbey on Wednesday 28 January before going on to St George's Chapel at Windsor for the interrment. Franco would have been able to practice some of the English he had been learning in his thrice-weekly lessons. A keen golfer, he planned to return later that year for a golfing holiday in Scotland. The new left-wing government was wary of Franco. His behaviour in Asturias had revealed in no uncertain terms the way he felt about the left and how, given the power, he would deal with it. For this reason the new administration posted him as far away as possible, in the Canary Islands. When the rising began Franco was cautious about joining it. The right-wing conspirators had to make it as easy as possible for him. They decided to collect him.

In the gardens beside the River Segura in the heart of the city of Murcia is a memorial to Juan de la Cierva, the local man who invented the autogiro, the forerunner of the helicopter. In 1936 he was working in London when Luis Bolin, the London correspondent of the right-wing Madrid daily *ABC*, contacted him. Bolin had been asked by the paper's owner to charter an aircraft to collect Franco from the Canaries. La Cierva recommended hiring a DeHavilland Dragon Rapide from Olley Air Services at Croydon airport. A retired army officer, Hugh Pollard from Midhurst in Sussex, his nineteen-year-old daughter Diana and her friend Dorothy Watson were to go along, posing as wealthy tourists. In the early hours of 11 July ex-RAF pilot Captain William Bebb started the plane on its fateful journey. After stops at Bordeaux, Lisbon and Casablanca, the Dragon Rapide landed in Gran Canaria on 14 July.

On 17 July, all across Spain, the military rising began. The following day Franco declared martial law. The two sides both represented a multiplicity of parties, factions and interests. Those that sided with the rebel generals were henceforth referred to as Nationalists or Fascists; their opponents who stood up in defence of the government were labelled Republicans or Reds. As fighting broke out locally Franco headed for the airport. Soon after two o'clock Captain Bebb lifted the plane and its new passenger into the air and headed for Morocco. After stopping the night at Casablanca the mission was completed with their arrival at Tetuan in Spanish Morocco. Franco stepped off the plane and took control of the Spanish army there. Meanwhile Captain Bebb and his passengers headed home. The Nationalists showed how grateful they were for the British tourists' contribution by decorating them after the war. That week rebel officers seized control of approximately one third of the country. Sections of the military and civil guard loyal to the government joined with large numbers of resolute and determined civilians to fight back. Such was their determination to defend the republic that the Spanish fascists could soon have been defeated but for help from their friends in Germany and Italy.

A fellow democracy was being attacked by its own army supported by those growing menaces to peace, Hitler and Mussolini. By doing nothing was Britain guilty of a shameful betrayal of the Spanish people? Did her failure to help another democratic government encourage fascist aggression? Many believed so and would claim later that, had fascism been defeated on those Spanish battlefields, it would not have been able to launch its assaults on Britain, France, the Soviet Union and the United States. It was called the 'sell-out of the century'. Britain and France did nothing as they perceived that the bigger threat to the West came from the Soviet Union and communism. Had Spain not shown signs of becoming a Soviet satellite? The socialist leader Francisco Largo Caballero had adopted red flags, the *Internationale* and clenched-fist salutes. The Foreign Office had received complaints from British firms in Spain forced by the Popular Front government to reinstate redundant workers. The left-wing government was clearly not good for business. Surely fascism's anti-Bolshevism and firm progressive government were to be admired rather than feared?

In Britain the average man in the street was unconcerned by events in Spain. Before starting at Oxford University, Chris Thornycroft had been sent to Germany to learn the language. Living in a society where citizens suffered intimidation and beatings, he soon learnt that fascism was a serious threat which should be vigorously opposed. Back in Britain he found people more interested in football matches than in what was happening on the Continent. If voters were not interested then association with a foreign Communist Party would not help the Labour Party win elections. Even they and the TUC did not advocate helping their Spanish comrades.

Britain had no desire to risk a war with Germany over Spain. Memories of the First World War were still fresh. The nation had been weakened by a worldwide economic depression; the armed forces and defence industries had been run down. Neither could Britain afford a conflict with Italy: that would have meant major commitments in the Mediterranean at the expense of her widespread imperial obligations.

For Britain and France a weak fascist Spain was the safest option.

It was important to them that Soviet influence was kept at bay. One must sympathise with leaders of the time who faced an incredibly delicate and complicated situation. In hindsight we know what Hitler planned but in 1936 his tanks were yet to start rolling; people did not know that an Austrian was about to try to repeat the efforts of a Corsican. It is interesting to speculate that, had the fascists been defeated in Spain, Hitler's tanks would not have stopped in France but would have carried on into what would have been enemy territory, following the route of Napoleon's troops all the way to Gibraltar and Lisbon. The Second World War might have started with a second Peninsular War. But in 1936 Britain and France did not think that helping the Spanish Republican government would encourage Hitler to occupy Spain because Hitler's expansionist policies were yet to be fully appreciated. Britain and France proclaimed that the Spanish war was an internal affair that should not be encouraged. Foreign nations should not sell arms to either side or send men or supplies. Britain, France, the Soviet Union, Portugal, Germany and Italy signed a Non-Intervention Treaty. This was a massive and unjust body blow to the Spanish government, depriving it of its right to buy arms to fight an illegal insurrection. Worse still, Hitler and Mussolini had no intention of keeping their side of the bargain. Fascist violations of the agreement were soon revealed but the Non-Intervention Committee was powerless to prevent them. Far from discouraging the conflict, the agreement became a screen for German and Italian support of the rebels.

If the British Government was uncomfortable about the situation, some of her citizens were outraged. If their country would not act, they would. People like Chris Thornycroft would take themselves to Spain and join the fight against fascism. Their sentiments were summed up by the Spanish communist deputy Dolores Ibarruri (La Pasionaria or Passion Flower) who warned, 'Stop the bombs on Madrid and Barcelona today or they will fall on London and Paris tomorrow.' The vast majority of volunteers were industrial workers who felt unhappy with the way their own society had failed so many people. Their suffering from poverty and unemployment heightened their repugnance of the right-wing threat. As C. Day Lewis said, 'They went because their open eyes could see no other way.' Felicia Brown was an artist, a thirty-two-year-old Slade graduate who had gone to Spain to attend the Popular Olympics in Barcelona, the games organised as a rival to Hitler's Berlin showpiece. Then the war started and as a committed communist she felt impelled to join a militia which was sent to the front in Aragon. She became the first British volunteer to shoot at Franco's rebels and the first to fall; she was killed on 25 August 1936. Other early volunteers made their own way to Spain but by October British recruitment and transport was organised by the Communist Party. It was a long train journey all the way to the International Brigade's base at Albacete in south-east Spain but at least the Party paid the fare. Of more than two thousand volunteers who went to Spain more than a quarter did not return.

Thirty or so Britons, who included the Cambridge student and poet John Cornford, joined the XIth and XIIth International Brigades which were sent to reinforce the defence of Madrid in November. Nationalist troops were already in the city, close to the centre. Two months later, after savage fighting, Franco realised that his triumphal entry into Madrid would have to wait. The human price for frustrating his advance was high. Of the thirty Britons, just five remained. On Christmas Eve 1936 a much larger group of Britons, the 145 men of No. 1 company of the English-speaking battalion in the XIVth International Brigade, were rushed south with other Republican units to check a Nationalist offensive coming from Córdoba and Granada. On 28 December No 1 company led an attack on the fascist-held village of Lopera. Heavy fire from machine guns, artillery and aircraft halted their advance and then forced them back. The following day they resisted a concerted Nationalist push but their position was compromised by the crumbling of the resistance on their flanks. The Republicans brought up reinforcements which persuaded the Nationalists to call off their push. No 1 company was then moved hundreds of miles to assist the Nationalist offensive to the north-west of Madrid. Initial progress was halted by fog, snow and enemy fire. After less than a week the 67 that remained of the original 145 from No. 1 company were withdrawn. Despite heavy losses the company had conducted itself extremely well, earning a hero's welcome back in Albacete.

The number of British in Spain was growing all the time. By the beginning of January there were four hundred and fifty. The XVth Brigade was formed from English-speaking volunteers and officially became part of the Republican army on 31 January 1937. This British Battalion was given a new home twenty miles away in the village of Madrigueras. The next month it faced its first battle. The government had left Madrid for València, three hundred miles to the east on the Mediterranean coast, well away from the front. With the Nationalists pressing the capital from the north and west, the road east to València became critically important for communications and supplies. Nationalist assaults had so far failed so they decided to go round to the south of Madrid then strike north to sever the vital València road. If they succeeded in doing this, supplies of food, arms, men and ammunition to Madrid would be cut off and it would be only a matter of time before the besieged and starving city fell into their hands. On 7 February the XVth International Brigade, consisting of the British, Balkan and Franco-Belgian battalions, was despatched to the front to help stop the Nationalist offensive. Two thirds of the seven hundred and fifty Britons in Spain prepared to go into battle.

The fascists had crossed the Jarama River and were only a few hills away from the València road. Early on the morning of 12 February, after an overnight stop at the village of Chinchón, the British travelled some way along the road and then left their trucks at a large farmhouse and set off across the broken hills. After about two miles they were descending towards the now visible Jarama River when they encountered ferocious enemy rifle and machine-gun fire. They withdrew to the crest of Suicide Hill where they made their defence. Fighting was heavy. The Franco-Belgian Battalion to the right of the British had been pushed back and a knoll was now occupied by Moors who were firing constantly at Suicide Hill. The British were unable to use their machine guns as they had brought the wrong ammunition; meanwhile German machine guns rattled away at their positions. With casualties mounting and the Moors and Foreign Legion getting closer, the British withdrew to the plateau. Seeing their chance, the Moors rushed over the ridge. Unfortunately for them, the correct machine gun ammunition had by this time arrived and eight Maxims reaped a grim and bloody revenge. The front had been held but at the cost of half the battalion. Amongst the dead lay Clem Beckett, a speedway champion who before the war had broken records at the Coventry, Manchester and Rochdale tracks all in one day.

Overnight the Nationalists moved up: first light revealed that they were uncomfortably close. The Maxims opened up, forcing the British back. Hours later disaster struck: No 2 Machine Gun Company was captured, its position having been exposed by the unauthorised withdrawal of a rifle company. The one hundred and sixty that remained of the five hundred took up new defensive positions around a sunken road. Next day they were pushed back again by the overwhelming numbers of infantry and tanks. The Nationalists would have reached the Madrid-València road but for one last effort by the battalion survivors and fighters from other broken units who rallied and marched back to the ridge. The Nationalists fell back. They had missed their opportunity. That night the Republican line was strengthened and both sides dug in. Madrid's lifeline had been successfully defended. The Republicans hailed it as a victory. The British Battalion was boosted by eighty-five new arrivals from Madrigueras. After ten tedious weeks in the trenches they were replaced and withdrawn to Mondéjar.

Glaswegian Alex McDade, who was killed later in the war, wrote a song about the battle and the long time spent in the trenches. It quickly caught on and was to be sung at veterans' reunions long after Franco's victory.

There's a valley in Spain called Jarama,
That's a place that we all know so well,
For 'tis there that we wasted our manhood,
And most of our old age as well.

From this valley they tell us we're leaving,
But don't hasten to bid us adieu,
For e'en though we make our departure,
We'll be back in an hour or two.

Oh we're proud of our British Battalion,
And the marathon record it's made,
Please do this little favour,
And take this word to Brigade.

You will never be happy with strangers,
They would not understand you as we,
So remember the Jarama Valley
And the old men who wait patiently.

In the spring of 1937 the Frontier Supervision Scheme and Naval Patrol were introduced by the Non-Intervention Committee with the aim of isolating the war in Spain. A hundred and five observers were placed on the border between France and Spain. Meanwhile all ships bound for Spain had to visit certain ports to pick up two of the three hundred and thirty inspectors which had been appointed by Britain, France, Germany or Italy; the inspectors travelled with them to ensure that nothing illegal was unloaded. The schemes were nice ideas but had so many loopholes as to be unworkable. They applied only to non-intervention countries so ships wishing to land an illegal cargo would simply fly the flag of another country. The schemes were further undermined by corrupt observers, the clever concealment of illegal cargoes, and by smuggling.

The Soviet Union sent military aid to the Republicans (she had to be seen to be supporting fellow communists) but nothing on the scale of aid sent by the dictators. Russia feared German ambitions in Eastern Europe and this was a way of keeping Germany busy elsewhere. Non-intervention was a farce but for Britain and France it reduced the likelihood of war with Germany and Italy.

At Jarama the British Battalion had defended Madrid's lifeline. Their next major battle was an offensive to cut off enemy troops that had penetrated the Madrid suburbs. The British formed part of a force that struck south from the Sierra Guadarrama north-west of Madrid and aimed to meet up with another Republican force coming from the south of the city. The XVth Brigade was ordered to take the fortified village of Villanueva de la Canada. They went into battle on 6 July 1937, a stiflingly hot day that was spent trying to silence the machine guns based in the church tower which poured a murderous fire on the rifle-bearing attackers. That evening the British sighted a party of women and children coming down the road towards them. From behind this human shield fascist troops opened fire. The British had little alternative but to return fire. Inevitably many of the women and children fell, hit by bullets from both sides. Later that evening the final resistance in the village was overcome. Republican troops elsewhere along the front had also successfully pushed forwards.

The XVth Brigade fought on towards the strategically important Mosquito Ridge. They almost got there but the final yards were denied them by an unending barrage of artillery, machine-gun and rifle fire. While this bloody drama was being played out on the ground, the ultimate destiny of the Battle of Brunete was being decided in the air, now dominated by German and Italian fighters and bombers. On 18 July the Nationalists launched a great counter-attack. It swept the Republican troops back and reclaimed Brunete before running out of steam. The British Battalion, exposed in a forward position, suffered a severe mauling. On July 25 the XVth Brigade left the front. The vast majority of the Britons lay dead, wounded or unaccounted for. Just forty-two of the three hundred that had gone into battle less than three weeks before returned to base at Mondéjar. The large number of casualties was repeated all across the Republican army. They had lost twenty-five thousand men.

The return of the wounded, the arrival of new recruits and the inclusion of many Spaniards (they were now the majority) enabled the battalion to recover strength. It was not long before it returned to the action. In the middle of August it was ordered to the north-eastern province of Aragon where the latest Republican offensive was attempting to capture the important city of Zaragoza. Approaching from further down the Ebro river valley, the main road to Zaragoza is overlooked by Pulburrel Hill. The British Battalion was ordered to take this hill and confidently began the ascent but their progress was suddenly halted by heavy machine-gun fire from what turned out to be formidable German-built fortifications. They suffered many casualties in terrain that offered little protection. The following day anti-tank guns pummelled the Nationalist gun emplacements before the troops once again set off for the top of the hill. After some resistance, the defenders surrendered, though they still had ammunition and many of their fortifications were intact. Despite the heavy losses the British were pleased with their victory. The defenders had overlooked the need to store water. After two days in the dusty heat surrender and all the risks that went with it was preferable to the continued agony of thirst.

Other troops of the XVth Brigade had taken the village of Quinto. This left just one more village on the road to Zaragoza, Fuentes de Ebro, but after three days it had still not be taken. The most savage fighting was taking place in Belchite where Republicans were fighting from house to house against the besieged Nationalist garrison. Some British units were involved. Such was the destruction that Franco ordered that Belchite be left in ruins for all time as a monument to the Civil War. The battalion moved on to take Mediana in order to prevent Nationalists from relieving Belchite from that direction. Mediana soon fell, followed by Belchite on 5 September.

With all the Nationalist strongholds in the area cleared, the Republican army again turned its attention to Fuentes de Ebro. The attack on 13 October against reinforced Nationalist defences was disastrous. Air support was minimal; the advance by forty tanks and the infantry was hopelessly uncoordinated. The British Battalion was unable to progress in the face of deadly machine-gun fire. After ten days in the trenches the XVth Brigade returned to base. At Mondéjar the British Battalion was built up again, heavy casualties having reduced it to just a quarter of its fighting strength.

With the fall of Gijón on the Biscay coast in late October, Republican resistance in the north was at an end. Two thirds of Spain was now in Franco's control. The Republicans occupied eastern Spain. Franco would now try to drive his forces through the middle of this sector, to the coast, dividing it in two. Before the initiative began, the Republicans struck at Teruel.

On 10 December, just days after a visit from future British prime minister Clement Atlee, the brigade returned to Aragon. The capture of Teruel was added cause for celebration on Christmas day in the village of Mas de la Matas. The new year 1938 began with the defence of Republican gains against an overwhelming Nationalist counter-offensive boosted increasingly by German and Italian manpower and arms. As the British Battalion positioned itself on Santa Barbara Hill, a Nationalist force of eighty thousand men with six hundred guns closed in on the snow-covered market town. The British guns were very effective against the enemy infantry and cavalry below. The three British rifle companies were ordered down the hill and across the river to join the successful stand there, the Nationalists concluding that Teruel would have to be taken later some other way. The British Battalion was moved north; there the brigade was to break through the front and cut one of the fascist supply routes to Teruel. Despite the attentions of artillery and bombers the brigade reached the road but the action did not, as had been hoped, relieve the pressure on Teruel. It was finally recaptured by the Nationalists on 22 February.

On 9 March Franco's army, supported by nine hundred aeroplanes, launched a massive thrust through Aragon and Catalonia. They outnumbered their opponents five to one and were able to roll back Republican resistance. The British, sent north through Belchite, were forced back through the town. There was a general retreat; stands could not be made due to open flanks. The Nationalists' encircling tactics meant that the battalion kept finding that villages it withdrew to had already been taken and that the only way out was across open country. In the chaos individuals and groups of men became detached and the battalion fell apart. An attempt was made to rebuild the XVth International Brigade at Batea: the realisation that if the Nationalists were not stopped soon then the Republic was doomed brought in more men eager to fight. They included British veterans of previous battles who were still recovering from wounds. The headcount in the British Battalion rose to six hundred and fifty.

The reconstituted XVth Brigade was ordered to the front to face another massive Nationalist offensive launched on 30 March. The British Battalion was moving down a road from Calaceite to the front when, turning a bend, it met a column of Italian tanks, armoured cars and infantry. The British broke for cover and fierce fighting ensued. A quarter of the battalion was killed or wounded, another quarter taken prisoner. Survivors made their way individually or in groups back through dangerous country to safety across the Ebro. The rest of the XVth Brigade had also broken up. Further south, on 15 April, the Nationalists reached the sea, and cut Republican Spain in two.

As the Nationalists were busy in the south, driving towards València, the Republicans launched an offensive back across the Ebro on 25 July. The British Battalion, with its hardcore of experienced veterans supplemented by new recruits, numbered 650, a third of them British. The battalion was ordered to take Hill 481, which would facilitate the taking of Gandesa. For six days they tried but the hill was strongly fortified and the terrain and vegetation offered no protection from the brutal rifle and machine-gun fire or from the blazing sun. They reached the top only to be forced back by machine-gun fire raining death from impregnable concrete pillboxes. Jack Jones, later to be General Secretary of the Transport and General Workers Union, was wounded in the shoulder and right arm.

The one-hundred-thousand-strong Nationalist army now sought to capture the Sierra Pandols overlooking the Ebro river crossings. The battalion fought a valiant and successful action to defend a spur of the strategically important Hill 666, but the Republicans now faced the heaviest bombardment of the war. In the Sierra Caballs ten thousand bombs a day poured down onto the Republican army. The XVth Brigade rushed along the front, filling cracks where they developed. As the front stabilised the battalion was withdrawn, but it was called back on two occasions.

Had the Spanish Civil War been fought exclusively by the indigenous population then the Republic might well have put down the rebellion by this time. That it was instead teetering on the edge of defeat was due to the great discrepancy in foreign aid to the two sides. Some forty thousand foreign volunteers from more than fifty countries went to Spain to fight for the Republic but they all needed to be trained, armed and organised into fighting units. In contrast the hundred and forty thousand Germans and seventy thousand Italians arrived in the form of an organized army – with a huge amount of hardware, including sixteen hundred aeroplanes, three hundred and fifty tanks, thousands of guns and millions of shells and cartridges. In the vague hope of persuading Franco to send the Germans and Italians home, Prime Minister Negrin announced, on 21 September 1938, that all foreign volunteers were to be repatriated. The British Battalion still had one more battle to fight and not all knew of Negrin's intentions. Ironically, it was to be one of the most costly.

If the Republicans still clung to the hope that Britain or France might come to their assistance they were to be bitterly disappointed when, eight days after Negrin's announcement, both accepted Hitler's annexation of the Sudetenland. Franco had been worried by Hitler's actions: the invasion could have precipitated a European war necessitating the withdrawal of German and Italian armed forces from Spain. The Republicans would have benefited, not least from France sending in supplies. Chamberlain's appeasement of Hitler, which allowed the Germans to stay in Spain, earned him Franco's 'warmest congratulations' for 'his magnificent efforts for the preservation of peace in Europe'. The Republicans had to face the bitter truth that there was no anti-fascist alliance out there prepared to act in the face of aggression. If Britain and France were prepared to accept Hitler's move into Czechoslovakia, what hope had they of assistance against a German- and Italian-sponsored Franco?

The people of Barcelona gave an emotional farewell to the International Brigades that paraded through the city on 29 October 1938. Cheers were raised and tears were shed. La Pasionaria addressed the people who had been prepared to give everything: 'We shall not forget you; and when the olive tree of peace puts forth its leaves, entwined with the laurels of the Spanish Republic's victory, come back!' On 7 December the three hundred volunteers that stepped off the train at Victoria Station were hailed as heroes. Of the two thousand three hundred British volunteers who went to Spain, 526 are known to have died. At least a hundred and seventy had volunteered for the medical services: the Republicans had faced a shortage of nurses because the nuns, who had traditionally fulfilled that role before the war, had sided with Franco.

Madrid fell on 28 March 1939. Three days later Franco declared that the war which had cost half a million lives was over. Internal tensions had led to the conflict but external forces had decided its outcome, making it the bitterest of defeats for the losing side, a defeat compounded over the next few years by a bloody repression which claimed the lives of a further two hundred thousand Reds.

After Britain declared war on Germany in response to the invasion of Poland she had to work hard to keep Spain out of the conflict. A shattered and starving Spain may not have been able to offer much fighting assistance but Spanish Atlantic ports could have been used by the German-Italian Axis and the strategically important Gibraltar could have been lost. Franco was convinced that there would be a German victory but he needed western credit, food and fuel, not a blockade of his ports. Both Spain and Germany believed that Britain would react to the seizure of Gibraltar by taking one of the Canary Islands. This prompted a German demand to station Stuka aircraft there. Franco declined; it would be creating another Gibraltar.

In June 1939 the Duke and Duchess of Windsor passed through
Madrid on their way to Lisbon. As King Edward VIII he had abdicated
the throne in 1936. His fascist sympathies have long been a matter for
speculation. If Franco wished to seek the duke's assistance in German
peace negotiations with Britain his cooperation was not encouraged
by Spanish news that the British secret service planned to kill him.

With memories of Russian intervention still fresh, Franco was
delighted when, on 22 June 1941, the Nazis invaded the Soviet Union.
His faith in the German Axis had been cooling; now he again believed
they would win. The Falange celebrated by stoning the British
Embassy. Spain remained neutral but forty-seven thousand Spanish
volunteers joined the Blue Division which went to fight alongside the
Germans on the Russian front in 1942. In the end, Spain would have
entered the war had Britain's collapse appeared imminent: Franco
would have sat on the right side of the peace negotiations table
demanding a share of the spoils of victory.

Franco ruled Spain until his death on 20 November 1975. He was
not a good leader; he was interested only in keeping power, not in
building a modern post-war Spain. In 1956 British Ambassador Sir Ivo
Mallet referred to Franco's two folders, 'One marked "problems which
time will solve", and the other "problems which time has solved", his
favourite task being to transfer papers from one folder to another.'

George Orwell's *Homage to Catalonia* made him Britain's most
famous Spanish Civil War volunteer. He was not at Jarama or Brunete,
he did not take part in the Aragon offensive or the crossing of the
Ebro; instead he spent the first half of 1937 with a Marxist militia in
a dormant sector of the Aragon front. Laurie Lee, whose classic auto-
biographical tale *As I Walked Out One Midsummer Morning* described his
travels through Spain before the war, wrote about his personal expe-
riences of the conflict in *A Moment of War*. None of the other British
volunteers has any recollection of his being there.

In the years that followed many memorials were erected in Britain
to those who went to Spain. In London there is a fine bronze sculp-
ture situated close to the London Eye, in Jubilee Gardens. It consists
of three figures protecting a fourth who kneels wounded. Another
impressive bronze memorial to volunteers is La Pasionaria on the
Clyde Walkway at Customs House Quay, Glasgow. On the plinth are
her words which summed up why fifty-three Glaswegians, two thousand one hundred altogether from Britain, went to fight against the
spread of fascism: 'Better to die on your feet than to live forever on
your knees.'

Epilogue

D URING WORLD WAR II, MI5 so effectively countered hostile German espionage in Britain that Abwehr, the main German intelligence service, started relying heavily on information from a less direct route – Spain. Two stories demonstrate how British intelligence exploited this to its own advantage.

Juan Pujol, who was born on 14 February 1912 in Barcelona, loathed the political extremism of both sides during the Spanish Civil War. This prompted him to give practical assistance to Britain in her struggle against Nazi Germany. He resolved to become a spy, but had considerable difficulty gaining acceptance from the British intelligence community. Thank goodness he persisted: he was to become one of their most successful agents ever. Failing to convince the British, Pujol made contact with Abwehr at the German embassy in Madrid. The Germans were almost as difficult to impress; he was told that they might be interested if he was able to enter Britain. Pujol went to Lisbon and began building up a reputation with Abwehr by filing fictitious reports. They were convinced that he was in England, that Lisbon was simply where his courier was entering the peninsula with his messages in order to avoid the closely monitored Royal Mail. After the British intercepted some of the Pujol 'intelligence' that the Germans wired from Madrid to Berlin, they were finally persuaded to recruit him.

He boarded a British merchant ship to Gibraltar; a Sunderland flying boat took him to Plymouth where he arrived on 24 April 1942. He was met by two men from MI5, one of whom was Tomás Harris, himself half-Spanish, who was to be Pujol's case officer. Within days the two were building an increasingly complicated web of deception that would severely undermine German military strategy. They recruited twenty-five fictional sub-agents to add to the two that Pujol had already created in Lisbon. This not only impressed the Germans but prompted them to send more money to finance them – $340,000 in total. When they had to kill one off, the deception stretched to placing an obituary in the *Liverpool Daily Post*. Pujol's fantasy spy team made its biggest contribution to the allied effort by confusing the Germans over the time, place and scale of the D-Day landings. There would have been far more Germans in Normandy had Pujol's intelligence not convinced them that the Normandy landings were a diversion, that the main invasion would be at Calais. Even after the landings the Germans did not redeploy from Calais to oppose the consolidation of the Normandy bridgehead because they still believed that they were in the right place to repel a much larger assault. Early on D-Day itself Pujol maintained his credibility with Abwehr by wiring them that the Normandy invasion was imminent, knowing it would be too late for the Germans to react. Germany was so grateful for the work of the man they regarded as their principal agent in Britain that in July 1944 he was awarded the Iron Cross in absentia. Five months later he was awarded an MBE. After the war, Pujol moved to Venezuela.

Then there was 'the man who never was'. In 1943 a Spanish fisherman discovered a body floating off the Spanish coast. German agents identified it as that of a Royal Marine who had probably died in a plane crash on his way to Allied HQ in North Africa. In the pockets of the deceased Major William Martin, amongst theatre tickets, a letter from his girlfriend and one from his bank manager, was documentation showing that the known allied plans to attack Sicily were actually a decoy to divert the German military machine from the real targets: Greece and Sardinia. After the posthumous search, Major William Martin was buried in Huelva where a local lady took to tending his grave and placing red carnations on it. Señora Isabel Naylor de Mendes was made an MBE for her devotion. It was only in 1996 that the truth emerged. The grave actually contained the body of one Glyndwr Michael, an alcoholic Welsh tramp who had committed suicide in a London warehouse at the age of thirty-four. In what was called Operation Mincemeat, members of British Intelligence dressed the corpse in a uniform and planted it with documentation prior to the Royal Navy submarine *Seraph* putting it in the sea off the Spanish coast. The German intelligence organisation swallowed Mincemeat whole. Thousands of allied lives were saved when Sicily was invaded.

Principal Sources

CHAPTER 1
Parsons, John Carmi. *Eleanor of Castile.* Palgrave Macmillan, 1995.
Powrie, Jean. *Eleanor of Castile.* Brewin Books, 1990.
Prestwich, Michael. *Edward I.* Yale University Press, 1997.

CHAPTER 2
Barber, Richard. *Edward, Prince of Wales and Aquitaine.* The Boydell Press, 1996.
Barber, Richard & Green, David. *The Black Prince.* Sutton Publishing, 2003.
Barber, Richard. *The Life and Campaigns of the Black Prince.* The Boydell Press, 1997.
Green, David. *The Black Prince.* Tempus Publishing, 2001.

CHAPTER 3
Fraser, Antonia, *The Six Wives of Henry VIII.* Weidenfeld & Nicolson, 2002.
Luke, Mary M. *Catherine – The Queen.* Frederick Muller, 1968.

CHAPTER 4
Erickson, Carolly. *Bloody Mary.* Robson Books, 2001.
Grierson, Edward. *King of Two Worlds.* Collins, 1974.
Kamen, Henry. *Philip of Spain.* Yale University Press, 1998.
Loades, David. *Mary Tudor.* Blackwell Publishers, 1992.
Prescott, H.F.M. *Mary Tudor.* Weidenfeld & Nicolson, 2003.
Ridley, Jasper. *The Life and Times of Mary Tudor.* Weidenfeld & Nicolson, 1973.

CHAPTER 5
Abella, Rafael. *Los Piratas del Nuevo Mundo.* Planeta, 1992.
Cordingly, David. *Life Among the Pirates.* Abacus History, 1999.
Cordingly, David. *Pirates.* Salamander, 1996.
Sugden, John. *Sir Francis Drake.* Pimlico, 1996.
Williams, Neville. *Francis Drake.* Weidenfeld & Nicolson, 1973.

CHAPTER 6
Martin, Colin & Parker, Geoffrey. *The Spanish Armada.* Mandolin, 1999.
Milne-Tyte, Robert. *Armada!* Wordsworth Picture Library, 1998.
Whiting, Roger. *The Enterprise of England.* Sutton, 1995.
Williams, Patrick. *Armada.* Tempus, 2000.

CHAPTER 7
Perry, Margaret E. *Mousehole.* Margaret E. Perry, 1998.
Usherwood, Stepehen & Elizabeth. *The Counter-Armada 1596.* Bodley Head, 1983.
Wilkinson, John. *The Pirate and the Prophecy.* United Writers Publications, 1995.

CHAPTER 8
Parnell, Arthur. *The War of the Succession in Spain.* George Bell & Sons, 1888.

CHAPTER 9
Harvey, Morris. *Gibraltar.* Spellmount, 1996.
Hills, George. *Rock of Contention.* Robert Hale, 1974.

CHAPTER 10
Gregory, Desmond. *Minorca, the Illusory Prize*. Associated University Press, 1990.
Mata, Micaela. *Conquests and Reconquests of Menorca*. 1984.
Mata, Micaela. *Menorca Británica 1712-1727*. Institut Menorquí d'Estudis, 1994.
Sloss, Janet. *Richard Kane, Governor of Minorca*. The Bonaventura Press, 1995.

CHAPTER 11
Harbron, John D. *Trafalgar and the Spanish Navy*. Conway Maritime Press, 1988.
Terraine, John. *Trafalgar*. Wordsworth Military Picture Library, 1998.
Schom, Alan. *Trafalgar*. Penguin, 1992.
Trafalgar. Phoenix, 2003.

CHAPTER 12
Díaz-Plaja, Fernando. *La Guerra de la Independencia*. Planeta, 1994.
Esdale, Charles. *The Peninsular War*. Palgrave MacMillan, 2003.
Fletcher, Ian. *Craufurd's Light Division*. Spellmount, 1991.
Flethcher, Ian. *In Hell Before Daylight*. Spellmount, 1994.
Fletcher, Ian. *Voices from the Peninsula*. Greenhill Books, 2001.
Gates, David. *The Spanish Ulcer*. Pimlico, 2002.
Hathawy, Eileen. *A Dorset Soldier*. Spellmount, 1993.
Paget, Julian. *Wellington's Peninsular War*. Leo Cooper, 1990.
Weller, Jac. *Wellington in the Peninsula*. Greenhill Books, 1999.

CHAPTER 13
Chant, Roy Herman. *Spanish Tiger*. Midas Books, 1983.
Duncan, Francis. *The English in Spain*. John Murray, 1877
Holt, Edgar. *The Carlist Wars in Spain*. Putnam, 1967.
Somerville, Alexander. *History of the British Legion*. London, 1839.

CHAPTER 14
Noel, Gerard. *Ena – Spain's English Queen*. Constable & Robinson, 1999.

CHAPTER 15
Alexander, Bill. *British Volunteers for Liberty*. Lawrence & Wishart, 1982.
Alpert, Michael. *A New International History of the Spanish Civil War*. Palgrave Macmillan, 1998.
Fyvel, Penelope. *English Penny*. Arthur H. Stockwell, 1992.
Gregory, Walter. *The Shallow Grave*. Five Leaves, 1996.
Mitchell, David. *The Spanish Civil War*. Granada Publishing, 1992.
Norris, Christopher (ed). *Inside the Myth*. Lawrence & Wishart, 1984.
Preston, Paul. *Franco*. Fontana Press, 1995.
Ranzato, Gabriele. *The Spanish Civil War*. The Windrush Press, 1999.
Thomas, Hugh. *The Spanish Civil War*. Penguin, 2003.
Williams, Colin; Alexander, Bill & Gorman, John. *Memorials of the Spanish Civil War*. Alan Sutton, 1996.

EPILOGUE
Seaman, Mark (intro). *Garbo – The Spy Who Saved D-Day*. Public Record Office, 2000.

GENERAL
Borrow, George. *The Bible in Spain*. J.M. Dent, 1843.
Ellingham, Mark & Fisher, John. *Spain*. Rough Guides, 1997.

Index of Spanish Place Names

The 8-volume Who's Who in British History Series ... a Biographical Companion to British History

Who's Who in Roman Britain & Anglo-Saxon England
Richard Fletcher
ISBN 0 85683 089 5 · £27.50 hardback
ISBN 0 85683 114 X · £13.95 paperback

Who's Who in Early Medieval England (1066-1272)
Christopher J. Tyerman
ISBN 0 85683 091 7 · £27.50 hardback
ISBN 0 85683 132 8 · £14.95 paperback

Who's Who in Late Medieval England (1272-1485)
Michael Hicks
ISBN 0 85683 092 5 · £27.50 hardback
ISBN 0 85683 125 5 · £14.95 paperback

Who's Who in Tudor England
C.R.N. Routh • revised by Peter Holmes
ISBN 0 85683 093 3 · £27.50 hardback
ISBN 0 85683 119 0 · £14.95 paperback

Who's Who in Stuart Britain
C.P. Hill
ISBN 0 85683 075 5 · £27.50 hardback
ISBN 0 85683 110 7 · £14.95 paperback

Who's Who in Early Hanoverian Britain (1714-1789)
Geoffrey Treasure
ISBN 0 85683 076 3 · £27.50 hardback
ISBN 0 85683 131 X · £14.95 paperback

Who's Who in Late Hanoverian Britain (1789-1837)
Geoffrey Treasure
ISBN 0 85683 094 1 · £27.50 hardback
ISBN 0 85683 137 9 · £14.95 paperback

Who's Who in Victorian Britain
Roger Ellis
ISBN 0 85683 095 X · £27.50 hardback
ISBN 0 85683 138 7 · £14.95 paperback

The 8 volumes which make up the *Who's Who in British History* series range from Roman to Victorian times, presenting history as biography, complementing the conventional approach. The authors give us more than the bare facts of their subjects' lives: they place them in the context of the age, evoke their personalities and evaluate their achievements.

Each biographical entry is a complete essay, skilful in its selection of evidence and its methods of assessment. The authors have all been teachers, but it is their view that history which is instructive can also be entertaining.

The range of personalities is wide and embraces royalty, politicians, poets, playwrights, inventors and artists. The sequence is broadly chronological rather than alphabetical, making it easy for the reader to browse from one contemporary to another, building up a living picture of the age in which they lived. The index, with its cross references, facilitates the tracing of further information.

'Readers ... will be instructed, stimulated and ... entertained'
TIMES
LITERARY
SUPPLEMENT

Published by SHEPHEARD-WALWYN (PUBLISHERS) LTD
Suite 604 • The Chandlery • 50 Westminster Bridge Road • London SE1 7QY
Telephone: 020-7721 7666 • Fax: 020-7721 7667
e-mail: *books@shepheard-walwyn.co.uk* • www.shepheard-walwyn.co.uk